Dollars & Events

Dollars &
Events

How to Succeed in the
Special Events Business

Dr. Joe Jeff Goldblatt, CSEP
Frank Supovitz

John Wiley & Sons, Inc.
New York   Chichester   Weinheim   Brisbane   Singapore   Toronto

Library of Congress Cataloging-in-Publication Data:

Goldblatt, Joe Jeff, 1952–
   Dollars & events : how to succeed in the special
events business / Joe Goldblatt, Frank Supovitz.
       p. cm.
   Includes index.
   ISBN 0-471-24957-2 (cloth : alk. paper)
   1. Special events industry—United States.   2. Special
events—United States—Marketing. I. Supovitz, Frank. II. Title:
Dollars and events
   GT3406.U6 G65 1999
   394.26'068—ddc21   98-39937

Printed in the United States of America.

10 9 8 7 6 5 4 3 2

With love we dedicate this book
to our children
Max and Sam Goldblatt
and
Matthew, Ethan, and Jacob Supovitz
and to our wives
Nancy Lynner
and
Catherine Supovitz

Contents

Foreword

Over the years I've discovered that generally entrepreneurs come in two varieties—those who are and those who plan to be. Notice I said plan to be, not want to be; planning is crucial to the success of any entrepreneur, whether or not they've already started their businesses. Chances are if you're reading this, you either own or plan to start a special events planning business. Whichever category you fall into, buying this book is a smart step.

Entrepreneurship has changed significantly in the past decade. Many entrepreneurs today did not set out on this path; due to a variety of reasons beyond their control they entered this entrepreneurial course reluctantly. If you started your special events planning business within the past several years, this could be you. And if you're wondering whether you really need a book to tell you about the business you're already in, it's very likely you do.

Like many others who start businesses, you probably started your special events business because it's what you knew how to do. In other words, you worked as a special events planner, so you thought it would be natural for you to start this type of business. That's good thinking. But if you think your former career prepared you for your current (or future) enterprise, you'd be wrong. You may know all there is to know about special events planning, but what do you know about running a business? Have you ever even written a mission statement or business plan?

Being an entrepreneur and being an employee are two very different things. Although you may have become an expert at planning events, how much do you know about doing research, finding capital, hiring (and firing) employees, preparing financial statements, or the zillions of details other people were responsible for? Chances are not enough. Now you're the boss, and you're responsible for everything. If you've already started your business, you've likely discovered this fact. If you're still in the planning stages, remember to take this into account. In fact, you probably don't even know what you don't know.

That's what this book is for. Many folks believe it is inherently risky to start a business. And while risks certainly exist at start-up, I believe the real risks, the big risks, come during the growth stage. After all, once you're in business, you have more to lose if something goes wrong. I was impressed when I received the manuscript for *Dollars & Events*. I immediately noticed the subtitle was *How to Succeed in the Special Events Business,* not how to start an events business. That's to your advantage. When you're finished reading this book, you'll have a better understanding of not only how to start, but, more important, how to sustain your business.

Thomas Huxley once wrote, "If a little knowledge is dangerous, where is the man who has so much as to be out of danger?" That person doesn't exist. To succeed at anything—in business or in life—you must constantly seek more. To learn truly is to grow. But Huxley also said, "The great end of life is not knowledge, but action." This book certainly gives you the knowledge, but it is up to you to take action. Go to it!

Rieva Lesonsky
Editorial Director, *Entrepreneur* Magazine

Preface

How do you define success in the business of special events? Is success measured in profits, lifestyle, or the acquisition of wealth? The seemingly endless infomercials that promote "get rich quick" schemes encourage you to believe that success is ultimately the result of "a simple method." In fact, achieving long-term success in business as well as life is a complex process that requires a carefully researched and well designed navigational system.

Consider the significant paradigm shifts that have occurred in the world of careers since the establishment of modern professions in the late 1800s. Previously, individuals worked for one organization and advanced vertically until retirement. Today, individuals work for many different organizations and often advance laterally before they are promoted vertically. Previously, individuals primarily sought financial security. Today, workers seek a package of career services including personal satisfaction, educational opportunity, as well as compensation. And finally, previously being a follower or good worker under the strong protective arm of a sympathetic boss was considered de rigueur. Today, employees are encouraged to become entrepreneurial, loyalty among organizations and individuals is rare, and employees (according to the U.S. Department of Labor) change jobs every 2.5 years. In fact, the U.S. Department of Labor predicts that the average U.S. employee will have not one but five careers during their working lifetime.

This book is a major navigational tool designed to successfully steer your life and career toward friendly waters. Just as the compass was used by ancient travelers to point them in the right direction and save time and effort, this book provides a system of proven methods to help you reach your destination in record time. To achieve long-term career and personal success, you must not only use this book initially to chart your course, but you also should use it throughout your career and life to regain your bearings and as needed to redirect your journey to achieve your personal and professional goals and objectives.

Through a series of interviews with outstanding special events entre- and intrepreneurs, you will meet successful role models. Using the best examples from the business literature you will learn how to adapt proven concepts such as "benchmarking," "best practices," "quality teams," and other methods to improve the growth of your special events business or career. Finally, by applying the activities at the end of each chapter, you will "learn by doing," which is the best way for special events entrepreneurs to understand and use the information contained in this book.

The authors wish to invite you to help us expand the canon of literature in the special events field by submitting your best practices in special events entrepreneurial thinking. Send us your success stories in marketing, management, or other event career or business operations and if we use them in the second edition of this book, we will send you a free book as our way of saying "thanks" for helping the industry grow. Send your ideas via e-mail to drevent@gwu.edu

Perhaps the best way to gain practical knowledge from this book is to share its contents with your employees, colleagues, or even family and friends. Take time to organize an informal discussion group to share, debate, and ultimately further illuminate the information contained in these pages. Through this dissection and analysis you will receive even greater value from your investment.

So, how do you define success in special events? Although success cannot be guaranteed in any life or career, one thing is for certain—a system for success is a valuable means of marking and measuring your achievements. As you open the pages of this book, you are beginning your journey as a modern special events entre- or intrepreneur. These uncharted waters can be treacherous in the days and years to come, so grasp this book as though it were the steering wheel of a powerful ship that represents your life and career. Hold tight, and as you look forward over the bow of your ship, see the horizon beginning to rise in the distance. With your talent, intuition, and the wisdom from others within this book, you will reach your destination in record time and appreciate this extraordinary journey. May you find the success you desire now and throughout your voyage into the new world of modern special events.

Dr. Joe Jeff Goldblatt, CSEP
Frank Supovitz

Acknowledgments

In a recent study of 1,000 of the largest businesses in the United States, *Success* magazine determined that *teamwork* was considered an important quality for promotion among executives. Since the early 1970s, the concept of creating and encouraging *quality teams* has been a central tenet of successful U.S. businesses such as Xerox Corporation and McDonald's. This book, the first in the emerging literary canon in the special events field, is also a sterling example of quality teams.

This project began with significant encouragement from our acquisitions editor Claire Zuckerman and continued with the wise counsel and enthusiastic support of JoAnna Turtletaub, the extremely talented hospitality editor of John Wiley & Sons. The entire editorial team at John Wiley & Sons provided continuous valuable support. Millie Torres-Matias was especially helpful in shaping the final manuscript into a format that is easy to read while at the same time very useful to the reader. Along the way, Erin McGee carefully and thoughtfully prepared the manuscript for this book and validated the Event Manager Entrepreneur Assessment Tool (E-MEAT) while earning her Master's degree in Event Management and working full time. She is a role model for all professionals in this field as she carefully balances her time to advance her career as well as grow professionally in service to the industry, as evidenced by her work within the pages of this manuscript.

Our families and colleagues have provided a support system that is essential to the completion of a lofty goal such as researching and writing a new book. Their unselfish devotion and encouragement has sustained us during the difficult days (and nights) required to produce this book. They are the very best example of a high-quality team and we are most grateful for their enduring support.

Finally, and certainly not completely, we wish to offer sincere appreciation for the many special events and business professionals who allowed their best practices to be used as role models in this book in order that the publisher, the authors, and the industry collectively could advance this emerging profession. These successful special events entre- and intrepreneurs are the shining beacons that thousands of future professionals will follow as they risk their capital, their time, and their personal lives for the once-in-a-career opportunity to use their entrepreneurial spirit to grow the business of special events. They know that this opportunity is much more than "Dollars & Events"; it is in fact the pursuit of success in the business of special events.

Our thanks go to the following members of our team:

Deb Belinsky
Shmoel Ben Gad
Jaclyn Bernstein
Gary Bettman
Tom Bollard
Jane Castan
Pam Cheriton
Mary Pat Clarke
Michel D'Angelo
Dr. Lisa Delpy
Dr. Douglas C. Frechtling
Scott Givens
Craig Harnett
Dr. Donald E. Hawkins
Rob Hulsmeyer, CSEP
David James
Shareen Joseph-Hernandez
Linda Higgison
Mitchell Kelldorf
Dr. Donald R. Lehman
Rieva Lesonsky
Barnett Lipton

Brian Low
Anna McCusker, CSEP
Erin McGee, MTA
Janet Meyers
Jack Morton
Eli Mundy
Ian Murray
Deborah Nielsen
Jim Palmer
Dean Susan Phillips
The Plaza Hotel
Paul Salvatore
Julie Rutherford Silvers
Stephen Solomon
Dr. Sheryl Spivack
Alexander Steinitz
Stephen Joel Trachtenberg
Don Whiteley
Joey Yaffe, MBA
Dr. Larry Yu
Richard Zahnd

About the Authors

DR. JOE JEFF GOLDBLATT, CSEP, is the Jack and Anne Morton Assistant Professor of Event Management and Tourism and Founding Director of the Event Management Program at The George Washington University, and served as the founding president of The International Special Events Society (ISES). He is the author of the first textbook in the industry, *Special Events, The Best Practices in Modern Event Management* and co-author of *The Dictionary of Event Management*, both available from Wiley, as well as other books. Dr. Goldblatt received the first and only Lifetime Achievement Award for service to the industry from ISES.

FRANK SUPOVITZ, is Vice President of Special Events for the National Hockey League. Prior to joining the League in 1972, he served as Vice President of Marketing for VENTURES and Director of Special Events for Radio City Music Hall Productions. In addition to having produced more than 100 events for the NHL, his prior event credits also include the We the People 200 Parade (the national celebration for the bicentennial of the U.S. Constitution), the Stanford University Centennial, the 1990 Goodwill Games Welcoming Ceremony, the U.S. Olympic Festival Opening Ceremonies, the 200th Anniversary of George Washington's Inauguration, the Operation Welcome Home Ticker Tape Parade, the Coca-Cola Centennial Finale Gala, and Polaroid's 50th Anniversary Celebration.

Dollars &
Events

Introduction

"How long did it take you to write this proposal?" "All my life."
—Julia Rutherford Silvers

Y ou have been preparing all your life to read and use the information in this book. Julia Rutherford Silvers, a special events entrepreneur located in Albuquerque, New Mexico, reminds us that learning is in fact a life-long pursuit. Therefore, as you begin reading this book, you must see it as an ongoing construction project. You are in fact constructing not only your career, but also your life in special events.

Under Construction

According to Joseph Yaffe, MBA, an instructor of the course entitled "Starting, Growing and Managing the Event Business" at The George Washington University, the vast majority of event management and event services organizations are either unprofitable or not achieving a satisfactory return on their investment. When a client asked Julia Rutherford Silvers why her proposal appeared to be a costly investment without recognizing the obvious benefit, Ms. Silvers immediately defined the work, study, experience, and of course "sweat equity" that produced the valuable ideas labeled innocently as "proposal." Ultimately, the investments the client or your employer will make are the event itself and all of the related resources required to research, design, plan, coordinate, and evaluate this temporary business operation. Therefore, the *return on event* (ROE) is critical to the future of every event professional.

What Is Your Property Value?

How does one measure the satisfactory return on event for a fundraising, corporate, government, sport, or other type of event? What criteria should be used as measurements to benchmark success? How should the sponsoring organization evaluate the outcome in financial, political, public relations, and other categorical methods? Perhaps most important, what other categories must be reviewed and included to provide a fair, accurate, valid, and reliable measure of success?

Breaking New Ground

This book represents the first attempt to apply the best practices of leading organizations to the special events industry. Through these pages you will learn how to consistently produce a satisfactory return on your investment. Furthermore, you will learn how to build a viable and sustainable event organization, whether it is a new company, an established business, or the special events arm of a larger corporate concern. Your organization will grow as a result of applying the principles found in this book to your daily operations. This growth in value may one day enable you to either sell your operation for a substantial profit, rise within the organization ranks, or by working smarter, reduce your daily responsibilities and allow you to enjoy more leisure time.

How This Book Helps You Construct Your Success

According to the U.S. Department of Commerce, nine out of ten new businesses fail each year. Those that survive the first year of operation usually succumb to a slow and often agonizing death the second or third year. Restaurants, a large and important part of the event man-agement field, have an even higher rate of failure than that of other businesses. Although no statistics are available on the rate of failure of event businesses, it may be assumed that many of these organizations suffer the same fate of other service businesses. Their struggles as well as many success stories are chronicled in this volume.

Entrepreneur or Entrepreneurial Employee?

Many future entrepreneurs got their first taste of running a business while working for others. While watching another businessperson experience the thrill of victory as well as the agony of defeat, these employees begin to make decisions regarding their own entrepre-neurial futures.

Successful employers increasingly encourage their employees to develop their skills in sensing, analyzing, achieving flexibility, and anticipating change. These skills are the prerequisites of successful entrepreneurs. Therefore, teams of entrepreneurial employees today often drive successful businesses.

In some cases these employees desire to "work for themselves" rather than others and contemplate starting their own special events businesses. In still other cases (the vast majority) these employees prefer to continue to let their employers assume the risk for the ven-ture and instead conduct themselves as entrepreneurial employees.

The primary difference between an entrepreneur and the entre-preneurial employee is best defined in the word *risk*. The classic entrepreneur assumes the financial, legal, and other critical risks for starting and operating the special events business. The entrepreneur-ial employee may contribute his or her sensing, analyzing, and antic-ipatory skills, but ultimately the business owner assumes the risk.

Whether you are a classic special events entrepreneur or an entrepreneurial employee, the proven practices contained in this book will help ensure your growth and enable you to make important decisions in a rapidly changing environment.

What Is the Super Industry: Special Events?

Although many businesses are in a state of rapid change, the special events industry is actually a multidisciplinary *super industry* comprised of many older, traditional industries. These industries include consulting, fund-raising, sports management, party supply sales and equipment rentals, lighting and sound rentals, audio-visual rentals, décor, catering, and many others. For the first time in the history of modern professions, many of these industries have banded together to form a new field of endeavor—which some would define as an emerging discipline—entitled Event Management. This professional field is comprised of tens of thousands of individuals and thousands of business organizations struggling to make a living from a vocation they love.

Surveying the Field

This book helps you replace the rose-colored glasses that may have brought you into the field with the clear-sighted twenty-twenty vision needed to be financially successful in both the long and short term. Event management is not unique in this struggle. Other professions have waged a similar battle as they have struggled to achieve recognition, raise their standards, and establish sound business practices that would help ensure their success. A careful examination of traditional professions such as medicine, law, and accounting reveal similar challenges during their formative years. Professions more closely related to event management, such as advertising, public relations, catering, and party rentals, further support the argument that this process of moving from an industry driven by enthusiasm to one that is both enthusiastic and profitable is essential to producing a healthy business environment.

Finding Your Critical Success Indicators

We have observed, from over 50 years of combined experience observing thousands of event management entrepreneurs as well as entrepreneurial employees, that there are five recognizable success factors. These five factors or indicators immediately transmit to others that the event management professional is authentically benefiting from the work he or she is doing. Figure I–1 lists these critical success indicators.

1. Doing What You Want to Do
2. Desired or Desirable Lifestyle
3. Satisfactory Remuneration
4. Personal and Professional Development Opportunities
5. Personal and Professional Validation

Figure I–1   Event Management Critical Success Indicators

Doing What You Want to Do

A wise man once described the ideal job as "that which you would do for nothing but ultimately master and [for which you] are well rewarded." In fact, the best jobs have little delineation between work and play. If you are going to achieve long-term success in the event management profession, you must do this for the simple reason that it needs to be done. In this regard, the art and science of event management is a healthy blend of ministry and profession.

Desired Lifestyle

The perfect blend of personal and professional life is growing more and more rare in our increasingly complex and demanding society. However, happy is the man or woman who occasionally finds a balance. This is especially true for the profession of event management, in which early burnout is unfortunately one of the liabilities often associated with the field. Therefore, it behooves the event management professional to determine early on personal and professional priorities and attempt to find a balance that can be restored when occasionally life gets out of kilter.

Satisfactory Remuneration

Regardless of your level of remuneration, every professional requires a certain income to meet daily expenses. In addition, according to salary surveys in most modern professions including event management, there is a median or mean salary that a trained and experienced event management professional should seek. Of course, if your salary is astronomically inflated but your work environment is mentally destructive, the wage is still too low for the ultimate damage that is caused in the long term. Therefore, balancing income with work satisfaction is important, as is seeking a financial affirmation of the value of your time and contribution to the organization.

Personal and Professional Development Opportunities

The successful event management professional seeks continuous opportunities to improve him- or herself throughout their careers. These opportunities may be through formal education, training, apprenticeship, or simply the school of hard knocks. Regardless of the avenue you select, you must commit yourself to staying green and growing throughout your event management career.

Personal and Professional Validation

Whether you are the recipient of an earned degree, an industry award, or a letter of commendation from your supervisor, everyone needs a pat on the back to provide tangible evidence of obvious accomplishment. Seek opportunities and organizations that recognize the importance of personal and professional validation and set goals for yourself to achieve this validation. These tangible and intangible symbols of your success will help you rise in your profession and will fuel your desire to continue your personal and professional growth.

Focusing Your Sights

These five critical success indicators may be seen through an equal number of lenses, much like the used by an optometrist to correct poor vision. As one ages, the musculature of the eye changes and often requires artificial correction to maintain perfect vision. Throughout your event management career, you will need to adjust these lenses to remain focused on the event management critical success indicators. Figure I-2 describes these important lenses.

---

1. Culture
2. Geography
3. Income Potential
4. Opportunity for Growth
5. Equity, Investment, and Financial Independence

Figure I–2   The Corrective Lenses for a Successful Event Management Career

Culture

Every human being works within a specific culture. Culture is best defined as the state of being at a specific time in one's life. The state of being may be related to geography (see below) or a historical period or specific events. However, it is essential that successful event managers remain focused upon their critical success indicators by constantly refocusing their cultural context to achieve the growth and opportunity they need for the future. In fact, the term culture is linked to the term "cultivate," as in "cultivate the soil." If your soil is parched, you may need to look for greener pastures in your career.

Geography

Since the beginning of humankind, people's lives have been dramatically influenced by geography. Some individuals are mountain people and others are desert animals. Still others long to live by the sea. Determine early on what geography provides the richest environment for you to nourish your career physically, spiritually, as well as professionally.

Income Potential

Once you have adjusted your lens, you may notice a slight blurring, which means it is time to refocus by determining how culture and geography may be influenced by income potential. For example, you may determine that you are most effective in a tie-less, ocean environment; however, the income potential as an event manager is severely limited in this location. Therefore, by readjusting the lens you may find that you are content to live within one or two hours of the ocean in a culture that is somewhat relaxed but enables you to achieve an income that will support your lifestyle requirements. You must constantly refocus the lens to make certain that each optic is in perfect focus, and to ensure that you maintain your clear view of the critical success indicators.

Opportunities for Growth

What opportunities are available for continuous growth through education, recreation, religion, and personal relationships? This important lens must be carefully polished to make certain that you are continually growing, as you stay focused on your five critical success indicators.

Equity, Investment, and Financial Independence

Finally, the ultimate reward is not financial; it is the total realization that through your labors you have achieved independence. Through independence comes freedom to pursue new goals and opportunities. Financial equity and investment lead to this achievement. They are not goals in and of themselves. The ultimate goal is to adjust these five lenses throughout your career to enable you to achieve independence while remaining focused on your critical success indicators.

Your Professional Viewpoint

Use the five lenses of culture, geography, income potential, opportunity for growth, equity, investment, and financial independence as tools to sharpen your view of those critical success indicators that will drive your event management career. In Figure I–3 you see a graphic illustration of how this viewing system can help you master your career and enjoy your life.

Figure I–3   The Viewing System for a Successful Special Events Career

Entrepreneur–Entrepreneurial Employee: A Common Purpose

Whether you are an entrepreneurial employee working within the government or private sector or a classic entrepreneur with a developing, new, or existing business, this book will help you put the best practices of some of the world's leading organizations to work within your strategic plan. These best practices may have required hundreds of thousands or even millions of dollars in research activities to improve the organizations in which they were discovered. Now, for the first time, you may freely adopt and adapt these practices to improve the profitability and overall operations within your organizations. Indeed, this book will help you maximize your return on each event to accelerate your pursuit of success.

Conquering the Bell Curve of Event Management

The entire business development cycle is profiled in this text. You will have the opportunity in the pages that follow to develop your organization's vision and mission statement and furthermore to craft a working applied strategic plan. If your organization has already accomplished this important step, you may wish to compare your current plan with the current principles and best practices shown here to further refine your strategy.

From research to marketing and human resource management, a thorough profile of the best operations strategies of event businesses are discussed in terms that are readily adaptable to your individual organization. Case studies of both U.S. and global event management organizations are given throughout this book. You may use these figures or blueprints for success to model your own organizational strategies.

Maturity and Reinvention

This book also describes how to sustain your success once your event management organization matures. Since the special events industry is moving from growth into maturity, this is a particularly relevant and timely section. In today's competitive environment only organizations that remain green and growing will survive. Techniques for growing your event management organization to the next level are described and a detailed situation analysis questionnaire is included to enable you to determine the position of your organization both internally and externally. Once you have fixed this position you may chart your course to the next level to ensure that you are continually advancing toward success.

Finishing Touches

The text concludes with ample resources to assist you in the future, including business development tools such as books, magazines, consultants, internet resources, and other critical elements to further ensure long-term success. Perhaps most useful is a comprehensive listing of standard contracts, planning forms, and other documents that are being published *for the first time* in an attempt to standardize this field. In addition, examples of the best practices in terms of marketing materials are included to further assist you with developing your marketing and promotion programs.

Step-by-Step Techniques to Help You Learn

Within each chapter a wide variety of figures provides a quick reference for the key concepts being discussed. Each chapter concludes
with a review of the relevant literature under the heading entitled
Tools of the Trade and a summary of the key points entitled The View
From Here. These sections allow you to review and at the same time
explore additional sources for further professional development.

Your Guides

The authors of this text bring a unique dual perspective to this subject.
One is the former owner of a successful event management business
who ultimately sold the firm and developed a lucrative consulting
practice. The other is one of the leading special events executives in
the multi-billion-dollar sports industry. Prior to joining the sports
management industry, he served as an executive with leading event
management firms responsible for producing such noteworthy events
as the Fiftieth Anniversary of Polaroid Corporation, the bicentennial
of the U.S. Constitution, and the opening ceremonies of the 1990
Goodwill Games. The two authors bring different perspectives—that
of an entrepreneur and of the modern entrepreneurial employee—to
comprehensively examine and reveal the previously hidden secrets of
success in the rapidly growing field of event management.

The Bottom Line: A Jump Start Toward Success

As a result of exploring and using the ideas presented in this book,
there is no legitimate reason why present or future members of the
event management industries should suffer the same fate of other
emerging professions. The proven techniques found herein will remove the land mines that have surprised others and will provide firm
footing for event management entrepreneurs and entrepreneurial
employees to climb to the highest level of success in this new and
growing profession.

How to Use this Book for Maximum Benefit

Make certain you allow sufficient time to study the techniques presented in this book and perform the recommended action steps. Too often busy business owners or overworked employees do not allow themselves the time that is absolutely essential for continuing education. Excuses such as "This is a luxury I can ill afford" do not hold up in today's fast-changing and increasingly competitive business environment. Just as you would expect your physician to stay current with the latest diagnostic methods, drugs, and treatments regardless of how busy she is, your employees and clients have the right to expect the same from you! Use the following techniques to stay on the cutting edge of your profession and receive the *added value* you deserve from your investment in this book.

At minimum, set aside a period of time each week for reading one chapter of this book. A total of ten weeks is ample time to digest this volume and practice some of the recommendations that are essential to understanding the principles that are described. Make certain that this study time is free from distraction and truly enables you to concentrate for a fixed period of time. Researchers believe that the average reader can effectively concentrate for up to 20 minutes and then requires a stretch break to further improve retention. Use the technique of 20 minutes of concentrated reading followed by five or ten minutes of relaxation, including physical exercise, to enhance your study periods and improve your overall comprehension.

Second, benchmark your accomplishments by maintaining a reading log that describes the related reading material (Tools of the Trade) you are reviewing. Reviewing trade magazines, newspapers such as the *Wall Street Journal,* and other periodical sources as well as books will broaden your understanding of these principles and their practical application. Each chapter of this text concludes with recommendations for further study. Use these additional resources to accelerate as well as expand your command of this subject. The reading log is simply a random listing of the sources you have studied and the key ideas you have gleaned. See Figure I–4 as an example.

Third, and finally, make certain you develop action steps at the conclusion of each chapter. Thoughtfully and carefully complete the assignments that will help you improve your practice by applying the ideas that are presented. As you develop your own best practices, you are simultaneously improving the event management profession

Example

Publication	Key Ideas
In Search of Excellence	Management by walking around (MBWA)
Clicking	99 lives syndrome and marketing opportunities
Dollars & Events	Develop viewing system
The Customer Comes Second	Reward your employees

Figure I–4   Reading Log

for others. Here is an example of how to complete the Breaking New Ground section:

Breaking New Ground

Example:

1. Rewrite the following mission statement: "We believe that our special events organization should be large and well known."

   Rewrite: "We believe our event management organization must achieve global recognition and serve specific markets worldwide."

Final Thoughts As You Begin Construction

These three important strategies will not only increase your enjoyment of this book but also greatly increase your command of the subject matter, and perhaps most important, guarantee that you maximize the return on event for this investment.

During the 1970s and 1980s, a long litany of business self-help books were published. Many of these books stressed the need for U.S. companies to adopt the successful Japanese system of building effective work teams or they championed the importance of total quality management (TQM). This book combines many of these business philosophies but also advances the discipline of management science one step further by proposing a set of strategies that new or developing fields such as special events may use during a critical formative time.

The event management field is in the adolescence of its development period and rapidly approaching maturity. During this challenging time (and anyone who has raised teenagers knows how challenging this can be), it is essential that professionals within this growing field make concerted efforts to examine ways they are currently doing business and endeavor to do better. Within this volume event management entrepreneurs and entrepreneurial employees will find the tools, techniques, methods, examples, and resources to improve productivity and profitability.

Your investment confirms your commitment to take your place among the top 1 percent within the event management profession. These are the individuals who not only do what they love but also are fairly rewarded for their talent and effort. You will find yourself in a new league as you apply the principles in this book. Some call them the captains of industry, or the barons of commerce, but regardless of your definition you will find yourself in the major leagues and headed for the event management hall of fame. Along the way, through the pages that follow, you will find the markers, the symbols, signs, mileposts, and personal guides to ease your journey and make your trip a successful one. How long will it take you to reach your destination, to complete construction? All your life. Now, use these tools and get started.

CHAPTER 1

Choosing Success

Step One: *Choose success through a careful analysis of your personal and professional goals.*

Obviously, success is not simply a matter of choice; otherwise, everyone would be successful. Achieving success in any field is a process, one that requires professional expertise, personal commitment, realistic expectations, an entrepreneurial spirit, and time. The degree to which one possesses these essential prerequisites, combined with the unwavering drive to apply them to the development of a career, separates those who truly choose to succeed from those who merely talk a good game.

Whether you are starting your own business as an entrepreneur, energizing your current position as an entrepreneurial employee, or are just starting out in the special events industry, you need a blueprint that will guide you through each step of constructing a successful career. A well-constructed house rests on a sound foundation, is separated from the elements by insulated walls, windows, and doors, and is capped by a roof that shields the interior from rain. Properly installed wiring provides the power to run appliances, and plumbing provides water and removes wastes. Regardless of how well the visible foundation, walls, and roof are built, improperly planned or installed wiring and plumbing can endanger the entire structure with the possibility of fire or flooding.

Building a successful business or career is much like building a new house. The visible foundation of expertise and experience can create an attractive structure, but all of the wiring and plumbing of running and operating a business, department, or project must also be carefully designed and constructed in order to avoid a conflagration that can engulf the entire effort. This chapter provides the first step in the process of choosing to achieve success—building your career with a carefully crafted plan, or blueprint, upon which all subsequent construction is based. There is, however, an even more basic step to be considered before drafting the first blueprint. You have to have a clear vision of what you want your finished house to look like.

Common Success Indicators

As the architect of your career, you have to have a clear and realistic concept of what your successful career will look like. While priorities and the definition of success will vary by the individual, there are five common "indicators" by which most people would measure success:

Doing What You Want to Do

You may most enjoy producing events, designing floral arrangements, managing talent, building props, or running transportation systems. Some might argue that money is the primary success indicator, but as Groucho Marx once said, "Money will not make you happy, and happy will not make you money." If you can love what you do, and do what you love, you have achieved the most basic and satisfying level of success.

Achieving the Lifestyle You Want

Lifestyle, or quality-of-life objectives, may include living or working in a particular geographical area, traveling only as much as you desire, being able to contribute to causes you hold dear, or providing yourself and your family with a home and the accoutrements of a "good life."

Achieving a Satisfying Level of Compensation

Earning a certain level of income in terms of cash, deferred savings, and perquisites that compensate you for the time, money, and effort invested in your business, is by most definitions indicative of success. If you own a business, increasing the value of your equity against the possibility of full or partial sale is an indicator of success.

Personal and Professional Development

You also build a successful career by increasing your level of proficiency in your chosen field, and developing your skills as a businessperson, manager, and marketer. Widely recognized development tools include earning certification as offered by professional organizations such as the International Special Events Society (ISES), or the International Festivals & Events Association (IFEA), among others.

Self-Actualization and Validation

Achieving a sense of fulfillment, feeling that you have succeeded in attaining much of what you set out to do, is the highest level of achievement. Earning awards and honors from your peers such as Gala Awards (*Special Events* magazine), being sought by media and academia as an expert, resource, consultant, or spokesperson contributes to this sense of fulfillment.

Years after you build your house, you may find that the original design no longer meets your needs. You may have to add a bedroom or bathroom, enlarge the dining room, or update the kitchen. It is similarly natural that your definition of success and the relative importance of each of the common indicators may change as your life and career develop. It is not unusual for those who approach their goals to reassess, refocus, and refine what they are really looking for out of their business, their career, and their life. While common, this need may come more rapidly for those whose career goals were focused primarily on the achievement of financial milestones, evidenced by hundreds of stories about those who have "made it" but are still unhappy and unfulfilled. For an outstanding self-help manual for those who look to regain the spark that drove them to seek success, Harold Kushner's *When All You've Ever Wanted Isn't Enough* is highly recommended (see Tools of the Trade at the end of this chapter).

Setting Goals

Once you have determined how you will recognize success, the process of attaining it begins and ends with the setting of goals and the achievement of those goals. As aspirations are a highly personal matter, there is no business standard for what your goals should be. You alone set the agenda, determine the methodology, and select the target. As there are a minimum of two sides to your life—the personal and the professional—it is a good idea to consider the effects of one upon the other, and strive to achieve the balance between personal and professional goals that is comfortable and right for you.

This book assumes that you are either an entrepreneur seeking to start or re-energize your own business, or an ambitious "entrepreneurial employee" who exhibits many of the same qualities of an entrepreneur while in the service of an employer (the qualities and distinctions between the two will be discussed later). If you are an entrepreneur, the blueprint you will use to set and attain your professional goals is a business plan. Your goals will include levels of gross sales, net income, share of market, rate of growth, and the timetable for expansion of your product line. If you are an entrepreneurial employee, your goals may include the corporate level to which you wish to rise, and the size and types of projects you will be trusted to manage, among others.

There are also goals that are more personal in nature, such as the level of annual personal income, recovery of capital, time spent with your family, the ability to acquire a new home, car, or other personally important possession and having the time to enjoy it. While these goals are not normally contained or analyzed within the printed pages of a business plan, they are important considerations when you determine the feasibility and desirability of starting a new business, or actively pursuing career growth. They must be balanced against the demands on your time set by your professional goals. Many successful businesspeople are miserably unhappy because they have been unable to balance their personal desires and their corporate goals.

Personal and professional goals are not always distinct from one another. There are also those that fall somewhere in between, which are either primarily good for your business, good for you personally, or sometimes equally good for both. Figure 1–1, the Personal/Professional Goal Balance, illustrates how trying to achieve balance between professional and personal goals will compete for your time,

Professional	Personal
Net corporate income	Personal income
Stable opportunity for growth	
Gross annual revenues	
Reasonable working hours	Time spent with family
Share of market	Respect of your peers
Recovery of capital	Recovery of capital
Growth in company value	Personal savings (children's education, house, car)
Leadership position in industry	Sense of self-fulfillment
Organizational stability	Happiness
Opportunity for training and development	Education
Work location is nearby	Leisure/recreational activities

Figure 1–1 The Special Events Personal/Professional Goal Balance

attention, and spirit. As entrepreneurs will discover, the balance will heavily favor professional goals in the first years of any new business. It is difficult to achieve many, or perhaps any, of your personal goals during this start-up phase. During your personal audit of goals, it would be wise to consider how long you are willing to live with your life out of balance.

Enhance Your Chance

While you can not truly guarantee success, you can choose to greatly enhance your chances at achieving it. And, you have taken the first step by demonstrating that you want to achieve success in your chosen industry—special events—enough to invest in tools such as this book, or this course. If you are considering starting a new business, you have to beat some formidable odds. If 90 percent of all new businesses fail each year, you have to ensure that you have what it takes to be among the other 10 percent.

If your reaction to the last statement is that being in the other 10 percent is not good enough—rather, you want to be in the most profitable and successful 1 percent—you are exhibiting some of the most essential attributes of which successful entrepreneurs are made—drive and determination. Entrepreneurial employees, those who aggressively take the initiative to pursue opportunity on behalf of their employers, exhibit many similar characteristics. Their measures for success are slightly more complex. Their short-term goals involve achieving success for their employer, which benefits them financially and in the form of career advancement and salary growth in the long run.

Of course, sheer determination is hardly enough. You could be single-mindedly determined to be the best hockey player in the world, but if you cannot skate, shoot, and score, your chances for success are severely limited. You first need a base of knowledge, skill, and experience that will enable you to compete against the masters already established in your field, as well as an entire spectrum of characteristics that will help push you toward your goals. A candid self-assessment of these personal and professional attributes can help you evaluate your strengths and identify areas on which to concentrate for improvement.

The Event Manager Entrepreneur Assessment Tool (EMEAT) in Figure 1–2 was developed to help those wishing to launch a new event business or career evaluate those professional abilities and personal characteristics which define the successful event entrepreneur. EMEAT seeks to identify the presence of key entrepreneurial determinants through the scoring of responses to 25 questions. These determinants, as summarized in Figure 1–3 and discussed below, fall into four general categories: expertise (technical, experience, business, financial, marketing, planning); self-confidence (willingness to take risks, determination, independence, and decisiveness); self-discipline (adaptability, time management, focus, and proactivity); and leadership and motivational skills (salesmanship, persistence, and vision).

Technical Expertise

You may already possess the technical expertise to provide an outstanding product or service to your clients or employer. This book assumes that you either already have this expertise, or have a realistic plan on how to procure it from others established in the field.

Statement	A: Disagree Strongly	B: Disagree Somewhat	C: Neither Agree nor Disagree	D: Agree Somewhat	E: Agree Strongly	Point Value
1. I regard myself as being among the most expert in my field.						
2. I believe that others within my industry regard me as being among the best in my field.						
3. It is not common to find someone in my business with as much experience and expertise as I have.						
4. I successfully plan and manage my personal and business finances.						
5. I am able to create realistic, well-organized budgets.						
6. If I develop and maintain my client base, there is no compelling reason to actively pursue new clients.						
7. I consider myself to be an organized individual.						
8. I view failure as a learning experience.						
9. I would be prepared for the possibility that I could lose everything I invest in my business.						
10. I could not survive if I lost money in the first 3 to 5 years of my new business.						

Figure 1–2 The Event Management Entrepreneur Assessment Tool: A 25-point inventory of event entrepreneur traits and characteristics (*Continues on next page*)

Statement	A: Disagree Strongly	B: Disagree Somewhat	C: Neither Agree nor Disagree	D: Agree Somewhat	E: Agree Strongly	Point Value
11. I am driven to make my business succeed at all legal costs.						
12. I am willing to invest as much of my personal time as is necessary to ensure that my business succeeds.						
13. I prefer working in a business environment that I can control.						
14. If the details of running a business keep me from producing my product, or providing my service, I would rather work for someone else.						
15. I prefer not depending upon others to provide direction or support.						
16. I find it easy to make decisions and follow through on them.						
17. I take pride in being able to provide new and innovative solutions to my business challenges.						
18. I am able to detect changes in the business environment and can adapt to these changes by adjusting my business or marketing plans.						
19. Even when there is more work than can possibly be completed in a day, I budget my time to maximize my productivity every day.						
20. I find it easy to get sidetracked by activities that do not help me directly manage, market, or execute my business.						

21. I am always looking for a new opportunity, and when I find them, I "go for it."

22. I regard myself as one who can motivate people to do their best.

23. I find it easy to establish a rapport with a potential client, and can motivate them to trust me.

24. I am not deterred when I do not get a potential piece of business, rather I continually attempt to find ways to meet the client's future needs.

25. I know what I want my new business to be, and I can communicate my vision to my partners, employees, vendors, and clients.

Point Values

For Questions 1–5, 7, 8, 9, 11–13, 15–19, 21–25   (A) 0 points, (B) 1 point, (C) 2 points, (D) 3 points, (E) 4 points

For Questions 6, 10, 14, 20   (A) 4 points, (B) 3 points, (C) 2 points, (D) 1 point, (E) 0 points

Scoring

If you scored 85 or above, you are a strong candidate for success as an entrepreneur in the highly competitive special events industry.

If you scored 65–85, you should collaborate with partners whose talents and personality traits complement your own.

If you scored 65 or lower, there is a need to better develop your entrepreneurial outlook and skills.

Figure 1–2   Continued

1. **Expertise**
   - Technical
   - Experience
   - Business (Financial, Marketing, Operations)
2. **Self-Confidence**
   - Willingness to Take Risks
   - Determination
   - Independence
   - Decisiveness
3. **Self-Discipline**
   - Adaptability
   - Time Management
   - Focus
   - Proactivity
4. **Leadership and Motivational Skills**
   - Salesmanship
   - Persistence
   - Vision

Figure 1–3   Key Traits and Characteristics of the Successful Events Entrepreneur

As you will discover, successfully marketing yourself to potential clients or employers will involve convincing your prospects that you possess a higher level of expertise (or can offer better value) than your competitors. You will, therefore, repeatedly be called upon to demonstrate your expertise, and to execute your duties as a supplier to standards sufficiently high to ensure repeat business. Perhaps the easiest way to demonstrate a level of expertise is to point to the experience you have gained in the execution of projects in the past. Much like the well-composed resume you would prepare for any prospective employer, your experience will count for much in the sales process.

Most large companies started out with either a single or small group of entrepreneurs who combined their professional abilities and experiences with good business practices to grow their companies into the forces they are today. From Blockbuster's Wayne Huizenga to McDonald's Ray Kroc, these stories are well documented outside of

A Special Events Pioneer

Jack Morton, the son of a North Carolina sharecropper, began a 60-year career in the entertainment business at the age of 12, working in a small silent movie theater taking tickets, changing rolls for the player piano, and posting bills. But Jack was first bitten by the "entrepreneurial bug" a year earlier while selling soft drinks and candy on commission at a minor league ballpark. By age 18, Jack gained his first experience as a manager, overseeing operations for an 850-seat silent movie theater at about the time that "talkies" first appeared. His compensation at the *Carolina* included a percentage of sales over the theater's breakeven point. To maximize his commission and compete against theaters already showing sound films, Jack hired neighborhood kids to create behind-the-screen sound effects to accompany the feature.

A few years later, Jack Morton was booking bands for dances held in hotel ballrooms across Washington, D.C. Seeing an opportunity to build upon his experience and increase his cut of the profits, he began promoting his own dances. As his reputation grew, musicians sought him out for bookings, and hotels looked to him to fill dates for their ballrooms. Jack Morton Enterprises—now Jack Morton Productions—continued to build on experiences and expertise to grow its business.

After World War II, trade associations and corporations began to discover the value in staging conventions and large business meetings. Reading the trend, Jack was able to combine his expertise in working with the hotel and music industries to pioneer the new entertainment form of corporate events. The company has since used the same strategy to continue building its sales and client base, moving into audio-visual and new media to keep pace with market demand. Although marketing Jack Morton Productions is a never-ending process, success through 60 years of expertise and experience helps to perpetuate the company's leadership position in the field.

the events business. While less known to the average person, stories like these abound in the events business as well.

As the special events industry continues to mature, the number of highly skilled professionals working in the business increases every year. "This field is made up of hundreds of technical geniuses, who so often lack the practical know-how in business and entertainment," observes Morton. "It is a field that requires not only technical skill, but good business sense and a lot of creativity." We couldn't agree more, Jack.

Business Expertise

Business expertise can be separated into several key components. In no particular order, they include: finance, marketing, operations management, human resources, and strategic planning. Richard Stevenson, in *Fundamentals of Finance,* defines finance as "the means by which funds are obtained and the methods by which these funds are managed and allocated." An understanding of bookkeeping, budgeting, capitalization, payroll, and taxes, among others, is an essential underpinning to founding and maintaining a business. Many of these issues will be examined in Chapter 5.

Marketing (Chapter 8) is often confused with one of its component parts—sales. While sales are essential to the survival of a business, it is an understanding of underlying marketing principles, that is, identifying and delivering a solution to a client's wants and needs, that closes the sale. Advertising, publicity, promotion, and direct sales are all parts of the marketing process, the integration of which will comprise the essence of your marketing plan. An understanding of how they work together to bring you and your clients together is essential to any successful entrepreneurial effort.

Operations management addresses the ability to set up systems to design, manufacture, and/or deliver your product or service to your clients. Questions you will need to consider may include:

- Will you need to manage your clients' projects in a linear fashion (one project at a time taken from conception to completion), or will you have to manage many projects in various stages of development simultaneously? If so, how will you manage these projects to ensure on-time and on-budget delivery of your product or service?

- Will you maintain a large inventory of equipment or supplies, or will you source what is required on an as-needed basis?

- What length of turnaround time can your customers expect between the time they place their order and when your products reach their destination?

The systems required for each type of events business will differ, but each process must be dissected and analyzed in their component parts to effectively plan how you will run your business.

An understanding of human resources (Chapter 9) is also among the essential business expertises one must bring to a new business. Human resources issues can be examined on two levels: the technical (e.g., hiring and firing practices, payroll and benefits programs, lawful employment practices), and the personal (e.g., team building, motivation, leadership, employee retention). Special events is often described as a "people business"; therefore, knowing how to motivate clients, co-workers, and suppliers to their highest potential is an essential part of expanding your career.

Planning Reduces the Risk of a Risky Business

Webster's New World Dictionary defines an "entrepreneur" as "a person who organizes and manages a business undertaking, assuming the risk for the sake of the profit." As previously mentioned, if you are a true entrepreneur, you will never be completely satisfied with whatever measure of success you do achieve. The standard you set for success will always move a little farther away every time you approach it. Just like a successful commissioned salesperson who has their sales quota raised each time they achieve it, you will always elevate your expectations of yourself.

If you are entering the market as a first-time independent, you should be realistic in those expectations. It is difficult to achieve success on the sole basis of a great track record or a good idea. While it is the essence of the entrepreneurial spirit to take risks, it is essential that you increase the odds in your favor by spending the time required to consider all aspects of your new endeavor with your eyes wide open. The questions are many and varied—from how you will generate sufficient capital to sustain your new business to how you will compete with established suppliers, from how you will manage your business administratively to how much you will charge for what product or service. Considering and codifying all of these, and other important issues, is the process of building a business plan.

"Lack of capital is the primary reason that new businesses fail," says Rieva Lesonsky, editorial director of *Entrepreneur* Magazine. "And, the reason a new business usually finds itself without capital is due to poor planning. New entrepreneurs are used to coming from larger companies with support systems behind them, systems they take for granted. They don't consider what's needed before they get into it, right down to buying pencils and paying for electricity. They know what they know, but they don't know what it takes to run a business."

Lesonsky stresses the need for creating a thorough and realistic business plan to avoid the perils and pitfalls of starting a new business *before* committing to getting started in the first place. If you have never created a business plan before, there are many new tools available to help you. You are holding the first such tool in your hands right now. This book is filled with the answers to the specialized questions to be asked for start-ups in the special events industry, along with a business plan outline in the Appendix. While this book also endeavors to analyze the "macro" questions common to every business plan regardless of industry, there are excellent additional resources worth investigating to help you create the kind of professional business plan required for review by lenders, investors, and even some clients.

If your business experience is limited, a computer-assisted plan is highly recommended. One such recommended resource is Palo Alto Software's *Business Plan Pro,* available from *Inc. Magazine. Business Plan Pro* takes you through both the philosophies and the technical aspects of writing a professional plan, and is accompanied by an outstanding, easy-to-understand 200-page guide to the successful development and implementation of a simple business plan preceding the actual software guide. Step-by-step on-screen instructions ensure the creation of a business plan suitable for presentation to investors, partners, and key staff. Those equipped with Lotus Smart Suite on their personal computers can also find a business plan template in Lotus Freelance Graphics, an ideal graphics package for those not requiring as basic a starting point in the construction of a business plan. On the other end of the spectrum, for those with little experience and who are uncomfortable with computers, IDG Publishing offers *Business Plans for Dummies,* available at most bookstores.

Since even a computer-assisted business plan is only as good as the information you provide and the assumptions you make, how do you know that your assumptions are realistic? First, if you are expecting profits, particularly spectacular profits, in the first 12 to 18 months, it is unlikely that you have a realistic business plan. Reality checks are essential. Don't be afraid to reach out for professional help, because the time and money you spend now in pursuit of realistic expectations can save you thousands of dollars and months of futility. If your segment of the industry has a trade organization, arrange a personal or telephone meeting with its director. Find out what the industry norms are for return-on-investment, the state of the industry, and competitive pressure (you may even find out where you can get professional help in starting your new endeavor). Another good resource is SCORE—the Service Corps of Retired Executives. While it is likely that its members can not be of significant service to the specifics of your business, they can help you to understand many of the general business issues that may be eluding you.

Finally, if you are starting a business, it is likely that you have retained an attorney to help you organize the legal, regulatory, and tax implications of your business (if you have not, run—do not walk—to your attorney's office to do so). Most attorneys charge on an hourly basis, so get an estimate on what it would cost you to have them review your business plan with an eye toward its value to financiers or investors. If your attorney has been involved in a number of start-ups, he or she can probably point out weaknesses in your plan or assumptions. A corporate accountant can also help in this regard.

Achieving success should be a cornerstone of your strategic business plan. Remember that you should consider success on two levels—the corporate and the personal. What you may consider successful for your company may not square with your concept of personal fulfillment. Your corporate goal might be attaining a certain level of sales, perhaps $250,000 in your first year, perhaps $350,000 in your second.[1] Your goal might be expressed in terms of market share—the achievement of 1 percent, 10 percent, or 20 percent share of market in your segment of the industry after some length of time. Your sales goal might well be coupled with a net income goal, that is, what would be left in the till after deducting all expenses and write-offs. And, your financial goals might be combined with more altruistic milestones—perhaps the ability to contribute to the community, attaining a certain level of respect from peers within your field, or retaining high-profile clients.

"People build this up to be mysterious and out of reach. If you attack it in small steps, it is both reachable *and* understandable," says Rieva Lesonsky. "It's like trying to lose 60 pounds. It sounds like a difficult task, but start out by trying to lose 20 pounds, then another 20

---

[1]Note: The median gross earnings for special events businesses in 1996 was $750,000, according to a survey conducted by The George Washington University Event Management Program for the International Special Events Society.

pounds, and then another 20. That's how you attack a business plan, one piece at a time."

Willingness to Take on Risk—No Guts, No Glory

As previously mentioned, the essence of the entrepreneurial spirit is the willingness to assume risk. The classical entrepreneur puts his or her own money and reputation squarely on the line in the pursuit of establishing and nurturing a new business. While entrepreneurial employees risk their employers' money, there is no lesser risk to their own reputations. After all, there is real risk to one's career if one gambles with their employer's funds and loses.

Pick up any business or special events trade publication, and success stories abound because people talk loudly about successes and shy away from relating their failures. Because no one wants to be thought of as a failure, it is rare to read about that majority of businesses that did not succeed and why. There are certainly far more failures than successes, and many more slow, steady corporate performers than meteoric rises and explosive, sudden success stories. As David James, of Panther Management Group, a multi-faceted event and entertainment company in Vancouver, British Columbia points out, "the year Babe Ruth set a record for home runs, he also set a record for strike-outs. He was willing to fail more than anyone else was. If you want to increase your level of success by 10%, you need to be willing to increase your rate of failure by 1000%."

"Most people would rather read about—and learn from—the folks who made it instead of the wannabes," writes Rieva Lesonsky in *Entrepreneur* Magazine. "This, however, is a disservice, since I truly believe that all of us can learn from failure." As failure provides us with perhaps the best remembered of lessons, there is great wisdom in this point of view. While no one sets out with the goal to fail in order to achieve such wisdom, don't be afraid to fail. You should be prepared to take your lessons from whatever failures you endure and move on. But don't be afraid to target success, either.

Willingness to take on risk should not be confused with recklessness. Strictly speaking, betting your retirement savings on a single spin of a roulette wheel is a willingness to take on risk, but it is hardly entrepreneurial. Entrepreneurs believe in their ability to succeed and take the proper steps to increase their chances of a payoff. Taking on a manageable level of risk is more prudent than investing your last dollar in a business that still has a significant chance to fail. Leaving

yourself enough personal capital to recover from a total financial disaster is a wise move for an entrepreneur. For then, even if you do fail,
you will at least have the option of beginning anew.

Getting Personal

As previously discussed, it is wise to assess your personal goals while
writing your first business plan or considering a career move. What
are the limits, if any, to which you are willing to sacrifice to ensure
that you meet your corporate goals? How many hours are you willing to work? For how long? How much personal income will you
require in your first few years when it is likely that you will be supporting your business more than your own family? What will you
need to keep in personal savings to ensure that a business failure does
not become a complete financial disaster for you and your loved ones?

This is an area where real self-examination is of significant
importance. If you have a family, it is essential that you involve your
spouse and/or children in the evaluation process. It is probable that
the first 3 to 5 years of your new business or career will require you
to spend significantly more time away from home. While considering
their opinions, be sure you will have their continuing support as you
pursue your professional goals. Without the support of your loved
ones, the road you will travel will seem lonely indeed. And success, if
achieved, will not seem very fulfilling without them there to help
you enjoy it.

Personal happiness at the office is also critically important. Of
course, no one is always happy at every minute of every working day.
In fact, during the formative years of a start-up business, happiness
may be generally elusive and sacrifice the general rule. Feeling the
pressures of running a business is normal, but if you are unable to
derive some happiness from your daily pursuits, you may be in the
wrong business or job.

Independence—A Splash of Cold Water

One of the qualities on which many corporations evaluate their employees is "initiative," the quality of looking ahead to new businesses,
new methodologies, and new challenges. In an entrepreneur, this
same quality is called "independence." Not only do entrepreneurs

have to constantly look for new opportunities, they have to stand on their own two feet.

Most people relish the thought of being independent. If you have previously worked for a corporation, and you strike out on your own, be prepared to be overwhelmed with details you never before considered. Corporations provide support functions that many managers take for granted, from the purchasing of office supplies, to the provision of equipment such as copiers, fax machines, and computers, to accounting and bookkeeping services, tax preparation, legal services, telephone coverage, reception, mail, and freight handling. All of those "automatic" and seemingly mundane corporate functions that once took no more than a quick phone call suddenly become your problems to resolve. And, when you do, it will inevitably steal valuable time from your more productive, revenue-generating activities, namely marketing, sales, creative development, and production.

The desire to be independent, however, is what gets most businesses started. After working as freelancers for several years, the three partners that founded Panther Management Group in Vancouver, British Columbia saw that the fruits of their labor were enriching their employers, and not necessarily themselves. As a result, they were encouraged to strike out on their own by both their clients and suppliers. David James recalls the initial euphoria and the slow dawning of reality: "This is perfect, we thought. All we do is set up a company. We take our services, sell them to our clients, and we'll be rich and famous. Suddenly, and for the next three years, we learned the realities of what it really takes, and all those little problems and accountabilities that come in."

What the three partners discovered is that independence does not necessarily mean going it alone. With each providing their own area of expertise and unique inventory of personality traits, Panther's principals provide a mutual support system for one another. One partner is stronger in financial matters, another in marketing, and a third in production. (Collectively, they would score higher on the Event Management Entrepreneurial Assessment Tool than they would individually.) Apart from the strength of a broad base of expertise, the partners offer one another psychological support, as well. There are those inevitable "bad days" when, after working 80 hours a week for months on end, one or the other loses his ability to see the forest for the trees, and understandably forgets why they stepped away from a corporate culture to establish an entrepreneurial business. Partners become a support mechanism, helping their colleagues recover their perspective, and setting them back on the rails toward their mutual goals.

Determination

Using practical knowledge born of experience and/or training as your guide, and with your eyes fully open to the risks involved in starting a new business, you have to maintain the hunger to keep moving toward the achievement of your goals. With this perspective, obstacles are no longer sheer cliffs that are impossible to scale, but trails that can be negotiated over time. There is more than one way to the top, some sloping slowly and gently over surer ground, others that climb more quickly and steeply at the expense of looser footing. There are side trails; some of them are even more difficult to navigate, some which lead to a sudden precipice, others that are dead ends.

Sometimes the trail you ultimately select is a matter of personal choice and style. Other times, the choice is made for you by the economics of your business. Regardless, an underpinning of dogged determination is the common denominator. Choose your path to success, and let no challenge—large or small—keep you from reaching the top.

Decisiveness

After all the time spent researching, planning, and evaluating, you have to *do* something! These first three activities will help you maximize profitability, but by themselves they will not generate revenues. Action without planning is foolhardy; planning without action is wasted effort.

One of the maxims of event planning is "make the plan, then execute the plan." In the special events industry, there may be millions of details involved in providing your product or service to your clients, but there are millions more involved in running your company profitably. The successful entrepreneur has to act quickly and decisively in order to handle the enormous workload of running a business. Quickly does not mean arbitrarily. It is more important to make a slower, more deliberate right decision than a quick wrong one, and to do so, anything more than a simple decision must be made after an evaluation of the issues. But, don't wait too long to act lest opportunities be capitalized upon by your competitors. And, once

An Empire in the Making

Jaclyn Bernstein was determined to make it in the special events business. President of her class for four years at the State University of New York at Albany, Jaclyn caught her events bug while serving as the sole student representative on the search committee for a new dean of the university's school of business. She observed that all of the details of one committee meeting at a New York City office building—from the room setup to audio-visual support to catering—were all being handled by a woman to whom she mused: "You know, I think this is what I want to do."

Jaclyn sought counseling from the University's career development office, which at the time had no practical advice for entry into the field. Affable and gregarious by nature, she determined to meet everyone, and learn everything, she could about the events industry. Ultimately, Jaclyn succeeded in arranging numerous courtesy interviews through family, friends, and acquaintances, and arranged to receive back copies of various industry publications from one interviewer. Perhaps hundreds of introductory calls, then resumes, and follow-up calls later, Jaclyn made contact with Pamela Tudor, the owner/president of Tours de Force Events, a New York-based destination management company. The initial conversation between Jaclyn and her future employer did not materialize into a position at first, so her job search continued. In the interim, she attended industry functions such as a Meeting Professionals International (MPI) Greater New York chapter meeting and the first meeting of the fledgling International Special Events Society (ISES) in 1987. The 22-year old Jaclyn, a natural networker, met dozens of leaders in the special events profession who would later figure prominently in the development of her career, and who one day would look to Jaclyn as an industry leader herself. She made it a point to introduce herself to the principal of Tours de Force Events, to whom she had spoken on the telephone weeks earlier. At that first ISES event, she also met her future business partner, Robert W. Hulsmeyer, at that time owner of his own company, Snow H Productions. With Jaclyn constantly popping up at important industry functions, Ms. Tudor was apparently intrigued, offering her an opportunity to interview, and eventually a position.

That Tours de Force Events occupied a small one-room office with a total staff of three did not deter Jaclyn. Neither was she dis-

(Continues)

couraged when offered a position on an unusual "trial basis," without compensation for 30 days (after which she was reimbursed for one-half of that period). Jaclyn viewed this period as her own personal "investment" in her career. Over time, her entrepreneurial spirit helped to increase the company's image and business by offering better, and more personalized, service to their new and existing clients. While Jaclyn's experience and level of responsibility within the company expanded steadily over the next five years, her modest salary barely kept up with inflation. To skeptical family and friends, she explained: "I am not working at a job. I am investing in my career!"

In 1992, when Tudor mentioned that she was considering selling the company, Jaclyn determined to realize her dream. She and her trusted friend and ISES colleague, Robert Hulsmeyer, had already been exploring business opportunities together, so the company appeared to be just such a possibility. But business had taken a downturn. During the turbulent 18 months of negotiations to buy the business, Jaclyn was told she could no longer be paid to work at Tours de Force Events due to insufficient revenues. Nevertheless, she remained at the office as long as possible, servicing clients and attempting to expand the business she wanted to buy.

Jaclyn kept her pager active, and continued to keep appearing at industry functions, convinced that her time to acquire the company was right and close at hand. Robert transitioned his own career into event production, but Jaclyn was without meaningful income for more than a year. Finally in 1994, seven years after joining the company, Jaclyn and Robert purchased the business assets of Tours de Force Events, and became Empire Force Events, a destination management and event production company. Now, the challenge of expanding the business would begin.

In the last half of 1994, Jaclyn and Robert worked around the clock to re-establish the company, and wrote more business in their second year than had been realized by the firm in any of the previous twelve. Three years later, their sales reached a level of five times the gross of Tours de Force's last year of operations. Today they are determined to pursue a strategy for growing the business based on leveraging the relationships with existing clients to capture more of the revenues spent by those companies. "We don't want to just create relationships with a lot of different people," says Rob. "We want long-lasting relationships with the great companies with whom we do business."

the decision is made, move on, with an occasional glance in the rearview mirror to ensure that it was made correctly.

Decisiveness does more than match challenges and problems with solutions. It also instills in your employees a sense of trust in your leadership ability. A vacillating manager is a difficult leader to follow. When employees can count on the staying power of an upper-level decision, they understand their marching orders and can better do their jobs.

Adaptability

A third, often-overlooked postscript to the "make the plan, execute the plan" maxim is "adjust the plan." The companies that succeed are those that can adapt to the ever-changing economic and technological environments. In 1859, Charles Darwin's landmark scientific text *On the Origin of Species* first suggested that living organisms must have the ability to adapt to changing environmental conditions in order to avoid extinction. Darwin called this basic underpinning of modern evolutionary theory "natural selection," most often described as "survival of the fittest." Throughout the history of life of Earth, species evolved, flourished, and eventually diminished to extinction as environmental conditions shifted, or competition increased due to the introduction of more successful species dependent upon the same food supply.

Darwin's theory of natural selection as applied to biology operates over great spans of time. In the business world, the same theories operate with far greater rapidity. As technology (the environment) advances and competition dependent upon the same food supply (the dollars available in the marketplace) grows, some businesses grow and flourish, and others proceed directly to extinction. A detailed and thoughtful analysis of the competitive environment is a cornerstone of any sound business plan. However, because new technologies and new competitive pressures are difficult to anticipate, the need to adapt is a daily evaluation.

If your business is technologically based, it would be wise to reserve capital for your second or third year to upgrade the technologies that will keep you competitive and on the cutting edge. For example, if you are starting an audio-visual company, you will acquire various pieces of sound, video, and lighting equipment that you will rent to clients. Today, you would probably look to purchase standard and often-required video technologies that would include laserdisk recorders, betacam tape players, television monitors, and rear screen projectors. In a few years, after digital television is more readily available, many of your clients will own equipment in their homes more advanced than the inventory on which you now depend for your livelihood. You will need to stock new, high-definition monitors side-by-side with your current inventory while the technological transition takes place. You will need new playback equipment, new projection equipment, even new, wider format screens to replace the nearly square current-day standard. If your business plan does not anticipate setting aside sufficient capital to replace your current inventory a year or two down the road, you will most certainly find yourself competing against those who did, and as a result can offer more advanced solutions to your soon-to-be former clients' problems.

Effective Time Management

A graduate professor of marketing once gave his students three weeks to "create" a product and complete a marketing plan suitable for presentation to a fictitious executive committee. After the presentations were given and graded, the professor asked for student feedback. "There wasn't nearly enough time to do as good a job as we wanted to on this project," one student remarked. "Precisely," replied the professor. "But, that's the way the world works."

If you have ever worked on an event, you know that perfection is elusive. There is never enough time to do everything as thoroughly as you want to on any project. Running a special events business, either as an entrepreneur or an entrepreneurial employee, increases the competition of details upon your time. Managing the business will mean there is even less time available to do everything you want to service your clients, market to new prospects, and maximize your profitability.

Special events professionals have to exercise effective time management just to complete their projects on time. Special events entrepreneurs have to raise time management to an art form to juggle the demands of their business with the demands of their individual projects.

The special events department in the example below survived because there was a much larger organization supporting it, one which derived more than 90 percent of its gross revenues from sources other than outside special events. The all-too-common marketing/production seesaw can be fatal to smaller special events firms dependent

The Marketing/Production Seesaw

In 1985, New York-based Radio City Music Hall Productions (now Radio City Productions) was determined to enter the special events business by devoting a full-time staff of three to the marketing of the company's capabilities outside the world-renowned theater, as well as the production of those projects. Although a small number of event productions were mounted through 1986, these first 18 months were primarily devoted to sales. The concentration on marketing paid off, as the next 12 months would establish Radio City as a major force in the events industry. During that time, the company would add Polaroid's 50th Anniversary Celebration, the Pre-Liturgy festivities for Pope John Paul's Visit to Los Angeles, the We the People Parade (the national celebration of the bicentennial of the U.S. Constitution), and the Super Bowl XXII Halftime Show to its base of prestigious productions. During that period, the special events department was so consumed by the production of these enormous events that little time was devoted to marketing the company's capabilities going forward. As a result, 1988 was a leaner year, with the staff scrambling to sell enough business to regain the company's momentum in the industry. With the staff now single-mindedly concentrating on marketing, 1989 would be another banner year, with five cruise ship introduction events for Royal Viking Line, the ITT Worldwide Management Conference, the 200th Anniversary of George Washington's Inauguration, and the Wall Street Journal Centennial, among others.

upon event work for all or the majority of its revenues. Effective time management techniques could have helped to ensure that some amount of time would be devoted to marketing during the entire year, evening out the peaks and valleys of production activity.

Focus

The focused manager screens out those activities that steal valuable time and concentration from the attainment of their company's goals and objectives. Most college students who have studied for exams would agree that getting sidetracked from the pursuit of an "A" grade on a test or paper is very easy. There are so many academic diversions (apart from the purely social) that it is simple to lose focus. Concentration on the issues at hand is an acquired discipline, one on which your entire financial future might depend once you have gone into business for yourself.

Given that special events are a creative industry and that adaptability is a key component to success, there would appear to be a battle between focus and creativity. After all, creativity and vision are processes that require an unfocused, unfettered imagination. While true, events professionals usually apply their creativity to provide a solution to their client's well-defined objectives. It is essential that they also apply their creativity, vision, and adaptability to provide a

 ## A Mega-Shake-Out

There was probably never an enormous market for mega-event companies. In the 1980s and early 1990s, companies of varying size and specialty competed for a relatively small number of plum, large-budget and highly visible events against a small number of companies specializing in the production of mega-events (i.e., events with budgets of $250,000+). The advantages of pursuing mega-events are obvious—great exposure, prestige, and profits. With bottom-line contributions of 15–30 percent, a single $1 million budget mega-event can sustain a small company with low to moderate overhead for a year or more. For larger production companies, and those with greater overhead expenses, the appetite for mega-event budgets is insatiable. Like *tyrannosaurs*, they would have to consume a large number of large-fee events to survive. During this period, corporate spending on meetings and incentives were at a peak and sponsors parted with marketing dollars less discriminately for major statewide, national, and international celebrations. In the early 1990s, the environment changed in the wake of international economic upheaval. As a result, corporations tightened their internal spending as well as their sponsorship policies. Some of those *tyrannosaurs*, those that adapted in a focused and controlled fashion, still function today. But, those mega-event concerns that attempted to adapt in a haphazard, unfocused way have gone the way of the dinosaur.

(Continues)

One mega-event production specialist founded in 1989 successfully captured a sizable share of the already shrinking mega-event market during its first two years, but it was already apparent that expansion of their core business would be essential to their survival. Rather than selecting and concentrating on one or two related areas for growth, the company viewed every corporate dollar as a potential opportunity. Heedless of whether the company could compete against more established firms in every other event specialty, the partners spent significant money pursuing projects for which it was qualified only by its reputation, and not necessarily by its expertise. With a staff of seven full-time employees, and two devoted exclusively to marketing, the company attempted entry in the sponsorship sales business, the television production business, the incentive travel business, the business meeting and communications business, all while attempting to maintain its core business of producing mega-events. In each of these new service categories, the company found itself competing with well-established, better-qualified competitors, and was unsuccessful in convincing new clients that a mega-events company could service their business as well as their current vendors. Had the company focused on one or two new opportunity areas in which they could leverage their mega-event expertise to build a reputation, it might not have ceased operations entirely six years after its founding.

solution to their own problems—the pursuit of success for their business or department.

Focusing on your core business does not mean abandoning your ability to adapt to changing business conditions or miscalculated business plans. Focus keeps you from growing in too many directions at once, spreading yourself too thin, and rapidly depleting your resources.

Proactivity

There are two different kinds of management styles—reactive and proactive. The reactive manager solves problems as they present themselves, and provides their company with service as and when expected or requested. The reactive manager may be extremely creative, but that creativity is applied only when a problem or project is presented to them.

The proactive manager anticipates problems, recommends solutions, and suggests courses of action before problems or challenges present themselves. Proactive managers exhibit an entrepreneurial spirit, looking for opportunities to benefit their companies, and by extension, themselves. Unfortunately, while many managers strive for proactivity, their heavy workload does not always allow them the creative time or space to identify new opportunities and present a reasoned strategy to management, partners, or investors to seize those opportunities.

But, the world moves too fast for business-as-usual. A business will take on either a proactive or a reactive persona, often based upon the personal style of its owner, partners, or chief executive. A reactive

Selling Solutions

When the National Hockey League's special events department surveyed the city of Vancouver, British Columbia, for the 1998 NHL All-Star Weekend, it came up dry in finding a suitable site for a large post-game party. In previous years, the NHL had to source unorthodox venues to accommodate the same event, from the hangar deck of an aircraft carrier in Boston to a pre–World War II blimp hangar outside of San Jose. With all of Vancouver's traditional event venues occupied by other groups, the special events department scoured the city, surveying museums, underground arcades, shopping centers, ferries, even airplane maintenance facilities, but nothing usable could be found.

Word of the NHL's search reached Panther Management Group, a local destination management company. Deborah Nielsen, Panther Management Group's director of marketing, contacted the NHL not to sell their services, but to offer her assistance in finding a venue. Within a week, Panther Management Group had not only located a venue—a cruise ship terminal freight storage facility in use only during the summer—but had also surveyed the building, created floorplans, estimated the costs of constructing temporary weatherizing material and installing heating, and enlisted the partnership of the Vancouver Port Corporation in pursuit of the NHL's business. In return for their proactive, to this point uncompensated assistance in locating a suitable venue, the NHL awarded Panther Management Group a contract to provide production and logistical services for the event.

business spends most of its time responding to the environment. They often find themselves in a perpetual state of crisis management because they do not anticipate challenges. They search for solutions once confronted with them head-on. By contrast, proactive businesses are on the constant lookout for new opportunities, and are on full alert for potential crises at all times. Proactivity suggests, but is not synonymous with, aggressive marketing. Searching out new opportunities and aggressively pursuing sales are certainly proactive pursuits. But, proactive managers also work hard to pre-empt potential crises through thorough planning and having their fingers on the pulse of the marketplace.

Leadership

Another key trait of a successful event entrepreneur is leadership, the ability to inspire and motivate your permanent, freelance, or volunteer staff to greater achievement. More than 2,000 years ago, Chinese warrior Sun Tzu defined leadership as "a matter of intelligence, trustworthiness, humanness, courage, and sternness." To put it in more modern terms, leaders know what they are doing, can be taken at their word, care about their people and clients, are unafraid of the unknown or taking risks, and can make the tough decision. National Restaurant Association former president Herman Cain, a more contemporary student of leadership principles, echoes Sun Tzu's observations with twenty-first-century sensitivity. In his book *Leadership Is Common Sense,* Cain agrees with the notion of leadership as a series of principles and characteristics rather than a single trait, a combination of determination, ambition, self-control, forward thinking, imagination, independence, intelligence, and honesty, among others. Interestingly, these are many of the same traits that define the successful entrepreneur. Therefore, one can surmise that the better a leader, the more likely that an entrepreneur will succeed.

Leaders must have someone to lead in order to be successful. In the 1967 Robert Aldrich film *The Dirty Dozen,* actor Lee Marvin trains and leads a group of convicts to victory against an impregnable enemy stronghold. While it is a great moral lesson that just about anyone can achieve greatness if led along the proper path, it is the stuff of Hollywood and not the reality of the business world, particularly not for small business owners and start-up enterprises. It is essential that you surround yourself with the right people to reach your goals (see Chapter 9). Once you have gathered your hand-selected team, be they full-time, part-time, or project-specific, it is your job to motivate, inspire, and direct them toward the achievement of your goals and/or the completion of your project.

Filling out your company with the right people starts with a candid assessment of your own strengths and weaknesses. The success of your entrepreneurial company is a direct reflection of your own entrepreneurial characteristics, as well as those of your employees. Create your own job description, and determine your ability to fill the job you have created for yourself. Characteristics in which you feel you are weak are those that you should seek out in others.

Salesmanship

In its most common application, salesmanship is the ability to communicate to a client that you understand their problem, you have a solution, and that they should invest their time and money in you to deliver the solution to their problem. At its most basic level, salesmanship is closely akin to leadership, that is, inspiring and motivating people who are not your employees to respond in a way that is advantageous to the growth of your company—to wit, selecting your product, or referring you to others. No matter how big your company gets, the best CEOs are great salespeople. Your sales force will do the groundwork to generate and qualify leads, but you, as the leader of the concern, must be the ultimate closer. A review of great special events sales techniques can be found in Chapter 8.

Persistence

To one of entrepreneurial spirit, the word "no" is rarely final. It only means "no for now." Persistence is not stubbornness. Stubbornness is steadfastly sticking to a position whether it is right or wrong. Persistence is the knowledge that your position is right, and that it is a matter of more effective communication, positioning, and the application of other entrepreneurial traits and characteristics that will influence a potential client, lender, or other target entity to respond as desired. Neither is persistence the quality of being annoying. Like many good things, persistence can be dangerous in too great a dosage. Calling a potential client every day builds no bridges—it's just off-putting. But, calling a potential client periodically with important insights and information that can influence future decisions or with invitations to other events you are working on can be helpful in measured quantities.

Persistence can change your profile to potential clients from "out of sight, out of mind" to "being in the right place at the right time." Even after losing a piece of business to a competitor, it is the quality of persistence that will position you at the head of the line of alternative suppliers for future projects. Coming in second is not necessarily defeat; it is a springboard for future opportunity. Finding out why you did not come in first may improve your odds the next time around. With proper positioning, the payoff can even come sooner rather than later.

Vision

Having a vision for your company is more than just setting goals. It is looking beyond the goals as set forth in your business plan, and visualizing what and where you want you and your company to be. In its simplest form, vision can be thought of as long-range strategic planning, beyond the horizon of your five-year plan. To many, the future is hazy and indistinct, but entrepreneurs with vision see themselves and their businesses five, ten, even twenty years into the unknown. Being able to articulate that vision to your partners, employees, and investors is a sign of leadership. Those who invest money or their careers with a visionary leader share the dream because they are as convinced that the future of that company holds amazing promise.

But, I'm Not An Entrepreneur! (What About Me?)

As previously mentioned, if you work in the special events department of a corporation, you are, by the strictest definition, not an entrepreneur. If you are fortunate, you work for a company that allows you to take risks within either explicitly or implicitly defined parameters. And, if you take advantage of that ability, and aggressively pursue goals—which accrue to the greater benefit of your employer—you show great entrepreneurial spirit. In recent years, a buzzword has entered the business lexicon (although it is not yet an annotated word in the *Webster's Dictionary*) to describe such a manager. The word "intrepreneur" has been used to describe corporate managers who exhibit entrepreneurial characteristics as they pursue the objectives of their employer. For the purposes of this book, however, we prefer to refer to corporate risk-takers as "entrepreneurial employees."

Entrepreneurial managers and employees may be risk-takers, but they are risking their employers' money. By extension, they are also risking their jobs and careers. In most cases, the more you can demonstrate an entrepreneurial spirit to your employer, the faster and farther your career and influence within a corporation will grow.

Because your company's competition is constantly snapping at your heels, you will feel increasing pressure to do something to maintain your company's reputation as a special events client, organizer, producer, or supplier. It is wise to begin much as an entrepreneur would—creating a business plan for your department, identifying your corporate and departmental goals, and organizing the proper human resources to get the job done.

If you are already an events professional working within a corporate structure, and you review the Key Traits and Characteristics of the Successful Event Entrepreneur, you will discover that many of these qualities are what landed you your job in the first place. As special events disciplines are highly creative, it is not surprising that an entrepreneurial spirit is a common trait amongst most events professionals.

The View From Here

1. It is important to evaluate your personal definition of success. Five common "success indicators" include: doing what you want to do, achieving the lifestyle you want, achieving a satisfying level of compensation, personal and professional development, and self-actualization and validation.

2. The process of attaining success begins and ends with the setting of goals and the achievement of those goals. The blueprint you will use to set and attain your professional goals is a business plan. It is wise to consider both your personal and professional goals, and to strive to achieve a balance between the two.

3. Key traits and characteristics shared by both entrepreneurs and entrepreneurial employees include: expertise (technical, experience, business), self-confidence (willingness to take risks, deter-

mination, independence, decisiveness), self-discipline (adaptability, effective time management, focus, proactivity), and leadership and motivational skills (salesmanship, persistence, vision). Entrepreneurs and entrepreneurial employees risk their reputations and careers, but only entrepreneurs risk their own capital or indebtedness.

Tools of the Trade

Cain, Herman. *Leadership Is Common Sense*. New York: Van Nostrand Reinhold, 1997.

Covey, Stephen R. *The 7 Habits of Highly Effective People*. New York: Fireside, 1989.

Kushner, Harold S. *When All You've Ever Wanted Isn't Enough*. New York: Pocket Books, 1986.

Morton, Jack and William Fuchs. *The Jack Morton (Who's He?) Story*. New York: Vantage Press, 1985.

Sun Tzu. *The Art of War*. Trans. Thomas Cleary. Boston: Shambhala, 1991.

Breaking New Ground

1. How do you define success? Assess your difficulties in balancing your personal and professional life. How would you propose to resolve those difficulties over time?

2. Self-administer the Event Management Entrepreneur Assessment Tool, and tabulate your results. Do you have what it takes to be an entrepreneur now? What skill or attitudinal areas would you have to develop to better launch your career?

3. Create an objective job description for your current or desired job. In what areas are you less than ideally suited, and how would you make up for those deficiencies in the short and long term?

4. Videotape yourself presenting your company's capabilities to an imaginary committee of investors or clients. Do not review upon completion, but record a second, revised presentation after you have completed reading this book, then a third after creating your first business plan. What differences do you notice?

CHAPTER 2

Vision, Mission, Strategic Planning

Step Two: *Develop the vision, mission, and strategic plan for building and sustaining your special events career.*

A train without a track to guide its journey will not be able to progress very far. In fact, when a train is derailed, it ceases to operate. The process of developing a successful mission and vision for your event organization will help ensure that you are able to achieve or exceed your goals or objectives. And as Harold Geneen often invoked to his troops at ITT, "There is no substitute for performance"— ultimately one must perform. Successful completion of the goals and objectives you set is the final measure of your performance as an event entrepreneur or entrepreneurial employee. The mission and visioning statements are the first phase of a comprehensive business plan. The remainder of this book will help you flesh out the additional phases. However, in this chapter you will learn *why* the mission and visioning process is critical to long-term event business success, how to conduct this process to achieve a desirable strategic plan, and *when* to revise and renew your plan to produce an event organization that is malleable, flexible, and enduring.

Many event organizations begin through programming activities rather than planning. Local community events are perfect examples of this process. In many small communities, the local parade or festival was started by one or two individuals who later convinced first a handful of others and then many more of the excitement of developing an event project. Unfortunately, excitement rarely is sustainable and does not often contribute to long-term event success.

During programming, the stakeholders develop ideas instead of strategies. Although this may provide the impetus needed to establish the event organization, it rarely sustains long-term growth. Research and planning are the tools that provide the solid foundation for an enduring and growing event business enterprise.

Step One: Formulating the Vision Statement

The first step is often taken by an individual. However, unless this single vision becomes a collaborative process, the event organization risks certain death due to tunnel vision. Therefore, it is critical that the process of visioning takes place with the input of a wide range of stakeholders. Remember that even small businesses (the majority of business enterprises in the United States are small businesses) also have stakeholders. The owner, the investors, the employees, the vendors, the customers, the trade and general media, the government and others are all stakeholders in even the smallest business. Figure 2–1 lists the typical stakeholders that should be considered for the visioning process.

Once you have identified the key stakeholders who will help create the event organization's vision, it is time to begin the formal process of visioning. Visioning is best defined as *the process that transforms abstract concepts into clear and attainable outcomes*. The term "event" is derived from the Latin term e*venire*. *Evenire* literally means "outcome." Therefore, the visioning process is in actuality an event or an outcome-based activity.

Step Two: Pre-work

Assign stakeholders tasks such as researching vision statements from comparable organizations. In addition, ask them to list those core values they would like to see the organization represent in the short-

- The event organization founder(s)
- The individuals involved in governance (i.e., board, committees)
- Internal personnel (financial, human resource, marketing, operations)
- Experienced volunteers
- New volunteers
- External supporters (i.e., key vendors, government agencies)
- Media representatives (both trade and consumer)
- Owners
- Investors
- Customers
- Prospective customers
- Trade associations
- Family
- Friends

Figure 2–1 Key Stakeholders in the Event Visioning Process

term, mid-term, and long-term stages. These values may include integrity, honesty, fairness, innovation, environmental sensitivity, or other beliefs they consider to be important to themselves personally, as well as to the future success of the organization.

Step Three: Finding and Selecting the Facilitator

The selection of this individual is perhaps the single most important decision you will make after you decide to develop your organization. An effective facilitator typically is an individual with the maturity, skill, and experience to guide the group toward achieving consensus regarding the vision and mission of the organization.

Step Four: Compensating the Facilitator/Consultant

The facilitator of your strategic planning session can very easily become a long-range consultant to your event organization. Therefore, it is important to determine early on the compensation structure for this important member of your organization's team.

Compensation arrangements with consultants vary; however, there are standard and customary practices that many professionals employ. Figure 2–2 describes these methods of payment. Later in this book you will see many similarities between the method of billing for consultants and event management professionals. Consulting predates event management as an established profession and therefore it is an accepted model to refer to when designing your billing practices.

Visioning: Session One

Directly related to the process for identifying the vision and mission for the event organization is the time frame that is required for this

---

1. **Comprehensive fee.** The consultant quotes a total fee not to exceed a certain amount. The fee includes all costs including deliveries, telephone calls, long distance charges, and transportation.

2. **Project fee.** The consultant quotes a total fee for your individual project. The fee includes time for professional services but does not include transportation or other variable costs.

3. **Monthly or annual retainer.** The consultant is retained by your organization for a fixed fee per month or year. This retainer includes an understanding or agreement as to the scope of work, or estimated maximum time to be spent on your business consulting activity. The fee does not include variable expenses and may increase if additional professional time is required.

4. **Weekly or daily fees.** The consultant quotes a flat fee such as $500 per day or $5,000 per week for professional services. This fee does not generally include variable costs.

5. **Fee plus percentage.** Some management consultants structure their fees to include direct compensation for their time plus they receive additional income (ranging from 1% to 5% of the gross income) from the event organization for a set period of time (usually for the length of the management contract). The consultant verifies the income from the business by receiving monthly copies of the bank statement and the balance sheet.

Figure 2–2   Methods of Payment for Consultants

phase. A good rule of thumb is to work in 90-minute blocks. Allow 90 minutes for formulating the vision statement and then take a fifteen-minute break. Then re-convene and allow 90 minutes for drafting the mission statement.

First, introduce the definition of visioning as described above. Confirm understanding and buy-in among the stakeholders. Ask for reports resulting from pre-work. Use a flip chart to list the values that each member of the group has selected. Group the values that are similar. Ask the group to prioritize the values from most important to not as important to help determine where you will focus your vision statement.

Once you have reached consensus on your core values, ask the participants to form groups of two or three persons and begin to draft the components of the vision statement. Set the parameters for writing the vision statement as shown in Figure 2–3.

As you can see from the examples above, the vision statement must not only reflect the philosophy of your event organization but also precisely describe the vision you wish to share with both internal and external event stakeholders. Therefore, once you or your committee members have completed the first draft, it is a good idea to test your communications ability by inviting a critical friend (someone from a similar noncompeting organization) to review your work and offer suggestions. This "editing" process is a critical step that should not be overlooked when you are building your event organizational blueprint.

---

1. Start each sentence with a strong statement such as "We believe" or "We value."
2. Keep it short, concise, in the active voice, and very specific
3. Keep it simple. If you are a first generation event professional, your grandmother should be able to understand what you mean.
4. Make sure it is defensible. It should be consistent with the actual values of the members of the group.
5. Make certain it is achievable. Can you turn these values into a central mission that the group can actualize?

Figure 2–3   A Guide to Writing the Vision Statement

Transformation

The next step is to transform the values of the event organization into a tangible, practical mission statement. This process of applied strategic planning is the process of transforming a general way of doing business into a series of specific goals and objectives that will help you efficiently achieve the desired outcome for your stakeholders. This phase is a natural evolution of the values scanning step. All mission formulations derive from the core values of the event organization.

For example, a not-for-profit event organization will exhibit different values than that of a for profit event organization. As a result, the mission statement will reflect these profound differences. Therefore, it is important that you carefully review the values phase and make certain that all of the stakeholders have sufficiently "bought in" before you proceed to develop the mission statement.

Key Questions

Just as there are key questions one must ask in the development of an event (why, who, when, where, what), similarly there are critical questions that must be answered in the formulation of the mission for the event organization. These three questions should guide the thinking for the development of your mission statement.

Who?

Whom do we serve? Who are the logical, available, and qualified customers (internal and external) for our event organization? See Figure 2–4 for examples of a wide range of event organizations.

As you can see from the example in Figure 2–4, in some cases an event organization may serve multiple internal and external customers. Deciding whom you serve and how you prioritize your service time and resources is a valuable exercise in formulating the mission statement. The event lighting organization may serve direct clients, event managers, audio-visual firms, and hotels. What is the primary business for this organization and what percentage of resources must be devoted to sustain its core business? These are important considerations when seeking the best way to allocate scarce resources.

Event Organization	Internal	External
Audio-visual producers	Technicians	Hotels, clients
Caterers	Staff	Event managers
Decorators	Designers	Event managers
Entertainment consultants	Talent	Clients
Event managers	Staff	Clients
Lighting	Staff	Event managers
Musicians	Artists	Clients

Figure 2–4 Examples of Event Organization Customer Groups

How?

The second question that must be answered is how will the event organization achieve the goals of delivering the proper resources to the customers? Whether your event organization is for profit or not-for-profit, many of the same issues will arise. Will you satisfy your customers' needs or will you provide high quality state-of-the-industry technology to satisfy your customers' needs? The event audio-visual organization, as well as the event management consulting practice, must carefully and thoughtfully answer these questions. The conclusions you draw will determine not only the final products you offer but your lines of distribution, as well as service quality standards. Figure 2–5 demonstrates how some event organizations answer these questions.

Regardless of the size or uniqueness of your event organization, you must answer "How" you will achieve your goals and objectives through your products and services. To answer this question you must first understand who you are serving and then what you are providing. The "How" determines how you will accomplish your mission as an event organization.

Why?

This commanding principle or core belief is at the heart of most event organizations. The majority of individuals who are employed in the event sector did not enter the profession to get rich quick. Instead,

Event Organization	How We Operate
Audio-visual	Sales, rental, consulting, staffing
Balloons	Sales, rental, design, training
Catering	Sales, rental, consulting, staffing
Decorator	Rental, consulting, staffing
Expositions	Sales, consulting, management
Fair/Festival	Sales, education, advertising, training
Hotel	Sales, rental, consulting
Library	Education, consulting, training
Musician	Entertainment, education, consulting
Professional Conference Organizer	Consulting, marketing, management
Video Producer	Consulting, staffing, design, equipment
Zoological Park	Education, training, staffing, rentals

Figure 2–5   How We Do Business

they decided to seek an opportunity to find something they would love to do so much that they would almost do it for nothing more than the sheer pleasure of going to work each day in a field they truly love. Unfortunately, prior to the publishing of this book and the establishment of formal educational programs such as those offered at The George Washington University, there was little available education to assist event professionals with accomplishing both challenges of finding a lifestyle they enjoy *and* earning a fair return on their investment of time and talent. By answering "why," the event organization can not only begin to describe their aspirations but also define in precise terminology their raison d'être (reason for existence). Figure 2–6 provides some examples of typical "Why" statements in a variety of event fields.

Each "why" statement is remarkably different. However, all of the event organizations shown in Figure 2–6 have one or more things in common. First, they start with an aspiration "to" and second, they precisely list both what they aspire to and whom they will attempt to serve. The mission statement, like an event budget, is a target, blueprint, or guide to help the event organization reach its destination using the most efficient route. Therefore, the raison d'être must reflect

- **Advertising Firm:** To achieve leadership in advancing marketing and communications through events for our clients worldwide.
- **Catering Firm:** To become the best event catering organization in our marketplace.
- **Event Management Firm:** To consistently provide on time, on budget, and high quality event management services and products for our clients and other stakeholders.
- **Library:** To use live events to support the acquisition and dissemination of knowledge to the widest possible constituency.
- **School:** To promote the use of events as a means to foster spirit, respect, and loyalty within our school community.
- **Special Effects Firm:** To provide state-of-the-industry technical effects and knowledge to enable our clients' projects to succeed.
- **Sport Event Management Firm:** To deliver exciting, safe, and effective sport events to the widest possible audience.

Figure 2–6   Why Our Event Organization Exists

the core beliefs or aspirations of its leaders and a sound methodology for achieving success as an event organization.

Critical Success Indicators

Whether you measure your success in profit, publicity, community awareness, or with a combination of other criteria, it is important to note that every event organization is accountable to their stakeholders. The mission statement is the first step in setting up the expectancy of accountability. By crafting the mission statement you are in fact determining how you wish to be measured as an effective event organization. Therefore, be careful how you commit your final words to paper. Although you must list precisely whom you serve, how you will serve them, and why you exist to serve, make certain you practice the old rule of thumb of under-promising and over-delivering. Even in the "Why" section of the mission statement you must avoid lofty goals that cannot be reasonably achieved by the event organization. Avoid sounding foolish by carefully auditing the strengths as

---

Event Management Consulting Organization: The Expert Event Planners' primary goal is to research, design, plan, coordinate, and evaluate consistently professional events to satisfy the unique needs of our clients. We intend to utilize global resources to enhance our internal capabilities and provide high-quality services and products to maintain our leadership role in the event management marketplace.

Catering Firm: The Good Taste Catering organization provides low-cost, high-quality catering products and services for social and corporate clients. We will maintain our leadership position by consistently exceeding customer expectations, while achieving a satisfactory return for our investors.

Technical Services Company: The Special Effects Company provides state-of-the-industry products and services, while delivering consistently safe, on time, on budget, and high value results for our customers. We will promote the expansion of the special effects industry through our continuous quest for improvement and will seek to identify innovative technologies and services to satisfy our clients' needs.

Figure 2–7   Sample Mission Statements

well as the weaknesses of your event organization before you finally submit your finished mission statement.

Figure 2–7 provides examples of mission statements from three fictitious event organizations. Use these examples as a blueprint from which to create your own example.

Understanding the Mission Statement

Once you have completed the first draft of the mission statement, the final test is to make certain key stakeholders as well as others can readily understand it. Therefore, use the following five-way test to confirm that your mission statement is easily understood.

1. **Brief.** Your mission statement should not exceed one typewritten page.
2. **Clear.** Avoid jargon or the need to define terms.
3. **Matches and supports the vision.** Re-read the vision statement.

Have you captured the vision within the mission? This may be compared to the "lightning within a bottle" test.

4. ***Philosophical and practical.*** Does the mission statement broadly define the event organization's philosophy and at the same time describe in practical language how you will accomplish this philosophical quest?

5. ***A rallying cry.*** Can you post your statement on the wall and generate excitement among the troops in your event management organization? The ultimate test must be the ability of your mission statement to help the troops motivate themselves to apply the principles you have described to improve the event management organization. Does your statement accomplish this important goal?

Constructing the Applied Strategic Plan (ASP)

Applied strategic planning is the process by which the event organization identifies the mission, vision, and critical success indicators to benchmark future performance. This process requires focus, discipline, and most importantly, consensus among all of the stakeholders to ensure widespread adoption. It should not be rushed. Instead, a reasonable time schedule should be established to allow each of the stakeholders to have time to contemplate and help craft a widely accepted final product. Applied strategic planning sessions may last from one full day to several days depending on the complexity of the organization.

The applied strategic planning session is preceded by the development of the mission and vision statement. Once this important task has been accomplished, the stakeholders must then establish a model to prepare the first draft of the strategic plan. Figure 2–8 demonstrates the typical steps for use in the strategic planning process.

The 21 tasks listed in Figure 2–8 need not occur in this exact order; however, to ensure that your plan is comprehensive, it is extremely important that you use this list to check and balance your progress. Some tasks will take longer than others. The mission and visioning process, as well as the SWOT analysis, usually take considerable time. It is wise to conduct these activities with the entire group of stakeholders. Individual task forces may handle the other phases best.

1. Identification of stakeholders
2. Establish time frame/schedule for planning process
3. Establish agreement on process
4. Audit internal and external environment
5. Mission
6. Vision
7. Review by critical friend
8. Audit industry and other competitive factors
9. Audit internal strengths, weaknesses, opportunities, and threats (SWOT)
10. Identify critical success indicators
11. Identify measurable objectives
12. Identify implementation stages
13. Review by a critical friend
14. Submission of plan for first review by stakeholders
15. Refinement of plan
16. Editing
17. Final review by stakeholders
18. Implementation
19. Periodic review
20. Evaluation and analysis
21. Re-engineering

Figure 2–8   Summary of Event Organization Applied Strategic Plan Steps

Identification of Stakeholders

The stakeholders are those who are invested in some way in the future success of your event organization. They may include financial investors, key employees, volunteer leadership, or others who are in search of a return on their contribution to your event organization. This investment need not always be financial; it can also be spiritual as well as emotional. Regardless of the type of investment, the stakeholders seek a reasonable return for their efforts. The strategic plan serves as the pro forma contract or blueprint that helps you provide that assurance.

Establish a Time Frame and Schedule for the Planning Process

Setting a realistic time frame is essential for the future success of your event strategy sessions. The length of time required will be determined by the experience of the stakeholders, the complexity of the organization, and the ability of the stakeholders to work together to achieve mutual goals. Once you have analyzed these three factors and established a time frame and schedule, add 25 percent. Most things that are done extremely well take longer than you planned. There is no need to rush this important process and therefore you should be liberal in the time that is assigned for the strategic planning exercise. Remember that the strategic planning process is hard work. Limit planning sessions to 90 minutes to make certain the stakeholders remain fresh and alert.

Establish Agreement on Process

Who will be the facilitator? Who will coordinate notification of the stakeholders? Who will be the scribe (recorder) of the decisions that are made? How will notice be given about the meetings? Who will provide mediation if there is a point that cannot be resolved through group discussion? These questions and many more must be resolved prior to beginning the formal strategic planning process. By agreeing on an acceptable process you will be better equipped to focus on the important work of designing and implementing the strategic plan.

Audit the Internal and External Environments

Are the stakeholders fully committed? Is political intrigue brewing among the stakeholders? What models are available in your industry? Do other industry businesses or organizations have strategic plans and can you review them? By auditing the internal and external environments, you are calibrating your event organization's radar screen to identify those impediments that may obstruct your process. Carefully and thoughtfully interview internal and external stakeholders to identify the temperature and barometric pressure that will provide the environment for the development of your strategic plan.

Review by a Critical Friend

Invite a critical friend to your meeting to provide his or her opinion regarding your draft plan. Carefully select someone who can provide supportive yet critical context for you to complete your strategic plan. The best critical friends are those with an understanding of your event organization but without a specific allegiance. This allows them to provide empathy as well as objectivity.

Audit Industry and Other Competitive Factors

What's going on in your industry? Are there mergers, acquisitions, consolidations, and public-private partnerships that you and your stakeholders must factor into the creation of your strategic plan? A review of the industry journals for the previous six months to one year will provide you with a snapshot of your profession. You must also examine general competitive factors, such as the financial markets, media, and political situations in countries or regions where you will be doing business. By reviewing these factors you will be able to comprehensively view the competitive environment in which you will create your strategic plan.

Audit Your Internal Strengths, Weaknesses, Opportunities, and Threats (SWOT)

Invite your stakeholders to help you explore the critical strengths, certain weaknesses, potential opportunities, and perilous threats within your event organization. By analyzing your organization from this multimodal perspective, you will be able to establish a better perspective from which to develop your strategic plan.

Strengths

The strengths of your organization may include a strong board of directors, experience, expertise, client base, or excellent capital resources. Other strengths may include the organization's reputation and buying power.

Weaknesses

The weaknesses are typically the opposite of strengths, but not necessarily. You may have a board with strong experience but little capital. On the other hand, you may have an organization with a good name but new and inexperienced leadership.

Opportunities

Opportunities include those predictable resources that may help you enhance your strategic plan, without requiring additional resources that you must fund or acquire yourself. For example, the board of directors may have strong connections with other similar but noncompeting organizations that will help your firm grow and prosper. These relationships spell opportunity for your organization.

Threats

Threats may be political, financial, or even physical (the age of your event organization offices or facilities). Understanding and assessing the magnitude and implications of threats to your organization helps you build an event strategic plan that will endure despite the fiercest challenges.

Identify Critical Success Indicators

How will you measure your future success? Financial reserves, attendance, volunteer participation, diversity, or succession of leadership? Whatever success indicators you select, they must have measurable results that may be qualified or quantified.

Identify Measurable Objectives

Right from the beginning you and your fellow stakeholders must carefully delineate how you will measure your success. Whether you look at percentage of profit, earnings per shareholder, growth in cash reserves, or other factors, you must determine methods for measuring your success or monitoring your setbacks in order to make corrections and then learn and grow.

Identify Implementation Stages

Knowing when you will implement your ideas enables you to phase in your plan and mesh your new strategies with that of the organization's normal business cycle. Make certain you interview any- and everyone who will be affected by your new plan to determine the best time period to put your ideas into action. One of the best ways to implement new ideas is through a thorough orientation and training period. By allowing sufficient time for learning and adoption, you are better assured of widespread acceptance of your plan.

Review by a Critical Friend

Once you have completed the final draft of your plan, it is wise to invite either the same or a new critical friend to review your plan. Allow sufficient time for your critical friend to review, ask questions, and then respond in writing as well as verbally to your draft strategic plan. Make certain you also allow time for the stakeholders to question the critical friend in order to clarify any unclear areas and then incorporate his or her best ideas into the final draft of your plan.

Submission of Plan for First Review by Stakeholders

This is where the bullets begin to fly. Print in large, bold letters "DRAFT" at the top of each page to remind the readers of the preliminary nature of these ideas. Begin the document with a statement such as ***Your Help is Needed Now to Perfect This Plan.*** Give the readers clear instructions such as "Please read, analyze, provide constructive advice, add, delete, or correct any part of this plan. Your input will result in the adoption of a plan that will work for all of us."

Refinement of Plan

When you receive the comments from your stakeholders, make certain you incorporate those that are relevant to the mission and vision the planning committee has established. Contact those stakeholders whose comments are particularly critical and try to find out how you can help them provide constructive advice that will improve the final plan.

Editing

Invest in a professional academic or business editor to clean up grammar and punctuation and help make your thoughts more readable to the lay reader. Remember, ultimately many people will read your event organization's strategic plan. You want to be sure that it communicates well to the widest possible audience.

Final Review by Stakeholders

Submit a final copy with the headline FINAL DRAFT to the authors of your document. Ask them to provide only minor changes at this point and then to sign their names at the bottom. Some organizations actually have a formal signing ceremony (a must for your event organization) where the authors actually pose for a picture while signing the final document.

Implementation

This is often the most challenging stage. However, by creating a phase-in system and schedule, this may become easier. Make certain you plan for contingencies. A typical challenge is when one or a group of stakeholders has been left out of the process and reacts negatively to the plan. Anticipate this and immediately establish contact to answer questions. Ask the opposing parties to give the plan time and then participate in the next phase, the periodic review.

Periodic Review

In this phase the authors as well as other stakeholders review the critical success factors to determine if the plan is working, what must be corrected, and how the course may be charted in the future to improve the ultimate success of your plan. Examine each step of the mission and vision statements and compare your plan to the measurable outcome you have established. Use percentages to benchmark your level of success in each area. For example, you may have stated in your plan, "We will achieve a 10 percent return on investment for all stakeholders." By assigning a specific percentage you can easily measure your performance.

Reevaluation

Following your periodic review, invest some time in critical reflection and reevaluation of your measurement criteria as well as the breadth and scope of your plan. One critical question is, "Is the plan helping us achieve what we envisioned during the mission and vision process?"

Revision

Obviously, all great plans require periodic revision to ensure final success. Whether you are Lewis and Clark or Admiral Byrd, failure to adjust your plan will almost guarantee peril. The process of revision need not be dramatic. It may only require adjusting the phase-in schedule or re-assigning tasks. However, having the courage to revise your plans to accomplish your mission is one of the most important steps you will take toward long-term success.

Re-engineering

The process of creating, implementing, and revising a strategic plan for your event organization is in fact the opportunity to re-engineer your mission and vision, and sharpen the focus for the future. By bringing your objectives into sharp focus and using sound reason to face the future, you have taken one of the most profound steps any organization can take. As change continues to accelerate, the successful event organization is that which can navigate the turbulent waters with a steady oar guided by a reliable compass. The strategic plan has become your compass and the strength of the oar is a commitment to move forward with persistence, courage, and the integrity that comes from within. The process of creating a strategic plan for your event organization has required a systematic study of your organization and the result is a balanced, stable, and secure craft that will be able to withstand the certain chaos that today's and tomorrow's business environment will continue to provide.

Do Strategic Plans Help Event and Other Organizations Perform Better?

According to Goodstein, Nolan, and Pfeiffer in their book, *Applied Strategic Planning, How to Develop a Plan That Really Works*, a survey sent to the Fortune 500 companies indicated that 88 percent did not have a mission statement. The 61 available mission statements were rated using ten criteria. According to the survey researchers (Pearce and David), *the corporate mission statement of the high-performing organizations significantly differed from the low-performing one on three of the eight components. More of the high performers included elements of corporate philosophy, corporate self-image, and desired pubic image.*

Although some may see corporate philosophy as a soft issue, it is important to remember that the author of *In Search of Excellence*, Tom Peters, once remarked, "Soft issues really determine the hard issues." Authors Terrence Deal and Allen A. Kennedy stated in their book *Corporate Cultures*, "Shared values define the fundamental character of their organization, the attitude that distinguishes it from all others." Indeed, a solid corporate mission statement can serve as the blueprint for future success for your event organization.

Whether you are an entrepreneur investigating the development of a new business or an entrepreneurial employee charged with heading up a strategic planning process, the first step must be to try to capture and expound upon the values, visions, and mission of your event organization. Once you have seized this "lightning in a bottle," the future direction of your event organization will be clearly defined. You will have found an enduring energy source that will help propel and sustain the future success of your event organization.

The View From Here

1. Event organizations must develop cogent, effective, and enduring vision and mission statements to achieve long-term success.
2. The first step in this process is to audit the organization to determine the key values of the stakeholders.
3. The next step is to transform these values into the mission (Who, How, What) of the event organization.

4. The final step is to use the five-way test to check the validity, reliability, and communications potential for the mission statement.

5. Successful event organizations use a powerful philosophical and practical mission statement to capture the driving forces for their organization. This "lightning in a bottle" is an effective energy source for all future planning and decisions.

Tools of the Trade

Goodstein, L., Timothy Nolan and William Pfeiffer. *Applied Strategic Planning.* New York: McGraw-Hill, 1993.

Deal, T. and A. Kennedy. *Corporate Cultures.* Reading, Mass.: Addison-Wesley, 1982.

Breaking New Ground

To better understand the principles and concepts in this chapter, complete one or both of the following activities.

1. Rewrite the following mission statement to remove the fuzziness and obliqueness: "The Electro Sound Company is the best in the world. We provide all things for all people all the time."

and/or

2. Write a mission statement for your organization and use the five-way test to confirm the integrity of your work.

CHAPTER 3

The Event Business Audit

Step Three: *Conduct a comprehensive event business audit.*

A lexander Steinitz is a musical conductor in Innsbruck, Austria. When asked to describe the most important tasks in his profession, one would expect him to mention composing, selecting the repertoire for his performances, and other typical tasks conductors must pay attention to in order to build a successful career. Instead, Steinitz says there are three critical areas that he believes are even more important to long-term success. Interestingly, each of these areas also helps guarantee success at each performance.

First, Alexander, also known as Sascha, says he carefully inspects the arrangement of the chairs for his musicians. Not only does he check the location, spacing, and other details but he also makes certain that each music stand light is functioning properly. He says that a good performance often begins with the arrangement of the chairs and the comfort of the musicians. This is a task that he does not entrust to others; instead, he arrives early and attends to these details himself.

Second, Maestro Steinitz does not hesitate to handle even the smallest detail before the performance, even if this includes standing at the photocopier and reproducing pages of the musical score if necessary. These details are the essence of a quality performance and sometimes cannot be delegated to others.

Finally, according to Sascha Steinitz, developing a point of view is essential to influencing others. Although he seeks the constant input of his musicians, ultimately it is his point of view (mission and vision) that must prevail. He does not hesitate to incorporate the attitudes or innovations of others into his point of view; however, he believes that those who will follow him (the musicians) are entitled to know and understand his philosophy or point of view.

These three tasks or rules for making great music can be easily adapted to the event management business you are leading or influencing through your entrepreneurial actions. Remembering to place the chairs in the right order, handling the details, and developing and expressing your point of view are all key ingredients when conducting the comprehensive business audit.

Situation Analysis

If your event business were a fixed position on a radar screen, how would you describe your current situation? Is your business firmly positioned? Is your business more fluid and changing course constantly due to outside or internal influences? Is your business moving forward, static, or perhaps even retrenching in your industry?

Whether you are currently operating or employed in an event management business or are considering starting a new venture, conducting the business audit is the next logical step toward success. Once you have determined your mission and vision, it is essential that you test your ideas within the actual and perceptual environment where your event management business will live and grow. Figure 3–1 describes the numerous reasons why and when you should conduct the comprehensive business audit.

Critical Decision Factors

Each of the five business decisions shown in Figure 3–1 requires a comprehensive and systematic analysis of your actual and perceptual business environment to ensure that your decision will result in a short, mid-term, and hopefully long-term term positive outcome.

Note: These times are optimal, but in many cases must be accelerated to meet rapidly changing business and competitive environments or potential business crises.

Reason	Timing
1. Starting a new business	1–2 years before operations commence
2. Adding a new line to your business	1 year before adding the line
3. Re-engineering your business	1 year before making changes
4. Expanding your staff	6 months to 1 year before decision
5. Reducing your staff	3 to 6 months before decision

Figure 3–1   Reasons and Timing for Conducting the Comprehensive Business Audit

Although the "when" is often driven by external factors such as a dramatic turn of events including new, unforeseen competition or a sudden economic recession, failing to carefully audit your business environment increases the chances of a sustained period of decline for your operation.

What Is a Comprehensive Business Audit?

The traditional audit conducted by an accountant or a taxing authority is in fact a thorough examination of every detail in your financial operations. The comprehensive business audit expands this process to include factors such as operations, human resource management, marketing, and customer perception of your service quality. The result of the comprehensive business audit should be a multifaceted, three-dimensional view of your business that will enable you to make informed decisions about your future.

When reporting to the doctor to have your ankle examined for a sprain, the medical professional will also order an X-ray to make sure there are no fractured bones. When conducting the comprehensive business audit, you must also look both within and outside the business organization to compare and contrast your business position with others who are your direct and indirect competitors.

Context: The Business Audit Plan Synergy

Before you conduct the comprehensive business audit, it is important to understand that this process is the critical precursor to developing the final business plan. The audit functions as the primary research phase that allows you to make valid and reliable conclusions in order to craft your business plan.

The relationship between the comprehensive business audit and the business plan is symbiotic. It is similar to the image of two raindrops slowly gliding down the pane of a glass window. At some point these divergent streams of water intersect and blend such that it becomes impossible to separate them. The goal of conducting the comprehensive business audit and the natural progression of creating the final business plan should be to achieve symbiosis between these two processes.

A Drama in Four Acts

The comprehensive business audit is conducted in four parts. Each part must take place in sequential order for the entire audit to prove fruitful. In fact, like a play with three acts, the business audit is evolutionary in nature and should result in a purposeful outcome.

Allow sufficient time to conduct the audit by allotting a period of time each week to participate in each phase. Make certain that the time periods for the audit are carefully scheduled so as not to interfere with normal business operations. This will provide time for uninterrupted contemplation by the key informants.

The key informants are those individuals who have access to the data or information that will help you make future informed decisions. These people should be high level or line operations individuals who are knowledgeable about the financial, human resource, and marketing activities of the business. They should include individuals who can provide you with day-to-day operational information, such as the chief executive officer, chief financial officer, key vice presidents, senior level managers. These people, as well as others, can provide you with sufficient history about the business organization, as well as give both the breadth and depth to place your findings in a historical context.

Part One: History and Organizational Structure

Knowing the history, organization, and culture of your organization is the first step in understanding your total business environment. Examine the organization's records to determine why and how the organization was established. Ask questions like, "Who were the initial stakeholders?" and "What challenges or crises did they face?"

For those organizations that are "start-ups" and must rely solely upon the institutional memory of employees who may have worked for other firms, this recall can be extremely important in identifying the best practices that will contribute to the future success of the company. Do not dismiss the rich experience of your colleagues; instead, use these professional histories as tools to enrich your own organization during this process.

The organizational structure can be of particular importance when you are trying to understand how the organization makes decisions. If the organization uses a top down management style with all decisions being driven by senior staff, then you will be better able to understand how long it will take for the organization to process critical decisions.

Furthermore, if the organization's culture requires a bottom up management style with all decisions being driven by line personnel or event users, the decision making will be more decentralized and may require more time for the implementation of new programs.

Part Two: Financial and Human Resource Operational Analysis

Once you have examined the qualitative values of the organization (history and organizational structure), you may turn your attention to the quantifiable aspects, including the financial and human resource operations factors. Every business, whether a for-profit or not-for-profit, must administer the financial requirements for the organization. All event businesses are highly dependent on human resources for the quality of operations. This fact behooves the entrepreneur or entrepreneurial employee to thoroughly review these critical aspects of the organization.

The financial audit should begin with determining the budgetary philosophy for the organization. Is the organization a for-profit or a not-for-profit corporation? What is the financial history of the organization for the past three years? What is the organization's record for accounts receivable versus accounts payable? What is the investment strategy? The comprehensive business audit should include a review of the most recent financial report, the profit and loss statement, and the annual internal revenue statement to best determine the financial position of the organization. In addition, interviews with key informants, such as the chief financial officer, treasurer, comptroller, or others, should be conducted to solicit the broadest range of input regarding the current and future financial position of the business.

Human resources are the principal capital of all special events businesses. Therefore, it is essential that your comprehensive business audit evaluate how human resources are acquired, trained, evaluated, and rewarded. Perhaps even more important, it is essential that you identify present and future needs for human resources within the context of parts one and two. Knowing the history and culture of the firm along with the financial position will help you forecast the appropriate level of staffing in order to provide consistently excellent service for your internal and external customers.

In fact, many special events businesses are one-person operations. Therefore, it is wise to involve external stakeholders, such as accountants, legal counsel, and successful business leaders in this stage of the audit process. It is not possible to objectively audit oneself in a comprehensive manner. Rather, one should draw upon the "brain trust" found in experienced and wise experts that can provide the objectivity and expertise required in helping your organization succeed.

Part Three: Marketing Plan Analysis

Whether your organization is a for-profit or not-for-profit business, you will be required to develop and implement a marketing plan to attract both internal and external customers. A systematic audit of the marketing plan will help you identify gaps that may be preventing your organization from achieving optimum success.

The organization must be probed to determine what markets are being served, how these markets relate (or fail to relate) to one another, what markets are not being served, and what secondary and tertiary markets may be served in the future. Probing marketing managers, senior managers, as well as internal and external customers, will help you begin to plot the radar screen that contains the markets that are critical to the success of your organization. Furthermore, you will be able to see where these markets bisect to help you strengthen your position through consolidating your marketing activities. For example, if you are serving both the social and corporate markets, there may be a synergy that can be achieved through concentrating on high income level social business, as these clients are likely to also be key corporate decision makers. Similarly, if your target market were national trade associations, a horizontal approach would be to begin to focus on the 50 state chapters of the same organization.

The marketing plan audit must certainly identify gaps that may be closed through future marketing activities. Specifically, a comprehensive business audit will seek to identify disconnects between present and future markets and the activities that are being utilized to reach these target markets.

Part Four: Short-term, Mid-term, and Long-term Future Plans

The final step is to identify specific plans that your organization has developed to improve your operations and profitability in the short-term, mid-term, and long-term future. Whether you are a not-for-profit organization who desires to improve your return on total investment, or a for-profit corporation seeking a better return for your stockholders, the primary way to accomplish this is through improving your planning and operations.

All businesses progress through a typical life cycle consisting of the entrepreneurial stage (startup, early growth), collectivity stage (assembling of people, resources, and processes), formalization and control stage (where control is centralized and all aspects of business operations are documented), and elaboration of structure/revitalization stage (the organization/business becomes more complex and there is a need to re-engineer certain systems). Therefore, it is a fact of your business life that you must look ahead to identify future challenges you may face in the mid-term and long-term life of your enterprise. Since most employees change jobs every two to three years (according to the U.S. Department of Labor) it is even more important for the entrepreneurial employee to plan in the short term and mid term as this may directly impact your career opportunities. As an employee you have the choice of becoming a victim of the lack of planning within your organization or taking responsibility for your future by controlling events through careful forecasting.

How can you predict in the short term, mid term, and long term when your event business may experience an economic shock that will drastically alter your operations and profitability? You can't. However, you can adjust the lenses described in the introduction to make certain that throughout the life of your business you stay focused on the key critical success indicators. For example, focusing the culture lens will enable you to see not only prosperity but also all the forces of change that may alter the way you do business. How is your field changing from a technological, human resource, and competitive point of view? What is the approximate time frame for 100 percent implementation of these changes? How are your customers likely to react to these changes? If you are a service business selling to event planners and a competitor ambushes your marketing plan by going directly to the customer with their product or service, how will you compete? Should an act of war be declared (as happened in the Persian Gulf crisis) or an oil embargo be put into effect (as in the 1970s) how will you maintain your operations when your customers are unable or unwilling to travel to attend events?

The only logical answer for forecasting the changes that are most likely to occur is to anticipate and plan. This process of anticipation and planning is known as scenario planning. It would be wise to sit down with your advisors (board members, investors, suppliers, and even customers) and devise a series of business scenarios that are likely to occur in the short term, mid term, and long term and then devise your calculated response to each challenge. Figure 3–2 lists typical short-term, mid-term, and long-term business challenges that you should consider.

The Special Events Business Life Cycle

Simultaneously there are business life cycles reflecting the changes in the exogenous industry and general environment (see Figure 3–3). These phases include the industry life cycle (the birth—usually rocky), growth (typically a period of steady growth and formalization), competitive shakeout (where the events industry reacts to competitive forces and consolidates), maturity (the adulthood of an industry), saturation (the beginning of decline), and ultimately decline (changes that may send the special events industry into a downward trend).

There is a fundamental relationship between the special events

Short-term
Cash shortages
Labor shortages
Inability to obtain financing

Mid-term
Retaining employees
Recruiting senior employees
Increased competition
Need for expansion

Long-term
Retirement, illness, or death of founder
Succession
Maintaining freshness of product

Figure 3–2   Short-Term, Mid-Term, and Long-Term Event Business Challenges

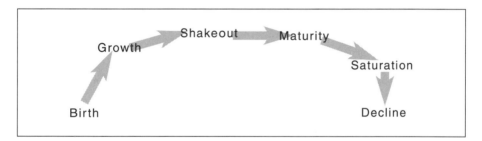

Figure 3–3   The Special Events Business Life Cycle

industry and your entrepreneurial event organization and therefore it is critically important to create your business plan with close attention being paid to the industry forces that will govern your future.

The Business Audit Process

Once you have identified the four parts of the business audit process, you must first set a time frame and develop a methodology for conducting this critical procedure. As with any important plan, you should know at the outset that it typically will take longer and cost more than you expect.

Therefore, do not underestimate the amount of time this will require and do not attempt to complete this as cheaply as possible. If you are a new business, you may prefer to handle all of the steps yourself. However, more mature business enterprises that are expanding their lines of business often hire consultants in the finance, marketing, or operations areas to assist them with the comprehensive business audit. Regardless of what resources you deploy to accomplish this important task, the senior person in the organization will need to be very involved in all aspects and should be prepared to devote significant time to this project. Figure 3–4 describes the percentage of time that is typically required by each member of your team.

This translates over a six-month period (typical for a comprehensive business audit) to three months for the senior managers, four to five months for the middle managers, and 45 to 90 days for the line managers. This is a substantial time commitment and must be carefully budgeted for when considering embarking on this process. Of course there are exceptions to every process, but in reality, as stated previously, if you are to err in terms of budgeting your time, you would be wise to allot more time than you believe will be required.

Managing the Business Audit

To produce good work you must manage each task carefully and strategically. One of the most common errors organization leaders make when embarking upon the business audit is trying to control all of the details and tasks through one or a small number of individuals. The administrative audit is a management process and requires the

Managerial responsibility	Time commitment %
Line managers (finance, marketing, operations)	15–25
Middle managers (supervisory)	40–50
Senior managers (executive, CEO, CFO)	25

Figure 3–4   Time Commitment for the Comprehensive Business Audit

same tools that you would use in managing other projects within your organization. The three basic tools are the organizational chart, the schedule, and the methodology.

The Organizational Chart

This important guide describes how each member of the audit team may effectively and efficiently contribute to the business audit process. The business audit process is participatory in nature; therefore, the organizational chart should reflect this culture and management style. Do not attempt to create a rigid autocratic structure. Rather, group responsibilities in a logical format that will promote teamwork among multiple stakeholders. Figure 3–5 provides you with a typical business audit organizational chart using a bottom up approach.

---

1. End Users: Customers, Vendors

   Role: Key external informants

   Scope: Provides line managers with external data to make informed decisions

2. Line Managers: Finance, Operations, Marketing, Human Resources

   Role: Key internal informants

   Scope: Provides middle managers with internal data to make informed decisions

3. Middle Managers: Coordinate Communications between Senior Line Managers and Senior Management

   Role: Data collection and filtering for senior management

   Scope: Collects data from internal and external stakeholders using interviews and focus panels

4. Senior Management: Set policies for process and monitor schedule

   Role: Match policies and procedures to achieve goals and objectives

   Scope: Set and monitor schedule

5. Owners: Investors

   Role: Establish goals and objectives

   Scope: Analyze, evaluate, and make appropriate decisions based on audit outcomes

---

Figure 3–5   The Business Audit Organizational Chart

Organization Size

According to a recent study by the International Special Events Society, 22 percent of event management organizations have over 50 full-time employees. Therefore, the vast majority of special event organizations may be classified as small businesses with fewer than 50 employees. Figure 3–5 demonstrates how a large, mature event organization may manage the business audit process. However, smaller organizations may use these same principles by simply consolidating the tasks and removing one or more layers of management.

Record Keeping

Throughout this process it is essential that you keep accurate records. Appointing one person as the organization's scribe is a way to centralize these activities. However, in most cases the records are first recorded on audiotape and then transcribed by a professional stenographer so they accurately reflect the full meaning of the key informants. Once you have reviewed the transcript, you may then reduce these comments to key findings or major points to help the readers and decision makers better focus their time. Each business audit journal entry should include the name of the organization, date, time, purpose-activity, participants, facilitator, and outcomes. Figure 3–6 demonstrates how your scribe may record a typical journal.

Five Forces that Influence Your Event Business

Within every business there are internal and external forces at work that can dramatically accelerate your success or bring your best efforts to a grinding halt. Imagine the image of the jet airplane with strong tail winds arriving a half hour early versus the same plane with strong head winds arriving one half hour late and you can quickly envision how important it is to identify and use business forces to best understand your business.

The five business forces include your customers, suppliers, industry rivalries, substitutes, and potential entrants. Although five independent concepts, each of these forces is dependent on the others to ensure a viable and sustainable event business.

ABC Event Company

January 5, 1999

Start: 4:00 P.M.

End: 5:15 P.M.

Purpose-Activity: Financial and marketing audit

Participants: Jane Doe, Mary Doe, Joan Doe, John Doe, Ron Doe, and Fred Doe

Facilitator(s): Dr. Joe Goldblatt and Frank Supovitz*

Outcomes: During this session the participants described the financial performance of the organization. According to the participants, the financial performance has been excellent for the past three fiscal years with annual growth each year of 5 to 8 percent over the previous year. There were no serious financial deficiencies; however, the participants described the lack of networked computers as a future gap that could reduce efficiency. Finally, the session concluded with a forecast of future income for the organization. The participants were mixed in their ability to confidently predict positive growth. One third of the participants were concerned about the competitive forces that were ramping up to offer lower priced goods and services at a discount, thereby securing some of the organization's traditional market share. Another third of the participants were confident that the reputation, experience, internal operational controls, and inability of competitors to respond as quickly would position the firm for a 10 to 15 percent increase in gross revenues next year. Finally, one third of the group stated that is was too early to tell and that only after the annual special event trade show could they confidently forecast the performance of the firm in the new year. They described this trade show as a chance to meet their customers and test the waters with new products and services.

*The facilitators led the discussion for this group.

Figure 3–6   Sample Business Audit Journal Entry

Customers

Identifying your primary, secondary, tertiary, and other customer target markets will quickly help you identify who your customers are and the power they hold. During the comprehensive business audit, ask your stakeholders the questions listed in Figure 3–7 about your current and prospective customers.

1. Who are they? (What are their demographics and psychographics?)
2. How many are there? (What is your total market share and growth potential?)
3. What are their needs, wants, and desires?
4. What is their buying history? (When, where, and how do they buy?)
5. Why do they buy from some special events organizations and not from others? (What is influencing their buying decisions?)
6. How much discretionary income do they have?
7. Where and how do they spend their discretionary income?
8. What do they value?
9. How do they prefer to buy? (By mail, phone, in person, Internet?)
10. How strong is their loyalty to their suppliers?
11. What event-related goods and services do they purchase?
12. What is their cash cycle? (When are they paid? When do they have to spend money or lose it?)
13. What is their potential for long-term cultivation? (Can their purchasing power increase? Will they develop loyalty to your organization? Will their purchases increase?)
14. Are there any negatives concerning your customers? (Are they exceedingly labor intensive, sensitive to certain economics, or combative? Do they possess other traits that may over time cause you or your colleagues to invest additional time and energy that may not be rewarded through profit?)

Figure 3–7   14 Questions that Help You Understand and Evaluate Your Customers

Suppliers

Suppliers to your event organization may be exclusive (you only contract with certain organizations), preferred (you will contract with others but you prefer to work with certain suppliers due to their service/quality record), or you may select the supplier to match the specific needs of the individual event. Knowing the capabilities and future availability of your event suppliers will provide you with the reassurance you need to make informed business decisions about the markets that you may potentially enter.

Industry Rivalries

The sometimes-contentious relationship between party rental dealers and caterers or between the event planner and his or her key vendors may contribute to disruption within the business environment. The special events industry is in actuality a super industry composed of dozens of well-defined industrial sectors. The U.S. Department of Labor assigns specific, well-defined industries with *standard industrialized codes* (SICs). These codes help quantify specific industries for the purpose of collecting accurate census and other statistical data. Therefore, given the unique nature of this super industry (similar to that of tourism), this fragmentation may lead to splintering within certain segments. It is therefore important to identify these potentially fractious situations and seek methods to monitor and where possible correct them.

Substitutes

Identifying those related services that customers may use instead of those of your event organization will help you anticipate future competitive threats. For example, instead of holding live in-person events, is it possible for some organizations to hold the same communications activity through the Internet? Instead of purchasing paper goods from your party rental store, is it possible or likely that some customer segments will use mail order or warehouse outlets to receive the same products at a cheaper price? By understanding the potential and probable substitutes, you will be able to anticipate these threats and develop strategies to combat them.

Potential Entrants

Those organizations and new technologies that are emerging as serious contenders within the events industry must be monitored to determine the level of threat in future years. Certainly the Internet, direct mail, cable television, direct broadcast satellite services and other distribution channels for event industry services will provide your current and future customers with more choices. As a direct result of these potential entrants, your event business may be challenged from a financial and operational standpoint. You must carefully assess all potential entrants and determine their viability in terms of whether they might evolve into competing organizations.

Customers, Capabilities, and Competitors within Your Event Business

The needs, wants, and desires of your customers, your personal and organizational capabilities, and the internal/external competitive pressures direct the methods you use to design your event entrepreneurial organization. You must carefully examine each of these issues and then use the findings from your business audit to construct or re-engineer your business.

Customers

Earlier in this chapter we discussed the potential characteristics of your customers. By carefully analyzing the profile of your customers you can begin to identify the needs, wants, and desires that will provide the foundation for future support of your organization's values. It is extremely important that there is no disconnect between your business values and those of your customers. Customer-driven businesses are those that rapidly succeed in the event industry.

Capabilities

Those event organizations that carefully assess their capabilities and realistically identify their core strengths will develop the laser-like precision needed to strike and conquer customer needs. Going right to the heart of an event organization is most difficult but also essential. Figure 3–8 provides examples of questions you may wish to pose to your internal and external customers to identify your event business capabilities.

Competition

The third and final issue that must be examined in comprehensive detail concerns competitive threats. These threats may or may not require identification of specific industry organizations that may ambush your plans. In the most common scenario some of the general forces that pose the greatest challenges to your business are technology, economics, or market confusion. Whether you are able to identify a specific competitor or must extrapolate from the larger business environment, a competitive threat is not the issue. The major consid-

---

1. What special skills differentiate you and your staff from other similar organizations?

2. What level of experience do you and your associates have and how does this differentiate your organization from others?

3. Are you or your colleagues certified or otherwise possess credentials by an objective third party in a specific body of knowledge such as Certified Meeting Professional (CMP), Certified Special Events Professional (CSEP), Certified Catering Executive (CCE), Accredited in Public Relations (APR)?

4. What is your organization's commitment to continuing education and training? What funds are invested in research and development for your event products and services?

5. What do your customers and suppliers tell you about your organization's unique capabilities?

Figure 3–8   Five Critical Questions to Identify Your Event Business Core Capabilities

eration is how these internal and external competitive factors will affect your ability to profitably develop your event business. This final analysis will enable you to anticipate challenges and assume the special events warrior position. You will now be able to mount a strategic offensive by stepping inside enemy territory and improving your position. This strength of position will help you and your business organization proceed confidently as you make future decisions. However, remember real estate tycoon Donald Trump, as well as Intel CEO Andy Grove; both are advocates of a healthy dose of *paranoia* to ensure that you do not become complacent with regard to your competitors.

 20/20 Hindsight

Linda Higgison, founder and CEO of the TCI Companies decided to refocus and reorganize her successful Washington, DC national meeting and event management company. Higgison, a finalist in the Ernst and Young Entrepreneur of the Year Awards, sensed that her mature firm was risking stagnation unless it identified new

(Continues)

growth areas. With the help of graduate students from The George Washington University Event Management Program, company president Valerie Sumner and staff conducted an administrative audit of the twenty-two year old firm. Through the process described in this chapter, TCI was able to identify the organization's core strengths and determine what market factors would support future growth. Using focus groups as well as survey research, TCI was able to qualify as well as quantify opportunities for growth and sustainability. This process, according to Higgison, created a new vitality within the company. The outcome was essential for the future success of the business. "The environment in which we do business is in a state of constant change. The customers are changing, their companies are changing, and our industry is changing. To be an effective partner, we found that we needed to become the constant amongst the clients' sea of change. The administrative audit process forces you to hold up a mirror to your meeting and event organization and see it for what it really is. Only when you know who you are and where you stand, can you effectively match your lines of business to those trends that are present or emerging within the environment in which you do business. By continually monitoring ourselves and the marketplace, we can seamlessly make the necessary adjustments in order to play the game where it needs to be played."

The View From Here

1. The comprehensive event business administrative audit is a critical strategic planning tool that allows you to assess the internal and external factors that control your future success.

2. The audit involves every stakeholder in the event organization and requires an organizational chart and schedule to ensure efficient and thorough implementation.

3. Customers, capabilities, and competition are three extremely important factors that must be carefully examined as part of the audit.

4. Financial performance and operations, marketing tactics, and potential new entrants provide a global analysis of the event business.

5. The audit must be documented in written form and the findings shared with appropriate stakeholders. This step, as all of the comprehensive event business audit phases, requires pre-planning to ensure the time, personnel, and financial investment is sufficient to guarantee optimum performance.

Tools of the Trade

Gerber, Michael. *The E Myth Revisited*. 1995.
Heskett, James L. *Managing In The Service Economy*. Boston: Harvard Business School Press, 1986.

Breaking New Ground

To improve your comprehension and understanding of the comprehensive event business audit, practice the following activities. This benchmarking/best practices exercise involves first practicing on another organization and then comparing the outcomes to those of your own organization. This comparison will not only allow you to practice your event business audit skills but will also provide you with a benchmark of business practices to contrast with your own organization.

1. Identify an event organization similar to yours. Make certain the event organization you identify is not a direct competitor. For example, a catering organization may wish to select a rental company or other nonfood and labor-supply company.
2. Formally request the opportunity to conduct a business audit of the organization you have selected. Tell the host organization what time and other resources will be involved.
3. Submit a draft schedule for approval by the host organization.
4. Offer to allow the host organization to conduct an event business audit within your organization.

Share your findings with the event host organization and then compare these results to those of your own organization once you have conducted your individual audit.

CHAPTER 4

Research

Step Four: *Conduct comprehensive research.*

Anna McCusker is a successful principal in the Toronto based firm entitled Décor & More. Ms. McCusker began her career as a florist and through professional networking met a colleague at an industry meeting. Their firm quickly grew due in large part to a thriving local economy, as well as their reputation for high-quality work. When asked about research activities their firm uses to identify their market, test new products, and otherwise reduce their risk of failure, Ms. McCusker smiles and says "Research is something we do every day."

In fact, most special events entrepreneurs and their entrepreneurial employees are constantly assessing, evaluating, comparing, exploring, and indeed conducting spontaneous informal research during their daily business operations. What is rare is the individual in this field that conducts formal, planned research as a strategic method for improving their operations, identifying new consumer demands, and finding ways to improve efficiency, quality, and innovation that will ultimately result in greater profits.

Ms. McCusker and her colleagues have recently retained a consultant to assist them with developing systems as well as exploring mid-term and long-range business planning methods. This process of identifying a consultant and collecting and evaluating data related to the consultancy is in fact a formal research activity. Therefore, Anna McCusker is part of a small percentage of special events entrepreneurs who are engaging in the important process of business strategic planning through research activities. This percentage is growing rapidly as members of this field recognize that systematic research reduces risk and ultimately may improve profitability.

What systematic special events research activities should you and your colleagues invest in? How will these activities improve your bottom line and grow your career? Figure 4–1 compares typical research activities with the outcome that may result from these practices.

Figure 4–1 provides only a small sample of the range of possibilities that await you through research activities. Research is so fundamental to the establishment and growth of an entrepreneurial enterprise and to your career that one would be foolish to proceed without investing time in this important step.

Focus Group

When attempting to determine the attitudes or underlying motivations of your customers, the focus group is the form of research activ-

Research Activity	Data Desired
1. Focus group	1. Customer attitudes
2. Written survey	2. Customer preferences
3. Telephone survey	3. Customer loyalty
4. Intercept survey	4. Customer buying habits
5. Tag and capture study	5. Product use patterns
6. Ethnographic study	6. Cultural changes
7. Direct mail test	7. Customer response
8. Delphi study	8. Industry trends analysis
9. Internet	9. Employment opportunities
10. Library, special collections	10. Comparable events

Figure 4–1   Research Techniques and Potential Outcomes

ity most frequently used. A focus group is not an informal meeting where you simply query the participants and record their thoughts. It requires a specific protocol to produce the quality information you need to make good business decisions.

A focus panel is comprised of eight to twelve individuals with one or more homogenous characteristics. For example, the panel may be mixed in gender; however, all of the participants are middle managers or politically conservative. In the case of event management business focus panels, the members may be both men and women; however, they may share the same salary level, the same religious affiliation, and even shop at the same stores for their party supplies. The purpose of this homogeneity is to identify traits within the group in order to compare and contrast their attitudes. For example, if the group were mixed in gender, yet shared shopping preferences, it would be interesting to find out whether men or women or both purchase certain products. Within the focus group setting you are in search of attitudinal preferences that may result from agreement as well as disagreement among the participants.

To select the panelists you may ask for volunteers (this is called self-selection) or select them yourself. Just as one would qualify a jury, you should further qualify the members of the focus panel by asking them to complete a brief written survey or by interviewing them individually. Once you have confirmed their qualification to join the panel, the next step is to offer an incentive to further confirm their participation.

When offering an incentive, be careful of biasing the panelists by offering too magnanimous a reward. Typical rewards or incentives include a free gift such as a book or in some cases a modest payment such as twenty-five dollars. It would obviously bias a panel of party rental customers to offer them a 25 percent discount on future orders. Instead, a twenty-five-dollar payment provides a strong incentive to show up without further strings attached. You should send each confirmed panelist a letter in advance describing what they are required to do as members of the panel, the importance of their participation, and the reward they will receive in return for their participation. Using a facsimile confirmation may provide a sense of immediacy and call more attention to your group. However, if you use a facsimile, make certain you ask the recipient to confirm their receipt by faxing back their signature indicating their desire and willingness to participate. Figure 4–2 depicts how to create a focus panel confirmation letter.

Focus Panel Confirmation

TO: Jane Doe

FROM: Joe Partystoreowner

SUBJECT: Confirming Your Participation in Focus Panel

DATE: January 1, 1999

ACTION REQUIRED: Confirm your receipt of this notice by signing below and returning by facsimile today to (410) 999-0000.

Dear _____:

Thank you for agreeing to participate in the focus panel scheduled for January 25, 1999 at 4 P.M. The session will be held at PartyLand Rentals, 2222 General MacArthur Highway in Anytown, USA. Should you need driving directions, please telephone (410) 999-0000. Free convenient parking is available in our parking lot. Your participation will help our firm provide better value to our customers.

During the focus panel you will be asked to respond to several questions and to view and use some new products we are considering offering to our customers. Joining you will be eleven other customers with similar backgrounds. The focus panel will conclude at 5 P.M. The session will be recorded on audiotape for later transcription. Your identity will remain anonymous. However, you will be asked to sign a permission form granting your approval of participation in this research activity.

In consideration for your participation our firm will provide you with a one-time payment of twenty-five dollars at the conclusion of the session. Should you have further questions prior to the focus group, please telephone me at (410) 999-0000.

Thank you for participating in this focus panel. I look forward to meeting you on January 25 at 4 P.M.

Sincerely,

Joe Partystoreowner

X

Accepted this date by Focus Group Panelist whose signature appears above   Date

---

Figure 4–2   Focus Panel Confirmation Form

Obviously the setting for the focus group session should be free from auditory or visual distraction. A conference table or individual chairs set in a semicircle is a satisfactory setting. It is important that each of the panelists be able to see and hear the other participants.

The moderator or focus group facilitator should be carefully selected. An ideal choice is someone unknown to the majority of the panelists. Therefore, using as the moderator the business owner or a salesperson who is well known to most of the panelists may bias the participants' responses. In some cases it is wise to invest in a professional focus group facilitator to ensure an objective approach.

The moderator will query the panelists about their opinions regarding specific issues or research questions that are important to your organization. It is extremely important that the facilitator not reveal his or her approval as the panelists respond to each question. Even a slight facial gesture by the facilitator may bias the next response from the panel.

It is possible to quantify some of the information gained from the panel by calling for a show of hands or asking each member to rate on a scale from one to ten their feelings about certain issues or products. The purpose of the focus group is to probe each panelist as well as the entire group to identify specific trends or attitudinal perceptions that may develop in the future. Therefore, the facilitator should feel free to ask follow up questions or ask participants to provide more specific information in order to clarify their preliminary answers.

Once the focus panel has concluded, the organizer should transcribe the audiotape to begin the process of data analysis. Using the raw data of the answers provided by the focus group participants, you must search for areas of agreement, disagreement, and strong opinions, as evidenced by a majority opinion or by repeated use of certain phrases, such as "too costly," "not convenient," and other key phrases that may appear several times in the text of the transcript.

The focus group research study concludes with a description of the findings and recommendations that have been derived from this activity. For example, you may find that the majority of your panelists do not agree that the new product you are considering offering is reasonably priced, or a large percentage of women shoppers believe extended store hours would provide added convenience and incentive to trade with your business. These findings may lead to recommendations that you revisit your plans to invest in the new product and consider staying open until 9 P.M. one or two evenings per week. Additional research, like using a written survey method, will further validate the preliminary information you have received from the focus group panel.

Focus group research does not employ the scientific method and therefore does not provide empirical data. However, using multiple focus groups can expand and further validate the information that is produced. For example, in 1993, the National Hockey League (NHL) conducted two focus group sessions to determine attitudes toward the All-Star Weekend being held in Montreal, Canada. The first session, in the fall of 1992, asked a panel composed of Montreal season ticket holders what they were expecting from the All-Star Weekend. They rated the All-Star Game itself as the element they most looked forward to. However, in the sessions conducted a month after the event, it became known that the Game was not the most enjoyed element, but rather the Skills Competition the night before.

The difference in before and after "satisfaction" ratings was striking. It can also be revealing to have "parallel" panels. For the above example, it would be interesting to determine how a panel of NHL fans who would be watching the event on television would rate the events versus those who would be watching live in the arena.

Although focus groups do not produce empirical data, they do provide an important element of understanding that supports traditional empirical research. For example, some focus group sessions actually take place in a room with a one-way mirror that allows the clients to view the physical reactions of the focus group participants without influencing those involved in the actual research. The focus group participants are told that individuals are viewing the session on the other side of the one-way mirror and within a few minutes typically the individuals relax and ignore this potential intrusion. The mirror allows the client to view subtle changes in body language as well as provides the researchers with a further opportunity to record minute reactions and to more precisely chronicle the attitudes and opinions of the focus group participants. Once analyzed, this combination of verbal and visual responses will produce a holistic picture of the overall feelings, attitudes, and opinions of the focus group participants.

Written Survey

The survey should be introduced with a brief letter or statement from the author describing the purpose and importance of the research. In

Dear Customer,

It is our desire to provide you with the highest level of service and the finest quality of products available in the special events industry. Please take a few minutes to answer the questions in this survey and return your completed questionnaire to our staff to provide us with the information necessary to continually improve our service and quality. Thank you for helping us become the kind of special events business you will continue to rely upon and recommend to others.

Sincerely,

Jane Eventmanager

Figure 4–3   Survey Opening Statement

this statement the prospective survey respondent must quickly be made to comprehend why it is worth his or her time to supply the information you require. Figure 4–3 provides a sample of this introductory statement.

A written survey should be brief and not include more than 15 or 20 questions. The questions may be closed (such as rate the following products) or open ended (such as describe your feelings about the following new services). An example of both types of questions is given in Figure 4–4.

As in the focus group, the results of your research will be directly related to the size and makeup of those you have sampled. Some researchers use a convenience sample and simply send the survey to everyone on a specific mailing list. Others will use a systematic random sample approach and identify a system for randomly selecting a specific sample for study. Sometimes a random number is assigned, such as every third or fifth person on the list. The number that is assigned may be selected by placing numbered slips of paper in a container and then randomly selecting a number that will become the method of enforcing the randomization process. In another common technique, a number is selected from a random number table that is found in many statistics or research textbooks. Regardless of what method you use, it is essential that you select one that will support and validate the desired outcome of your research.

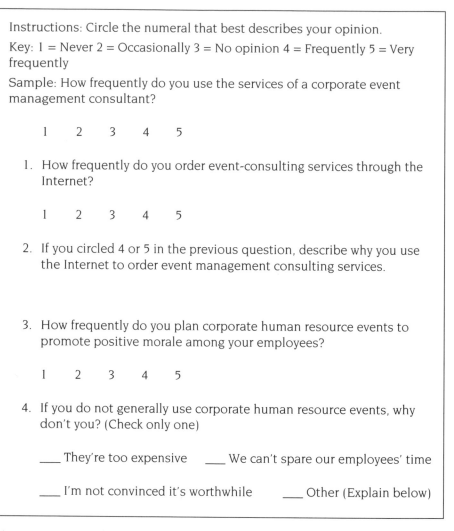

Instructions: Circle the numeral that best describes your opinion.

Key: 1 = Never 2 = Occasionally 3 = No opinion 4 = Frequently 5 = Very frequently

Sample: How frequently do you use the services of a corporate event management consultant?

        1   2   3   4   5

1. How frequently do you order event-consulting services through the Internet?

        1   2   3   4   5

2. If you circled 4 or 5 in the previous question, describe why you use the Internet to order event management consulting services.

3. How frequently do you plan corporate human resource events to promote positive morale among your employees?

        1   2   3   4   5

4. If you do not generally use corporate human resource events, why don't you? (Check only one)

        ___ They're too expensive   ___ We can't spare our employees' time

        ___ I'm not convinced it's worthwhile   ___ Other (Explain below)

Figure 4–4   Typical Survey Questions

Increasing the response to your survey requires a variety of proven techniques. The most often used technique is to offer a small reward such as a one-dollar bill or to agree to share the findings with the participants in exchange for their participation. Ultimately, a well-written opening statement will do more to increase the participation than any cash or other incentive you may add.

Regardless of how hard you try to achieve 100 percent response, it is unlikely you will be successful. To further validate your research it is important that you use a nonresponse technique to increase your return. Some researchers use a reminder postcard, while others use the telephone to increase the response. By planning to improve the return, you are demonstrating that you desire to achieve the highest possible response to increase the reliability of your findings. In most social science research it is desirable to achieve at least a 40 percent response.

Once the data has been collected and tabulated, they can be reported as findings and then interpreted through recommendations for further action as with the focus group. Since survey research yields quantitative information, this may be reported as follows: "Over 75 percent of the respondents stated that they frequently use the Internet to identify event management consulting services. This response may indicate future growth opportunities through this communications medium for this type of business."

Telephone Survey

The telephone survey is similar to the written survey, although the collection process is very different. The interviewer uses a written form to query the respondent and may or may not choose to probe for clarification for further information on specified questions. Typically telephone interviews occur during dinner or early evening hours when consumers are likely to be readily available to receive the phone call.

The telephone interviewer, similar to the focus group moderator, must be carefully trained not to inject bias by deviating substantially from the written questionnaire. Showing approval with a subtle verbal compliment may encourage the respondent to give a more positive response and may ultimately skew the final results of the survey. Finally, remember that telephone surveys need to be brief in order to not be intrusive. If the telephone interview includes more than four or five questions, it is wise to let the respondent know approximately how much time is required before questioning begins. Also, although you may have staff available to conduct the survey, most organizations contract with professional tele-research firms due to the intensive effort required for this methodology.

Intercept Survey

The intercept survey is used when a large number of respondents must be surveyed. By intercepting a randomly assigned number of customers, the event management entrepreneur may be able to infer certain findings and make recommendations that may represent the attitudes of a much larger group. The intercept survey may be conducted by distributing a written survey to every third, fifth, or other randomly assigned number of persons who enter your business or by taking a few minutes and conducting a live interview with these customers. Once again, a small reward will help encourage the customer to participate in the research activity. When the intercept survey is conducted using a systematic random sampling approach, the findings can be very conclusive and save you substantial time and money that would be required in trying to survey a larger population. One noticeable limitation of an intercept study is that it only includes people who are attending the event or walking in the door of your event business. It does not include your competitors' customers or disinterested customers.

Tag and Capture Study

What if you wish to determine the buying habits of customers at a suburban regional shopping mall during a special event you have organized? Using sophisticated computer programs, you are able to track sales by credit card as the customer moves from one cash register to the next. However, what about the customer who prefers to use cash or check? Most special events rely on cash purchases and these may be difficult to track for research purposes. First reported in *The Journal of Festival and Event Tourism,* the tag and capture technique allows the special events entrepreneur to track consumers at larger events who primarily use cash for their transactions. In this methodology, the researcher randomly selects individuals who agree to wear a special tag or button that identifies them to trained spotters at the event. The spotter records the time, location, and amount of the transaction as it occurs. The participant is given a small reward for agreeing to participate in this research activity. This technique has not been widely used but shows great promise in solving the dilemma of how to track, record, and interpret the behaviors of cash customers at larger events.

Ethnographic Study

Anthropologist Margaret Mead may have been responsible for popularizing the type of research known as participant-observer. The ethnographer is actually a scientist who not only participates but also objectively observes in the culture he or she is studying.

 20/20 *Hindsight*

In Prince William County, Virginia, there is a little town called Haymarket. The Walt Disney Company conceived the idea of developing an attraction tentatively entitled "Disney's America" in this small rural community 35 miles from Washington, D.C. Disney real estate experts conducted studies to determine the cost/benefit ratios of land purchases and also conducted other types of research, including focus groups, to determine the viability of this major project. The focus group may have been composed of individuals who, due to the small-town nature of the community, would not openly reveal their negative sentiments regarding the project out of fear of reprisals from their friends and neighbors.

Ultimately the project failed. Disney was unaware or chose to ignore a strong undercurrent of opposition from a highly vocal group of conservative citizens who felt that the development would encroach upon the historic values and quality of life of this area. The resulting negative publicity doomed this project and prevented further development. Disney reportedly lost millions. So what went wrong?

Perhaps if Disney had invested in an ethnographic study to probe deep into the culture of the Haymarket community, they would have identified the early objections and developed a course of action to overcome them. Instead, Disney focused their research on the more traditional quantitative financial studies and attitudinal research resulting from focus panels and surveys. What may be learned from this experience is that the research strategy must match the desired outcome. If the researcher must understand both the economy and the culture of the community, the research activities must be deeper and broader than merely an economic study.

As a special events entrepreneur you may wish to identify a future location for your office or store. By merely relying on statistical information from the local chamber of commerce you may miss important cues from the local culture. Therefore, it may be necessary for you to participate and observe in some of the activities or rituals of the local community to determine first hand if your business location is a good fit. Missing this important investigative step may cause you to miss a major cue that could spell success or failure for your investment.

Direct Mail Test

Direct marketers often use a split test to determine the effectiveness of mailings. A split test requires that you use a different type of vehicle, color, or text for two or more mailings and then measure the response from each one to determine which is more effective. Figure 4–5 demonstrates how this works.

A two- or three-way split test is an excellent way of measuring effectiveness against cost per thousand (CPM) impressions. Direct marketers use CPM as a means of determining the cost versus benefit of various advertising and promotion strategies. For example, if mailing number three produces the highest yield in terms of response and it requires the least cost (design, printing, postage), then this may be the format that you wish to use consistently in the future to increase your sales in a cost-effective manner.

Mailing number one: A postcard with a direct response phone number. The person calling is told to ask for extension number 500, which codes the incoming call as coming as a result of the postcard.

Mailing number two: A letter with a direct response postcard is enclosed. The postcard includes the following code to indicate the source of the response: *Mail code* XYZ.

Mailing number three: A self-mailer with a perforated card for direct response. The card uses the following code to indicate the source of the response: *Mail code* ABC.

Figure 4–5   Split Test Examples

Delphi Study

When you want to find out what experts are thinking regarding changes or future changes in your business environment, the Delphi study is the best approach. A Delphi study requires identifying an expert panel. Each panelist agrees to review your research questions and provide comments at least three different times. Unlike the focus panel, the Delphi panelists will never meet in person. Instead, they will independently review the questions you have submitted and try to achieve a consensus through several rounds of analysis. With each successive round the questions should become more narrowly defined until finally some sort of trend or forecast can be identified as a result of the expert inputs. The Delphi study is an excellent tool to use when you are considering developing a new line of business and are interested in comparing the general economic indicators to those of the demand side of your business.

One example of the Delphi methodology is the TEDQUAL (Tourism Education Quality) study conducted by Dr. Sheryl Spivack on behalf of the World Tourism Organization (WTO). In this study, Professor Spivack interviewed via mail survey dozens of experts in tourism education to identify trends as well as gaps in tourism education within higher education. Following several rounds of inputs from the experts, Spivack was able to draw conclusions that will help the WTO make informed decisions with regard to developing tourism industry education programs.

Internet

Perhaps the most prevalent research method in use today is the Internet search engine. Using Yahoo, Netscape Navigator, Internet Explorer, or a variety of other commercial search engines, literally hundreds of thousands of pages of information may be transmitted telephonically direct to your desktop. Some event business leaders find this process daunting due to the overwhelming size of the information database that is available. Therefore, one way to focus your search is to determine at the outset how you will use the information and then limit your search to focus only on data that serves those specific purposes. For example, if you are considering developing a new training program for your staff, instead of searching under education or event management education, first determine through what methodology your staff will receive their training materials. If you believe distance education through desktop computers is the best route, then limit your search to *event management distance education* or *continuing event management education and distance learning*.

By focusing on specific results or outcomes you will be able to navigate the information highway easily and efficiently. The key is to start with the end in mind and focus your search activities to achieve the desired result.

Library, Special Collections

Special collections at major university libraries such as The University of Houston Conrad Hilton Hotel School and The George Washington University Event Management Program are increasingly being formed to serve as a repository for important primary information in the event management field. These materials range from entire event planning documents to individual videos, audio tape interviews with leaders in the industry, to thousands of photographs documenting colorful and successful events worldwide.

These materials are available through interlibrary loan. You may contact your local public or university library and request that copies of specific materials are sent to you to review and use as research for an upcoming project. For example, if you need to develop a proposal for a future event, an excellent place to find a model is in the special collections division. In addition, if you are interested in benchmarking your current events against successful models you may find the best practices you need in one of these valuable repositories.

Presenting Your Research

Once you have successfully completed your research project, you will then have to present your findings to those stakeholders you must inform, persuade, or influence. To determine how best to do this, first consider the communications style of the stakeholders and next determine the location and time frame for the presentation. For example, if the time frame is short and the location does not allow for a formal presentation, you may prefer to present the findings in written form before the briefing and then use the group meeting to answer questions. In another setting with a longer time frame you may choose to use electronic media such as Power Point to graphically illustrate your findings. If the findings you are presenting are particularly controversial, you may wish to avoid sending a written report and present your data in person so that you can immediately respond to questions or concerns.

Regardless of how you present your findings, it is important that you solicit feedback from the stakeholders. Determine their reactions to the findings and recommendations and solicit their input regarding next steps. Finally, document the results of this reporting session in writing and distribute copies to all of the stakeholders to officially mark the next step in your business/career development process.

The View From Here

1. Research is integral to business and career development. It should be the first step in the preparation of any new business or career activity.

2. Research may be conducted in a variety of ways, from informal conversations to high-level scientific inquiry.

3. Match the research to the outcome. Always start with the end in mind. What are the goals and objectives of the research project? What questions do you need answered?

4. Identify an appropriate data sample from which you will conduct your research.

5. Make sure you have a sufficient number of people respond to your survey to increase the reliability of the results.

6. Use rewards to increase participation in research projects.

7. Increase participation by planning additional activities such as reminders.

8. Your goal should be to achieve a 40 percent or higher usable response from your survey population.

9. Use both qualitative (focus panels) and quantitative (surveys) to establish authentic findings when conducting research.

10. Use participant-observer (ethnographic) research to deepen and broaden the meaning of your research activities.

Tools of the Trade

Ritchie, J. R. Brent, and Charles R. Goeldner. *Travel, Tourism, and Hospitality Research*. New York: John Wiley & Sons, 1987.
Smith, Stephen L. J. *Tourism Analysis*. New York: John Wiley & Sons, 1991.

Breaking New Ground

To improve your research procedures, practice the following tasks:

1. Identify three research questions that you would like to know the answer to and use the Internet to conduct your search. Use at least three different search engines and then refine your search to narrow your findings.

2. Design a focus group to determine your customers' attitudes regarding introducing a new event planning service. Select the types of participants that will provide the most accurate information to help you make the required decision.

3. Create a written survey to determine attitudes regarding the need for your event business in a new shopping center. Determine whether you should use a specific population, convenience sample, or a systematic random sample.

4. Use a telephone interview survey to sample ten prospective customers regarding their future needs for event management services or products. Design the questionnaire and analyze the results.

5. Determine what would be the best methodology for presenting your findings to a group of potential event industry investors who are flying into the airport for a one-hour meeting in the conference center. How will you gauge their reaction to your findings?

CHAPTER 5

Dollar Wise

Step Five: *Create a realistic budget and financial contingency plan.*

For some special events entrepreneurs, money may not be the primary motive for going into business for themselves. It may be the promise of a more independent lifestyle, a desire to breathe life into products or productions of their own creation, or perhaps an insatiable drive to provide entertaining life experiences to a variety of audiences. No matter how lofty, altruistic, or ethereal your actual inspiration for starting your special events organization, without money—and enough of it—you will not be in business for very long. The very best idea simply can not survive without the money to bring it to market and sustain it until it achieves profitability.

As discussed in Chapter 1, insufficient capitalization is the primary reason that new businesses fail. And, the most common reason that these new businesses are undercapitalized is the lack of proper planning. Successful special events entrepreneurs invest the time required for projecting all of the expenses necessary for their new endeavor, identifying the sources of revenue they will require, and sourcing the capital needed well in advance to maximize profitability. Comprehensive financial planning also helps the entrepreneur set appropriate and competitive prices for their products and services at levels that will return the revenues required to offset expenses, and ultimately, generate profits.

Another frequent contributor to the failure of new businesses is the inability of the owner to control spending once in operation. It isn't necessarily that the owner is a spend-thrift. Just as likely, he or she may not be in touch with how their money is being spent, the depth of their current liabilities, or what steps need to be taken to ensure there is always enough cash around to fulfill their obligations. Financial documents such as budgets, forecasts, income statements, and balance sheets are the essential tools used to track financial performance for an established business. Frequent review and revision of these instruments can help provide an early-warning system for impending crises.

But, first things first. Let's get your event business up and running. If you have had experience in managing special events, you are probably quite familiar with the concept of a budget. In its most basic form, a budget is a three-part planning document: how and when you will receive *revenues,* pay for *expenses,* and the *net contribution* (i.e., profits or losses) that will result from these activities. The events industry is by its nature detail-oriented, so you probably already have the discipline to methodically and painstakingly think through all the elements that will be necessary to create a master corporate budget for your new company or department. If you have managed an event or project budget, the principles for developing a budget for your business are the same, just more comprehensive. In fact, most special events businesses are project-driven, in which the financial performance of your individual event budgets will each serve as a component of the firm's overall financial health.

Successful events entrepreneurs treat budgets like living documents, using them on a regular, sometimes daily, basis to track how many dollars remain available to spend on given *line items,* and whether or not cash reserved for one type of purchase needs to be reallocated to other, more acutely needed areas. A line item is a grouping of like expenses summarized and expressed as a single line on your budget. If your budget is properly organized, looking at line items rather than individual purchases can help you to continuously analyze the amounts of money being spent in various areas and enable you to adjust your subsequent spending accordingly. The fineness of detail reflected by the line items in your budget will depend upon the type of special events business you are operating, but in general, the greater the detail, the more useful and versatile your budget will be.

Creating a realistic budget is of paramount importance in the development of your business plan. If you are providing your own capital, or involving your friends and family in the funding of your start-up company, you want to be sure that your collective investment has the best possible chance to succeed before it runs out of money for personal reasons, if no other. If you are counting on investors to provide start-up capital, lenders such as banks, venture capitalists, and other specialists know what it takes to make a small company operate in any industry. They will look carefully at your income expectations, and if they appear too rosy or speculative, they may go no further. Prospective capital partners will also look at your expenses. If you have, in their opinion, seriously underestimated expenses, they will also demur.

In the event that your assumptions appear realistic and the balance of your business plan suggests a good chance for success, many lenders will require you to provide some form of *collateral* for their loan. This may be some personal asset of value which the lender would have the right to seize in the event that you later run short of cash and default on the loan. As this collateral may include equity in your home, car, IRA and 401k funds, or other personal assets, you want to be doubly sure that your financial assumptions are realistic.

A realistic budget is equally important to ensure that you are not overcapitalizing your company with borrowed cash. Assuming you are successful in securing funding, you will be required to pay interest to the lender over the life of the loan. Careful financial planning will help you borrow enough money to get your business off the ground without overburdening it with unnecessary levels of interest debt.

The financial stress on a new business is the most severe in the first 24 months; therefore, it is wise to try to secure loans with a repayment schedule over three years or more to keep monthly interest and principal payments at the lowest levels possible during this critical period. Since lenders and other investors will be out-of-pocket until you have completely fulfilled your financial obligations to them, they will be keenly interested in the long-term earnings potential of your new business. For this reason, your business plan must project budget estimates for a minimum of three successive years, or for at least as long a term as your financial obligation to the lender.

Don't be surprised if you find yourself continually adjusting your budget assumptions as you craft your business plan. The very process of creating these documents will help you to determine whether your profit expectations are realistic. Fine-tuning these documents before presentation to potential investors will help you to convince others of the same. Adjusting revenue or expense assumptions up or down to improve the profit or loss expectations of your company is almost always necessary. But, while reducing expenses in your budget may mean that you *want* to spend less, it doesn't necessarily mean that you *will* spend less. Similarly, increasing your revenue expectations does not mean that you will earn more, only that you want or expect to earn more. So, when fine-tuning budget numbers, you must make sure your underlying assumptions are based in reality, or you are more likely to wind up with a shortfall at the end of the year. The bigger the divergence between your expectations and reality, the harder it will be to convince your lender that you have set realistic assumptions. If after the first year, your financial performance is significantly lower than expected, you could face the unpleasant prospect of having your lender "call in" the loan, or ask for full repayment ahead of schedule—a potential death blow to your young company.

Depending upon which segment of the special events industry your company will operate in, you may or may not decide to include pro forma, or sample, project budgets in your business plan. In most cases, it is not necessary to include actual project budgets in your business plan. What is important, however, is to understand how the revenues, expenses, and net contributions of each project budget will flow into your master corporate budget. To do this, you will need to develop intelligent and realistic assumptions regarding how many projects, and of what scale, you expect to sell and execute in a given fiscal year, and how minimally profitable each needs to be to support your company.

Assuming that whatever expectations you have made are realistic, you should also be sure that your budget is as complete and comprehensive as possible. Figure 5–1 provides an example of a master corporate budget for Most Excellent Events, a hypothetical special events company which will be referred to throughout this chapter. The budget is comprised of line items grouped into major revenue and expense categories further detailed below. Recognizing how diverse the special events industry is, we are not suggesting that all of these line items will apply to your business. To help you prepare the most detailed budget possible for your new company or department, a more comprehensive checklist of the most common types of revenues and indirect expenses encountered by a special events company is provided in Figure 5–2.

Revenues

Revenues are the lifeblood of your business. Simply put, revenues are all of the sources of income for your business. The term *gross revenues* includes all of the cash or cash equivalents that are paid to you to provide your products or services to your clients, without deductions for any costs you encounter in the process of delivering that product or service. Specific sources of revenue will depend upon the type of business you are in, and may include: ticket sales, product sales, sponsorship sales, equipment rental and leasing income, subleasing of warehouse or office space, management and creative fees, goods and services received on a barter basis, gross dollars received against project expenses, even interest on the cash you have on deposit. The key to a successful business is maximizing these various sources of income, sometimes referred to as *revenue streams,* and where possible, diversifying the sources. A trade show display company, for example, may make a primary business of selling portable exhibition display units. To create a new revenue stream, the company might also offer to store the units they have already sold for clients with insufficient storage facilities, and provide service to "prep and clean" the units before shipment to the next location, both at a cost to the client. An event consultant that derives his or her primary revenue stream through management fees earned in the staging of sports events may be able to leverage relationships with other corporate clients, and in the process earn sales commissions on sponsorships as a secondary revenue stream.

   Another strategy to increase profitability is to expand the business you are already doing with current clients. That doesn't mean charging them increasingly more for doing the same work—that is a sure way to lose clients. As you build relationships with your clients, find out what other pieces of business they contract to others in the same or related disciplines, and try to capture some of that additional business. If you are an event producer who has earned the trust of a client while managing their annual stockholder meetings, you may be able to increase your revenues by convincing them to award you a

I. Revenues

	1st Quarter	2nd Quarter	3rd Quarter	4th Quarter	Line Total
Gross Event Revenues	$ 100,000	$ 275,000	$ 175,000	$ 350,000	$ 900,000
Less Direct Event Expenses	70,000	192,500	122,500	245,000	630,000
Less Commissions	3,000	8,250	5,250	10,500	27,000
Net Event Revenues	27,000	74,250	47,250	94,500	243,000
Other Revenue	2,000	3,500	3,000	5,000	13,500
Total Net Revenues	**$ 29,000**	**$ 77,750**	**$ 50,250**	**$ 99,500**	**$ 256,500**

II. Indirect (Operating) Expenses

1. Permanent Staff

	1st Quarter	2nd Quarter	3rd Quarter	4th Quarter	Line Total
President	$ 17,000	$ 17,000	$ 17,000	$ 17,000	$ 68,000
Sales Manager (Base Salary)	8,000	8,000	8,000	8,000	32,000
Sales Assistant	7,000	7,000	7,000	7,000	28,000
Receptionist	6,000	6,000	6,000	6,000	24,000
Payroll Subtotal	**$ 38,000**	**$ 38,000**	**$ 38,000**	**$ 38,000**	**$ 152,000**
Payroll Taxes	3,500	3,500	3,500	3,500	14,000
Health Benefits	1,750	1,750	1,750	1,750	7,000
Total Permanent Staff	**$ 43,250**	**$ 43,250**	**$ 43,250**	**$ 43,250**	**$ 173,000**

2. Marketing and Promotion

	1st Quarter	2nd Quarter	3rd Quarter	4th Quarter	Line Total
Advertising	$ 7,500	$ 3,000	$ 5,000	$ 3,500	$ 19,000

	Q1	Q2	Q3	Q4	Total
Brochures & Flyers	$ 8,000	$ —	$ 500	$ 500	$ 9,000
Presentations & Portfolios	$ 2,000	$ 2,000	$ 2,000	$ 1,000	$ 7,000
Corporate Video & Dubs	$ 5,000	$ —	$ 500	$ —	$ 5,500
Public Relations	$ —	$ —	$ 3,500	$ 3,500	$ 7,000
Travel & Entertainment	$ 1,500	$ 3,000	$ 1,500	$ 1,500	$ 7,500
Gifts & Premiums	$ 500	$ —	$ —	$ 1,000	$ 1,500
Total Marketing and Promotion	**$ 24,500**	**$ 8,000**	**$ 13,000**	**$ 11,000**	**$ 56,500**
3. Administrative/Office Expenses					
Office/Warehouse Rent	$ 1,250	$ 1,250	$ 1,250	$ 1,250	$ 5,000
Stationery and Supplies	$ 2,500	$ 750	$ 1,000	$ 1,500	$ 5,750
Telephone	$ 1,200	$ 1,200	$ 1,200	$ 1,200	$ 4,800
Postage, Messengers, Shipping	$ 750	$ 1,250	$ 1,000	$ 1,250	$ 4,250
Insurance	$ 500	$ 500	$ 500	$ 500	$ 2,000
Dues & Subscriptions	$ 500	$ —	$ —	$ 250	$ 750
Total Administrative/Office Expenses	**$ 6,700**	**$ 4,950**	**$ 4,950**	**$ 5,950**	**$ 22,550**
Subtotal Expenses	**$ 74,450**	**$ 56,200**	**$ 61,200**	**$ 60,200**	**$ 252,050**
Contingency Allowance	**$ 7,445**	**$ 5,620**	**$ 6,120**	**$ 6,020**	**$ 25,205**
TOTAL EXPENSES	**$ 81,895**	**$ 61,820**	**$ 67,320**	**$ 66,220**	**$ 277,255**
NET PROFIT (LOSS)	**$ (52,895)**	**$ 15,930**	**$ (17,070)**	**$ 33,280**	**$ (20,755)**

Figure 5–1 Most Excellent Events Master Budget: January 1, 2000–December 31, 2000

REVENUES

Creative Fees

Consulting Fees

Production Fees

Ticket Sales

Sponsorship Income

Retail Sales/Merchandise Income

Sales Commissions (Received)

Investments

INDIRECT EXPENSES

Personnel Expenses

Wages & Salaries

   Salaried Staff

   Hourly Staff

   Overtime

Employee Benefits

   Medical

   Dental

Errors and Omissions Insurance

Liability Insurance

Payroll Taxes

Office Expenses

Office Rent

Office Furniture*

   Desks*

   Partitions*

   File Cabinets*

   Storage Cabinets*

Office Equipment

   Computers*

   Printers*

   Copiers*

Fax Machines*

Postal Meter*

Postage Scale*

Telephone Equipment

   Service Contracts and Repair

   Office Phones*

   Cellular Phones*

   Pagers*

Telephone Service

   Office Phones

   Cellular Phones

Office Supplies

   Letterhead, Envelopes, Labels

   Business Cards

   Business Forms (e.g., invoices, statements)

   General Supplies (pens, clips, tape, staples)

   Copier Paper

Travel & Entertainment

   Air & Rail Transportation

   Car Rentals

   Personal Mileage

   Hotel

   Meals

   Business Meals

   Business Entertainment

Professional Expenses

   Dues

   Subscriptions

   Conventions & Trade Shows

Postage

Freight & Express Shipping

Figure 5–2 Checklist of Revenue and Expense Line Items

Messengers

Business-Specific Equipment
Leasing
   (e.g., lighting, sound, etc.)

Other Operating Expenses
   Vehicle Lease
   Vehicle Gasoline
   Vehicle Maintenance

Marketing & Promotion

Advertising, Creative

Advertising Placement

Public Relations

Brochures

Portfolio(s)

Videos & Dubs

*Potential capital expenses, if purchased

"800" Number Service

Gifts & Premiums

Other

Legal Services

Bookkeeping/Accounting Services

Insurance

Miscellaneous

Capital Expenses

Office Build-out

Business-Specific Equipment

Other Expenses

Loan Interest

Capital Depreciation

Operating Contingency

Figure 5–2   Continued

contract to manage their board meetings, new product introductions, or trade events. Quantify the cost efficiencies a client could realize by sending more business your way. Demonstrate that they could spend less by centralizing more work with you, and you may succeed in getting more work from them, thus maximizing the revenue streams already flowing from an established relationship.

Direct Expenses—Cost of Goods or Services

In the special events business, there are two types of expenses—direct and indirect. A *direct expense* is one that you encounter in order to fulfill your contractual obligations to your client. In some service businesses, direct expenses are also known as "out-of-pocket" costs; in the retail world, direct expenses are also known as the *cost of goods sold*. If you would not incur an expense were it not for a specific piece of business performed on behalf of your client, it is generally regarded as a direct expense. Direct expenses are the costs that you directly pay for products or services in fulfilling the client's needs at the cost that you pay for them, not necessarily what you ultimately charge your client for these same services. The sum total of what you charge your client is known as *gross event revenue,* and includes reimbursement of expenses, markups, and fees. Subtract direct expenses from gross event revenues and you are left with *gross profit on sales.* Gross profit is what you are left with in the bank before you begin to deduct those pesky indirect expenses to determine your company's overall profit or loss.

In contrast, *indirect expenses* are the costs that your company would encounter without regard to any specific sale, project, or other revenue-generating piece of business. In many industries, indirect expenses may be variously known as *overhead, fixed costs,* or the *cost of doing business.* Experienced event professionals starting their own new business may be very familiar with, and adept at managing, direct expenses. But, as will be further explored later in this chapter, indirect expenses represent hidden demons for experienced professionals turning rookie special events entrepreneurs.

To successfully manage your own business, you will be expected to successfully manage your client's projects. This book can not provide you with the practical knowledge necessary to manage your company's specific responsibilities in the execution of a given event. When you hang out your shingle as a special events professional, it is your responsibility to be the expert in your field that you purport to be. As a caterer, you would already know that your direct expenses must include at-cost bills for food supplies, beverages, centerpieces, rentals you incur such as linens, props, and equipment, and labor, as needed. If you produce media events, you are already familiar with such direct expenses as risers, lighting, sound, talent, teleprompters, power distribution, writers, technicians, and setup/dismantle crews.

As it is the objective of any business to generate profits while delivering a valuable product or service, it is essential to identify, in advance, *all* direct expenses pertaining to fulfilling a contract with your client. Clients expect to be asked to recompense their vendors for expenses encountered and satisfied on their behalf.

You can not afford to subsidize their projects out of your profits, and no reasonable client would ever expect you to. That is why it is so important to identify not only the obvious direct expense items, but some of the "hidden" direct costs a special events businessperson encounters while servicing their clients. Consider allocating some of your project budgets to reimburse your company for consumable office supplies, telephone and fax long distance charges, copier usage, and other easily documented out-of-pocket expenses that would not have been utilized had you not been working on that project. Public relations agencies, lawyers, and other businesses have been following this practice for decades. You may find it worthwhile to repay yourself for these hidden costs and discover that while doing so may have a minimum impact on your project budgets, it could have a larger, additive effect on your indirect expenses at the end of the year.

As you design your master corporate budget, also be cognizant of costs that may be attributable to a given piece of business but can not be reasonably classified as a direct expense. For example, if you pay commissions to your sales force, your client would not expect or be pleased to pay this as a direct out-of-pocket expense. The commission payable on a piece of business will have to come out of your gross profits, as might other expenses such as research and development conducted prior to your selection as a vendor.

It is important to keep track of direct expenses as they are incurred by your various projects to ensure that you have enough cash on hand to meet your obligations. While a deposit or advance you receive from your clients is cash-in-hand, it is not an asset that belongs to you. It really still belongs to your client. As unearned income, advance payments are considered as liabilities, since you will either use these funds to satisfy bills on behalf of your client's project, or be obligated to return them if you do not complete the project. It is not money you should use to run your business. Rather, it should be physically separated to deliver on your promises to your clients. Many special events businesses achieve this separation by maintaining two types of bank accounts—a *production account* into which advances are deposited and drawn upon to fulfill client obligations, and an *operating account* into which gross profits are deposited, and out of which overhead costs are paid.

Gross Profit on Sales

As discussed earlier, gross profit on sales is the result of deducting direct expenses and other applicable charges, such as commissions, from gross revenues. Because you have so far only accounted for direct expenses at your own cost, gross profit on sales includes any fees, markups, and administrative charges you have charged the customer in fulfilling your obligations. It is essential that your fees, markups, administrative charges, or whatever other methods you will use to generate revenues not only exceed the direct costs of your projects, but also provide enough additional cash to cover all of the indirect costs of operating your business as well. Otherwise, you will lose money, and over time you could lose your business.

For most businesses, the rule of thumb is to ensure that no more than 70 percent of gross event revenues be earmarked for direct expenses, leaving a *margin* of at least 30 percent to cover your general operating costs plus profit. You can extend this 30 percent margin for your company by developing ancillary revenue streams, as previously discussed.

The way you get to your 30 percent margin depends on the exact nature of your business and the types of clients you service. Many mature special events companies attempt to allocate 15 percent, or half of their gross profit, to cover the indirect expenses of operating their business, leaving the other 15 percent for pure profit. But, in the formative years of your business, do not be surprised if you need all 30 percent of your gross revenues—and in the very beginning, maybe even more—to cover operating costs.

Generating Profits: Fees and Pricing Structures

Some special events businesses charge clients a *package price* for their products or services. The budget or cost estimate the client receives contains a single figure for the work performed or the products provided. In this case, it is up to the entrepreneur to estimate the scope of the work and the amount that must be charged to generate the revenues required to cover direct expenses plus some percentage of indirect costs and a profit before work commences. A package pricing structure works well for companies providing nontechnical products through retail or wholesale channels, highly technical or specialized services for clients with little or no sophistication in the industry, and in markets where competition is relatively low or nonexistent. If competition is high, a simple price comparison could put your business at a distinct competitive disadvantage. A low-ball price from your competition could be based on providing inferior product, or a less complete list of services. Since a package price provides the client with no points of comparison, they may decide to buy from your competitor solely on economic grounds, and shortchange themselves in the process.

If your events business sells hard goods, such as décor, catering, or transportation, the prices you quote must include a markup to cover your operating costs. If you have additional revenue streams available to you, such as the sale of service contracts, you may be able to reduce your margin on the sale to offer a purchase price low enough to be competitive. Clients with a greater familiarity with the product frequently expect a cost breakdown—a list of precisely what they will be expected to pay for defined products and services within the total charge. In this way, an educated client can determine whether two competitive bids are comparable in terms of comprehensiveness and product quality. The degree of detail you provide in a cost breakdown will not only depend upon the type of business you operate; it will also depend on the client you are servicing, and your own assessment of what your clients want or expect to see in their cost estimates. In some cases, you may find it best to provide a moderate amount of detail to your client, with each budget line *marked up* by the 30 percent margin you need to run your business. In other cases, the budget might outline direct expenses at your cost, with your fee and administrative charges added in as a separate budget line. In still others, a blend of 15 percent markups and a 15 percent fee might be most appropriate.

The blended fee and markup format may make the most sense if your business offers intellectual, technical, or creative services. In these cases, it is common for the project budget to include a charge of 15 percent (or more) for creative development or as a production fee, with the remaining 15 percent spread as a markup across all other budget lines. A variant involves showing a 15 percent fee, plus an additional 15 percent for "administrative" or "overhead" costs to cover the services of company staff members who were not charged as a direct expense to the project budget, routine photocopying, postage, faxing, telephone service, project bookkeeping, and payroll administration expenses. Some clients do not raise an eyebrow over recompensing you for your overhead, but in most cases, it is best to minimize the perceived impact of recovering your indirect expenses by modestly marking up other budget lines. It is not very important to be consistent in how you represent your margin in project budgets or estimates from client to client. Assess what pricing structure will best win you the particular piece of business you are competing for, but be sure to recover the margin you need to survive and flourish.

From time to time, you may be tempted to reduce your margin in order to win a particularly prestigious client or piece of business. Think very carefully about whether you can afford to commit yourself to lowering your income requirements on a plum project. In most cases, it is ill advised. Rarely will you be able to recover these lost revenues by the end of the year, without increasing your margin on other projects and decreasing the value given to your full-paying clients.

Indirect Expenses—Overhead

The gross profits generated by the work you perform can be significant, but if your indirect expenses are high, you will have to charge your clients more or allocate a higher percentage of their project budgets to ensure that you will be able to cover your overhead expenses. Since maintaining higher prices when compared to your competitors can put you at a distinct disadvantage, it is important to keep your overhead as low as possible to ensure you can work at the lowest possible margin.

If you are an experienced events professional, you know direct expenses like the back of your hand. But, for the experienced professional turned new entrepreneur or department head, the "indirects" can cause nightmares. In the special events industry, indirect expenses are those costs that are not directly attributable to a particular project. Indirect expenses can be grouped into several major categories, including personnel, office and administrative expenses, research and development, non-event-specific travel and entertainment, marketing and promotion. In short, any expense you encounter in running a company that does not relate to providing a service, acquiring products for resale, or for which your clients do not directly recompense you, may be classified as an indirect expense.

As previously mentioned, indirect expenses are often called fixed costs in other industries. In the special events industry, we prefer the term *indirects* because most of our businesses are project-oriented. In our industry, what are usually thought of as fixed costs are all of those expenses that are indirectly related to the earning of our revenues. Because the flow of projects—and consequently, cash flow—is usually unpredictable, special events firms should not look at indirects as truly fixed. Frequently, expenses need to be adjusted down on a short-term basis to cover shortfalls, and in happier instances, may be adjusted up on a short-term basis to cover a large temporary influx of work.

As mentioned, indirect expenses have to be paid with the net profits generated by event projects or sales. As there is no direct revenue stream to offset indirect expenses, it is generally wise to project every possible indirect cost in your master budget, and to keep them as low as is feasible. Use Figure 5–2 as a checklist of major indirect expense categories you should consider when creating your first budget. Think carefully about what you think each item is going to cost, and then add a little more to it. Things will usually cost more than you expect, and if they don't, it is far more pleasant to put money back into your pocket unexpectedly than to have to pull some more out. If you are able, set aside an overall contingency factor of 10–15 percent over your total indirect expense budget to account for unforeseen expenses. If you can not afford to do this, you are probably undercapitalized and in danger of running short of funds before the end of your budget year.

People Costs

For many businesses, the most capital-intense expenses are those costs relating to personnel. Personnel expenses include salaries (including your own), overtime, taxes, payroll services or administration costs, and benefits such as life insurance, medical and dental coverage, and retirement plans. Frequently, start-up companies do not offer even the most rudimentary employee benefits. Other than payroll and social security taxes, there is no legal requirement to offer your employees such benefits, although the presence of at least some will make you a more competitive employer in the future.

It is generally wise to employ the fewest number of permanent full-time employees possible. If your business is seasonal or project-oriented, you may be best served by hiring "freelancers" on a project-by-project basis (see Chapter 9 for a full discussion of freelancers and other seasonal employees). Because you are not carrying the costs of providing employment to project-specific staff all year long, you may be able to incorporate their salaries into your project budgets as direct expenses and thereby better control your indirect payroll costs.

In addition to freelance project team members, using a commissioned sales manager or sales force can ensure that personnel costs stay in line with the revenues they generate. As can be seen in Figure

5–1, the costs of maintaining a salesperson can be divided between direct and indirect expenses. In this example, the sales manager's base salary of $32,000 is an indirect, fixed cost for as long as he or she keeps their job. In today's competitive marketplace, it may not be realistic to expect a salesperson to work on the basis of just their base salary, certainly not such a modest one. A base-plus-commission structure enables you to keep your costs commensurate with the revenues they generate, while providing a powerful personal incentive to the employee to deliver more, and larger, sales. While the rate at which commissions are earned will differ from company to company, our budget example for Most Excellent Events assumes a 3 percent commission rate on total sales of $900,000, or direct expenses against sales of an additional $27,000. Therefore, at year's end, the salesperson is budgeted to earn a total of $59,000, but in fact may earn far more if they are successful in increasing gross sales. From a managerial standpoint, since the salesperson's income grows with the revenues they generate for the company, this structure also assists you in compensating the salesperson to the level of their true worth.

Office Expenses

The second most common indirect expenses are those relating to providing your company with a place to do business. While personnel expenses can be adjusted, albeit painfully, in times of economic crisis, the financial terms for the rent for your office, warehouse, or other facilities are usually less flexible.

The costs of moving your business can also be dear. It is therefore very important that you invest great forethought in selecting the location for your place of business. Think about the clients you will be serving. Does your business require a premium address in the heart of downtown, or will a suite in a suburban corporate or industrial park suffice? Will you often be inviting current or potential clients to your facility? Will physical accessibility for your clients be important, or are you most often going to be visiting your clients? Will you be maintaining a showroom? Who will be visiting your showroom? Do your facilities allow room for expansion? Will your lease permit you to sublet portions of your space should you need to downsize? Can you afford the cost and amount of square footage? How long a term do you have to commit to? How many months in advance must your initial payment cover? How many months security deposit do you need to put down? Answers to all of these questions will need to be addressed before you lease a space.

Some start-up events entrepreneurs and consultants consider working out of an office in their home. The cost of maintaining a home office is attractive in that your space costs in terms of rent are already paid for. In many cases, there may also be tax benefits available, enabling you to deduct a percentage of your home's annual rent, or mortgage and real estate tax expenses, and utility costs, from your personal tax obligations. You should secure the services of a reputable accountant or financial advisor to evaluate the amount you may be able to deduct, if any. Their assessment will usually be based on the proportion of space in your home that is occupied by your office, and the percentage of time that space is used exclusively for conducting your business and generating income.

While a home office is often the most economical option available, it is not always the most practical. When your business, or the projects you are working on, require a staff beyond the physical capacity of your home office, you should consider at least temporary quarters elsewhere. You may want to investigate the feasibility of renting space in a corporate office suite. These cost-effective, short-term facilities commonly provide one or more private offices off of a common lobby shared by other small businesses, a receptionist to answer or forward your calls and take messages, and access to a conference room, secretarial services, and office equipment, among other services. If you do most of your work over the telephone, a corporate office suite is indistinguishable from having your own private facilities from the client's point of view. Short-term expandability may also be available should you require additional temporary staff for specific projects; however, you may pass these additional costs on to the project as a direct cost.

Whether you will be working from your home or leasing your own space, the details to be considered when creating your master budget are numerous. How much money will you need to invest in building out the space to your specifications? How much will the landlord contribute to the build-out? What furnishings will you need? Will you need to install drywall or partitions? Does the space need more overhead and task lighting, additional cabling for power, telephone service, or computer networking? Do you need to rent or purchase office furniture such as desks, workstations, file cabinets, shelving, and storage cabinets?

Once you have your physical infrastructure in place, you will also need all of the equipment required to make a business run. Consider your needs for telephones, cellular phones, pagers, computers, printers, copiers, fax machines, postal scales and meters, as well as any special equipment required to function in your segment of the special events industry. Think about whether you will opt to have service contracts for these items, or pay for maintenance and repair on an as-needed basis. Will you purchase or lease this equipment, and for how long?

Capital Equipment

If you decide to purchase your furniture and business equipment outright, you will have expended cash, but at first not really expended any capital. In the eyes of your accountant—and more importantly in the United States—the IRS, you have simply exchanged one asset (cash) for another (capital equipment). The value of that asset will diminish, or *depreciate,* over time. Let's say you purchase a desk. The useful life of that desk might be ten years. In the simplest case— known as *straight-line depreciation*—the value of that desk diminishes by one-tenth of its original value each year. After the tenth year, the asset no longer has any real value, and may be ready to be replaced.

The amount *amortized* each year (i.e., the amount that can be depreciated) depends upon the physical asset being considered. Copiers might only have a useful life of five years, and nowadays computer equipment may need to be replaced after three years at the latest. Even though this equipment is carried on your books as an asset, it does not have the essential liquidity of cash, the substance necessary for the payment of your bills. For the purposes of your cash flow, it is money spent and gone. The only financial value capital equipment has to your business is the amount of money you can generate by selling it on the used market, or trading it in for new equipment.

Most start-up companies will seek to minimize purchases, and choose to lease or rent capital equipment. This strategy leaves you with a predictable monthly expense for these items and requires far less up-front cash. In the beginning, it is wise to conserve capital to tide you over until you have established more predictable cash flow. So, in most cases, as little cash as possible should be invested in capital equipment. After all, when it is time to make payroll, you can't pay your staff in shares of capital equipment, even though it is carried as an asset on your books.

Another reason many companies lease equipment is the current rapid pace of technological advancement. After only a few years, for example, your computer equipment may be completely out of date and worthless except for a minimal trade-in value. But, if you have financed a purchase of the equipment, you may be obligated to continue using—and paying—for equipment you might rather replace. This explosion in innovation is not limited to office equipment alone. Innovation within the special events specialties also abounds. A lighting company may decide to lease equipment on a short-term basis on the belief that the introduction of new, advanced, computer-controlled lighting instruments are imminent. An audio-visual supplier may lease rear projection systems because of a belief that large, digital plasma screens, which do not require projectors at all, will soon become the client-preferred state-of-the-art. Or, a party goods manufacturer may lease packaging equipment with the thought in mind of procuring more advanced, high-speed equipment capable of processing greater volumes of goods as the company grows.

If, for whatever reason, you do decide to purchase capital equipment, you can frequently negotiate financing terms with your suppliers. An outright cash purchase is far less expensive in the long term, but it might also eat up a lot of cash that could be better used in other areas, such as marketing your new business or hiring necessary staff. Obtaining reasonable financing allows you to spend a manageable and predictable amount of money per year, although over the life of the loan you could be spending up to twice as much, or more,

Tom Bollard is one of the principals of Meeting Services, Inc. (MSI), an established special events contractor based in San Diego, California. MSI's broad range of services places particular emphasis on providing technical equipment and services to both corporate end-users and special events producers nationwide. Because this mature company conducts a high-volume rental business, Bollard prefers purchasing equipment that he can rent to others. "The essence of the rental business is: 'I own this piece of gear and you can borrow it,' " Bollard explains. But, when it comes back (a) I get the light back, and (b) I get money. Once the equipment pays for itself, it's all gravy."

before you pay off the lender. And, unlike a lease, you will own your equipment outright at the end of the term with no additional acquisition costs. (A note of caution: Start-up businesses will have no corporate credit history and therefore may have difficulty in establishing the credit necessary to secure the most favorable financing terms from a supplier.)

Administrative Expenses

You probably set aside enough money for pens, copy paper, tape dispensers, staplers, etc. But, did you consider the costs of designing and printing your stationery, envelopes, and business cards? If you are in a creative business, you might want to consider designing a creative logo and selecting a creative typestyle. Creative does not necessarily mean bizarre. In the 1980s, it was very fashionable to select exceedingly small fonts for use on business cards and at the bottom of letterhead. The theory was to involve the recipient in your collateral material—the harder it was to read, the longer someone had to study it to read it. While true, if the recipient had little or marginal interest in your company to start with, your collateral material more than likely landed in the trash pail before anyone could be bothered to read it.

Think carefully about your letterhead. While cost consciousness is always prudent, it is equally true that your stationery is often the first impression a prospective client has of your company. A creative logo, a well-composed layout, and good-quality paper are essential to positioning your company well. If you send a document that looks like rub-off lettering run off on a copy machine, you will give prospects the impression of a fly-by-night, undercapitalized supplier. Few reputable clients are likely to invest time and money in an operation they think has one foot in bankruptcy court and the other on a banana peel.

Telephones are also among the first lines of attack. Rent or invest in a good telephone system with enough lines to handle your business. Include productivity-enhancing features such as voice messaging, but be sure that someone is on hand to answer prospective clients' calls. There is nothing that arouses more suspicion than when a client's calls are consistently answered by a machine rather than a live human's voice. Rather than giving the impression of a busy office, frequent forwarding to voice-messaging gives savvy clients the impression of an office devoid of employees.

Marketing and Promotion

Later we will discuss the many ways to spend your marketing dollars, and just how to choose the best marketing strategies for your new special events company or department. What is important for the sake of the master corporate budget in your business plan is—did you remember to consider everything? For the new entrant into special events company ownership, the next few paragraphs outline a few perils and pitfalls to avoid.

Once you have answered the basic question of how you will go about promoting your company's products or services, you are ready to begin projecting how much it will cost. If advertising is important to your company, remember that there are two types of advertising expenses. The most obvious is the cost of placing your advertising in the media, whether on television, radio, or in print. The cost that many new entrepreneurs overlook in their planning is the cost of *creating* their advertising. Advertising creative expenses may include design fees, layout artists, copywriters, recording studio rentals, and talent fees (e.g., models, actors, voice-over artists), among others.

Creative costs are also inherent in the creation of flyers, brochures, and videotape demo reels. If you have never produced a video before, your new company's first demo is not the time to start. You may have to hire someone to write and produce your video, costs that exceed the actual time logged at an editing house. After creating and editing, leave enough money aside for dubs, or copies, of the videos. Be realistic in estimating how many dubs you need—after you have sent a copy to a prospective client, you will rarely get it back.

For some special events companies, public relations services are more important than traditional advertising. Public relations companies work on either a flat monthly fee or a "retainer plus" basis. The retainer represents the minimum payment per month for the firm's services, and the "plus" for those times when more than the quoted number of monthly hours is required. In either case, be on the lookout for *out-of-pocket expense* charges. Like your own direct expenses, out-of-pockets are those costs a firm undertakes on your behalf—postage, messenger services, couriers, copies and supplies, mileage, travel and entertainment, etc. It is wise to insist on your being able to pre-approve your out-of-pockets over a certain amount per month or per occurrence. You won't want to have to approve every postage stamp as needed, but surprises are things you don't want on the expense side of your ledger.

When completing your budget, think of all other possible bits of collateral material that may be necessary for the way you intend to market your business. Will you need to create attractive sales portfolios and leave-behind kits for your sales force? Will you be mailing cassette tapes or CD-ROMs? Do you think the establishment of your own website is essential to generating new business? Apply the same test to each of these questions—what will it cost to develop, produce, and duplicate these materials? Will you be sending cards and gifts at holiday time, or distributing company-identified premiums on qualified sales calls? Think about how much you wish to spend per prospect, then get it in the budget.

Think You're Finished? Think Again.

You owe it to yourself and your investors or shareholders to project budgets for a minimum of three, and preferably five, years into the future. You and your partners are in this for the "long haul," and a realistic plan for future growth inspires confidence and optimism among those who are investing time or money with you.

It is important to project when you expect to break-even, and more importantly, when you expect to be able to generate profits. As you estimate annual growth in sales, it is equally important to calculate the inevitable impact of this growth on your expenses. For example, when will you need new brochures and demo tapes? How many more staff will you need to add to your indirect expense budget to handle administrative functions as your company grows? By how much will you increase your staff's salaries? Will you need to expand into additional office space to accommodate more activity? What effect will inflation have upon your expenses from year to year?

Don't be overly worried if you find yourself reworking your budgets continually as your company searches for financing and approaches its grand opening. This is not only common, but also a happy consequence of your ongoing efforts to be as comprehensive as possible. As you continue to develop your business plan, a daily stream of new information will cause you to consider adjusting your ideas and approaches, and almost every new idea has a financial cost. Since your capital will be limited, costs for new ideas will necessitate downward adjustments in other areas.

Once your company is up and running, you will discover that it is a rare day, indeed, when your actual revenues and expenses match the figures in your budget. There are always unforeseen surprises—of both the happy and unhappy variety. Because a budget is a living document, the smart manager adds more columns to the original budget form for the purpose of periodic *re-forecasting*.

Many managers prepare a budget re-forecast on a monthly or, at minimum, a quarterly basis similar to the example in Figure 5–3. This budget worksheet analyzes the revenue and expense activity of Most Excellent Events after the first quarter. The column to the right of the 1st quarter line total shows *Actual To Date* activity. All of the revenues actually received and bills actually paid are represented in these totals. The third column shows the *variance* between budgeted revenues and expenses, and actual performance. The last column (*To Go*) shows how much of your budget remains through the end of the fiscal year, how much revenue the company will still have to generate, and all things being equal, how much remains to be spent in each area.

By re-forecasting your budget in this manner, you can determine whether you are ahead or behind on revenue projections and whether you need to take cost-saving measures due to greater than anticipated expenses or lower than expected revenues. If your expenses are generally regularly spaced throughout the year, and you have exceeded 50 percent of a budget line by the time six months have elapsed, you may want to begin considering how you will make it up in other areas. (This is a very simplistic view for the purposes of this chapter. Refer to Chapter 6 for a more thorough discussion of how a "cash flow" analysis is used to help in the re-forecasting process.)

Portraits of Financial Health

As previously mentioned, your budget provides you with a detailed guideline of how much revenue you expect to generate, and the expenses you expect to encounter. At year's end, the ultimate performance of your company against the budget is contained in an *income statement*, a document that provides a snapshot picture of your

I. Revenues

	1st Quarter Budget	Actual To Date	Variance	Annual Budget	To Go
Gross Event Revenues	$ 100,000	$ 85,000	$ (15,000)	$ 900,000	$ 815,000
Less Direct Event Expenses	$ 70,000	$ 59,500	$ 10,500	$ 630,000	$ 570,500
Less Commissions	$ 3,000	$ 2,550	$ 450	$ 27,000	$ 24,450
Net Event Revenues	$ 27,000	$ 22,950	$ (4,050)	$ 243,000	$ 220,050
Other Revenue	$ 2,000	$ 1,500	$ (500)	$ 13,500	$ 12,000
Total Net Revenues	**$ 29,000**	**$ 24,450**	**$ (4,550)**	**$ 256,500**	**$ 232,050**

II. Indirect (Operating) Expenses

1. Permanent Staff

	1st Quarter Budget	Actual To Date	Variance	Annual Budget	To Go
President	$ 17,000	$ 17,000	$ —	$ 68,000	$ 51,000
Sales Manager (Base Salary)	$ 8,000	$ 8,000	$ —	$ 32,000	$ 24,000
Sales Assistant	$ 7,000	$ 6,750	$ 250	$ 28,000	$ 21,250
Receptionist	$ 6,000	$ 5,500	$ 500	$ 24,000	$ 18,500
Payroll Subtotal	**$ 38,000**	**$ 37,250**	**$ 750**	**$ 152,000**	**$ 114,750**
Payroll Taxes	$ 3,500	$ 3,450	$ 50	$ 14,000	$ 10,550
Health Benefits	$ 1,750	$ 1,875	$ (125)	$ 7,000	$ 5,125
Total Permanent Staff	**$ 43,250**	**$ 42,575**	**$ 675**	**$ 173,000**	**$ 130,425**

2. Marketing and Promotion

	1st Quarter Budget	Actual To Date	Variance	Annual Budget	To Go
Advertising	$ 7,500	$ 7,000	$ 500	$ 19,000	$ 12,000
Brochures & Flyers	$ 8,000	$ 10,555	$ (2,555)	$ 9,000	$ (1,555)

Presentations & Portfolios	$ 2,000	$ 2,540	$ (540)	$ 7,000	$ 4,460
Corporate Video & Dubs	$ 5,000	$ 8,575	$ (3,575)	$ 5,500	$ (3,075)
Public Relations	$ —	$ —	$ —	$ 7,000	$ 7,000
Travel & Entertainment	$ 1,500	$ 2,250	$ (750)	$ 7,500	$ 5,250
Gifts & Premiums	$ 500	$ —	$ 500	$ 1,500	$ 1,500
Total Marketing and Promotion	**$ 24,500**	**$ 30,920**	**$ (6,420)**	**$ 56,500**	**$ 25,580**
3. Administrative/Office Expenses					
Office/Warehouse Rent	$ 1,250	$ 1,250	$ —	$ 5,750	$ 4,500
Stationery and Supplies	$ 2,500	$ 2,875	$ (375)	$ 4,800	$ 1,925
Telephone	$ 1,200	$ 1,440	$ (240)	$ 4,250	$ 2,810
Postage, Messengers, Shipping	$ 750	$ 675	$ 75	$ 5,000	$ 4,325
Insurance	$ 500	$ 500	$ —	$ 2,000	$ 1,500
Dues & Subscriptions	$ 500	$ 450	$ 50	$ 750	$ 300
Total Administrative/Office Expenses	**$ 6,700**	**$ 7,190**	**$ (490)**	**$ 22,550**	**$ 15,360**
Subtotal Expenses	**$ 74,450**	**$ 80,685**	**$ (6,235)**	**$ 252,050**	**$ 171,365**
Contingency Allowance	**$ 7,445**			**$ 25,205**	**$ 16,255**
Legal Fees	$ —	$ 5,000			
Temporary Personnel	$ —	$ 2,500			
Miscellaneous	$ —	$ 1,450			
TOTAL EXPENSES	**$ 81,895**	**$ 89,635**	**$ (7,740)**	**$ 277,255**	**$ 187,620**
NET PROFIT (LOSS)	**$ (52,895)**	**$ (65,185)**	**$ (12,290)**	**$ (20,755)**	

Figure 5–3   Most Excellent Events: 1st Quarter Master Budget Reforecast: January 1, 2000–March 31, 2000

firm's financial health by concisely summarizing all revenues, expenses, and ultimately profits or losses. For entrepreneurial special events department heads, profits and losses may be referred to as the department's *net contribution* to the company. Figure 5–4 is a sample year-end income statement for Most Excellent Events, the data for which would have been compiled by an accountant from the company's *general ledger*, a listing of all deposits and withdrawals by line item, or account.

It is tempting to attempt to save on the cost of preparing income statements by preparing them yourself. As an income statement is essentially a less detailed budget re-forecast, its preparation is certainly within the reach of owners of simple, small operations with no outstanding loans or plans for significant expansion. If, however, you share equity in your company with other partners or capital shareholders, owe substantial sums to a lender, or will seek to secure a loan in the future, it is strongly suggested that you hire a certified professional accountant (CPA) to prepare your income statement. Preparation by a CPA ensures a fair, accurate, and impartial portrayal to all of the stakeholders in your company who have an interest in the success of your business.

Income statements, together with the company's balance sheet,

INCOME		
Gross Revenues	$	785,000
Less: Direct Event Expenses	$	555,900
Less: Commissions	$	23,550
Gross Profits	$	229,100
OPERATING (INDIRECT) EXPENSES		
Permanent Staff	$	165,000
Marketing & Promotion	$	74,000
Administrative/Office Expenses	$	18,850
Total Operating Expenses	$	**257,850**
Net Profit (Loss)	$	**(28,750)**

Figure 5–4   Most Excellent Events Income Statement: December 31, 1999

provide an important early-warning system against financial disaster. A *balance sheet* is a list of all of your firm's assets and liabilities. Assets include cash, accounts receivable (i.e., outstanding invoices you have issued for which you expect imminent payment), and capital equipment less depreciation (see the earlier discussion on capital equipment). The sum total of all of your assets will equal the total of your liabilities plus the equity in your business. Liabilities include accounts payable (i.e., unpaid bills for which you expect to make imminent payment) and unearned income (i.e., cash you have received for work not yet completed). Equity is the amount of capital invested in the business by you and others. Figure 5–5 provides a hypothetical

ASSETS		
Current Assets		
Cash and cash equivalents	$	181,582
Pre-paid expenses	$	5,435
Equipment, furniture, and leasehold improvements[1]	$	24,873
Total Assets	**$**	**211,890**
LIABILITIES AND EQUITY		
Current Liabilities		
Accounts payable	$	51,635
Unearned income	$	54,005
Total Liabilities	**$**	**105,640**
Equity (Capital)		
Balance—February 8, 1999[2]	$	120,000
Additional capital contribution	$	15,000
Less: Net (loss)—year ended December 31, 1999	$	(28,750)
Total Equity	**$**	**106,250**
Total Liabilities and Equity	**$**	**211,890**

Notes:

[1] Figure is net of accumulated depreciation using the straight-line method over the estimated useful life of the asset.

[2] Company began operating this date. Future fiscal years will run January 1st through December 31st.

Figure 5–5　Most Excellent Events Balance Sheet: December 31, 1999

example of a balance sheet for Most Excellent Events. As is true of your income statement, it is wise to have a professional accountant prepare your company's balance sheet.

What Do I Do If I Was Wrong?

Financial difficulties are probably around the corner when your overall revenue variances are highly negative (i.e., your income is lower than expected) and/or your expense variances are highly positive (i.e., you are spending more than expected). What do you do when you see trouble looming?

Like anything else, an ounce of prevention is worth a pound of cure. If you believe that better times are ahead, and you are willing to continue or increase your level of financial risk, it may be time to consider drawing on a line of credit, asking investors for additional capital, or attracting new investors. Because it is, of course, easier to get a commitment from a lender when you don't really need the money, it is wise to talk to your lender while your finances are healthy. Rather than an outright loan when you don't need it, ask your lender for a *line of credit*. A line of credit does not guarantee a loan will be available when you need it. But, the longer you possess a line of credit without using it, the more likely it will help with a loan approval when you do need it, shrinking the amount of time you will need to hunt for new or temporary capital. It is much harder to shop for money when you are desperate for it and don't have the time to wait.

The first place to go for a line of credit, and ultimately a loan, is the bank which services your firm's checking account. If you have a history free of overdrawn checks, and have maintained a positive balance through the life of your company's relationship with that bank, you are more likely to get a line of credit. It is therefore a good idea to set up your banking relationship with an institution that specializes in servicing companies of your size in your geographic area. Your business will be important to them, and because they want to continue to service your business account, they will be more inclined to support your firm with a line of credit or loan, when needed. They would not want to lose your day-to-day banking business to a lender who is more willing to support your company.

There is another reason to have a line of credit in your arsenal for quick deployment when needed. Companies with which you do business may require credit references before they extend payment terms to you. This is particularly important for capital-intense operations like rental firms, lighting companies, and caterers. You will probably not be in a position to, or want to have to pay cash for the large quantities of equipment you will need to conduct your business. An experienced manufacturer, distributor, or wholesaler will often require credit references before they ship product to companies with whom they have not had a long business relationship. Prospective clients may also request credit references to ensure that once they begin sending your advance checks, you will not disconnect your phone and disappear. Likewise, you may, as part of your contract negotiation with a prospective client, request credit references from companies with whom you have no previous relationship, or familiarity. While it may seem generally unnecessary to acquire credit histories from well-established, publicly recognizable corporations, it is wise to check into any company's financial health before performing services or providing product for which you are not paid in advance or upon delivery. This information can be least expensively obtained from Dun & Bradstreet, whose "D&Bs" provide a wide variety of corporate financial data, as well as information on pending litigation for thousands of companies.

Should you automatically take that loan when you begin running short of cash? No, not until you have re-analyzed and prioritized your expenses. If you have budgeted well, you probably did not plan to spend money you didn't need to, so it may be very difficult to reduce your anticipated expenses. But, cutting or deferring expenses is far more preferable than taking a loan. Look at every expense line and see if you can reasonably put off certain discretionary purchases until such time as you do have sufficient cash reserves. Can you use the same brochure for another quarter- or half-year without affecting your ability to book business? Can you put off adding another clerical employee without damaging your ability to collect on receivables? Or, can you slow your payment schedule to vendors, with their advance agreement, to 45 or 60 days?

When taking on additional debt through a loan, remember that adding to your debt load means adding bank interest to your list of monthly expenses through the life of those new and all existing loans. And, you don't get something for nothing. You may have to put up even more collateral to secure that loan.

What If My Customers Are Not as Good a Customer as I Am?

Chances are that you depend upon your customers to pay you in order for you to pay your staff and suppliers. It is important for you to establish payment terms with your clients in advance that will provide you with access to their cash at the time that you need it to pay your creditors. A good practice is to attempt to receive deposits and advances in the amount of your direct project costs (depending upon your margin, perhaps as much as 70 percent of total project costs) ahead of the time you need to pay them. They may be paid in one or more installments, but most certainly before the day of the event. The final payment due from your customer would then represent your profit margin and overhead, and would most often be due on or just before the day of the event. As a buyer, your customer would be wise not pay you in full until services are fully rendered and found to be fully satisfactory. If you can get your money in full, in advance, great. But, if not, insist on being paid no later than the day your project is completed.

To ensure long-term success for your company, it is important that you maintain good credit. The easiest way to maintain good credit is to pay your bills on time. Savvy prospective clients will look into the finances of any company they wish to trust with their money, and many will utilize credit agencies to do so. Reports from credit agencies do not contain explanations that the reason you are occasionally late in meeting your financial obligations is because some of your clients did not pay you on time, or as promised. All they evaluate is whether you can be counted upon to pay your bills on time. Most events companies are small; if you have large companies as clients, they would be following good business practice to check you out. If you live too close to the edge, and your payment histories indicate delayed-, or non-payment, they might choose to look elsewhere for a special events contractor.

If you can not avoid late payments to vendors, honesty and disclosure is the best policy. If you anticipate running short on cash, but expect revenues within a reasonable amount of time, contact the suppliers you owe to discuss payment options. You may be able to agree to terms (e.g., pay half now, half in 30 days; another 15–30 days for full payment; or a down payment now and interest on the remaining balance), and avoid being reported to a credit agency as a reluctant bill payer.

Sometimes, even after doing all your homework, you may find it difficult to collect the money you are owed from a client. For large sums, you may opt to employ the services of a collection agency. A collection agency will use various legal means to encourage your debtors to pay you. The agency will receive a percentage of whatever they recover on your behalf, and typically you are paid once they are paid.

If you don't have the time to wait for a collection agency to go through the process of being paid, and eventually receiving payment, a factor is also an option. Factors purchase your receivables for a negotiated percentage of their full cash value, and then attempt to collect as much of the bill as they can. Your yield is far less with a factor, but once they take on the case, you are usually paid quickly, and without regard as to whether they will ever be paid. Factors, however, usually prefer working on large accounts with a large number of receivables, as they are taking the risk that some percentage of your customers will never pay. It is unlikely that the receivables for a small, service-oriented special events company will be valued very highly by a factor.

Regardless of whether you use a collections agency or factor, use these firms as a last resort. Letters from collections agencies can turn a slow-paying, but steady client into an antagonistic enemy. It is better, when possible, to use the same philosophy with clients as you do with suppliers. Call them to discuss whether extended payment terms are attractive to them. Perhaps they, too, are suffering a cash shortage. If you work with them to work out payment terms, your loyalty to them as a customer may result in gaining more of their business once their own financial situation improves.

What Should I Do If I See My Projects Going Over Budget?

As the majority of revenues and expenses for most special events companies flow from project budgets, the overall financial performance of the firm is closely tied to the financial performance of each project. Every special events professional has experienced budget overruns of some degree or variety. If you have written the contract or purchase agreement with your client wisely, your company could be protected against serious trouble. Most special event producers know to include a contingency factor for direct expenses of 10 percent or more into their event budgets. Frequently, clients will insist upon unforeseen changes in event specifications, and as we all know, most changes result in additional expenses. If your contract or purchase agreement includes the ability of the client to make some number or specific kinds of changes, you should build these additional contingencies into your project budget. If not, or for changes beyond those outlined in your client agreement, insist that your clients agree to a change order system. That is, if the scope, scale, or type of work changes at the client's request, provide them with an estimate of the overage immediately. Have them sign a change order, which includes a statement of estimated additional costs, and a stated agreement that they will be responsible for recompensing you for the overage. In this way, they will understand, in advance, that the overage was a result of their changes. It is best to have this understanding clear between the parties before the event so there are no surprises or reinterpretations later.

On rare occasions, you might find that a special events project has been delivered to your client under budget. If you occasionally find you have not used all of the contingency money set aside in your project budgets, how you treat this extra cash again depends on how you have structured your client agreement. Most clients would expect a refund on unused event contingencies. On one hand, it demonstrates how trustworthy you are. On the other, if the savings are significantly more than just the contingency allowance in your project budget, it suggests to a client that you do not budget realistically. One way to get value from a budget savings for both you and your client is to offer to credit it against future business for a mutually agreeable term (typically 12 months, to ensure you don't have to keep cash on hand as unearned income for longer than a year).

The View From Here

1. The master budget is the primary financial planning and tracking document for your business. It is composed of revenues, expenses, and the net contribution (profit or loss). A realistic bud-

get, in which the net contribution falls within industry norms, is also a key sales tool to attract capital investors.

2. Direct expenses are those that you pay to fulfill your contractual obligations to your clients. Indirect expenses are those that you pay to operate your special events business. You expect to be reimbursed for direct expenses, plus a profit margin, by your clients. You generate a profit through some combination of fees, markups, and/or administrative charges.

3. Gross profits are determined by subtracting your direct expenses from your gross event revenues. Net profits are determined by subtracting indirect expenses from gross profits.

4. Budgets are planning documents. Your actual financial performance should be tracked against the budget at least quarterly, and adjustments made as needed to achieve your financial objectives. Be sure that your budgets are comprehensive, estimating every type of expense you expect to encounter.

5. An income statement provides a snapshot of how your company actually performed with respect to revenues generated, gross profits, indirect expenses encountered, and your final profit or loss.

Tools of the Trade

Damodaran, Aswath. *Corporate Finance Theory & Practice*. New York: John Wiley & Sons, 1997.

Tracy, John A. *Accounting For Dummies*. Foster City, Calif.: IDG Books Worldwide, 1997.

Breaking New Ground

1. Combining personal savings, loans from friends, and the participation of a capital partner, you have access to $200,000 in capital. Create a master corporate budget for a small special events planning company expecting $500,000 in gross revenues in the first year. How much additional capital will you need? How will you get it?

2. What contingency plan would you follow if, after six months, it appears that you will generate only 75 percent of expected revenues at the end of the year?

3. Can you think of a situation when it is more advantageous to "write-off" the value of capital equipment all at once, rather than amortizing the costs over a period of three or more years?

CHAPTER 6

Finding Capital

Step Six: *Finding capital is essential to the start, growth, and sustainability of your event organization.*

Have you ever been in the uncomfortable position of having *too much month left* with *too little money* in your bank balance? Certainly every individual from time to time may experience this discomfort. Perhaps the most challenging period is the development and growth cycle of the entrepreneurial endeavor. In step six you will learn how to acquire sufficient capital to properly run your business or establish a budget within your organization's business unit that will adequately support your strategic objectives.

Whether your funding is derived from personal sources, family and friends, the bank, or even future customers and/or vendors, it is critical that you carefully identify how much money will be needed and for how long. Most small businesses are out of business within a year or two because they have literally run out of money. This does not need to occur, and step six may be seen as the second stage booster for your business rocket that will help ensure that you do not run out of fuel before you reach your destination.

Michael Gerber, in *The E-Myth Revisited,* states that, "There is a myth in this country, I call it the E-Myth, which states that small businesses are started by entrepreneurs risking capital to make a profit. This is simply not so. The real reasons people start businesses has little to do with Entrepreneurship." Gerber, who has worked with thousands of small businesses, knows that most individuals fall into one of three categories: technician, manager, or entrepreneur, and to be successful in the long term you must understand the importance and unique skills required of each role.

The manager within you must make certain that you are projecting revenues and expenses in a realistic manner that will enable you to develop a budget and financial plan to acquire the proper amount of capital with the appropriate terms for repayment. Too often the budget process becomes a "wish list" and is far removed from the actual reality of the business.

Types of Business Entities

Before you decide to identify sources of capital, you must first establish your business entity. The most common types of business entities are the sole proprietorship, the partnership, and the corporation. Each entity has different advantages for the entrepreneur.

The *sole proprietorship* is the least complicated business entity. If you are working from home, or just starting your venture, this may be the most prudent way to begin. The sole proprietorship is designed for one-person businesses that do not include multiple partners and do not distribute profits to investors other than the sole proprietor.

The *partnership* is an entity of two or more individuals who not only share the risk but also benefit from the profits of the business. They may or may not be equal partners, meaning that each partner may have a slightly smaller or larger share of the risk and reward.

The corporation is the most logical entity for those entrepreneurs whose businesses are likely to grow to a significantly larger size and where there are considerable risk management concerns. One of the major advantages of the corporate entity is that the corporation forms an invisible but often impenetrable veil between the business owner's personal and business assets. Should the business be sued for lack of performance or an error of omission, it will be difficult for the plaintiff to seize the personal assets of the business owner as a result of the action. In addition, there are considerable tax benefits (deductions) for corporate entities.

Determining the type of business entity will not only limit or potentially expand the type of financing that is available to you but will also have important tax and risk management ramifications. To determine the best type of business entity for your event organization it is important that you consult with both a certified public accountant and an attorney specializing in business law. In many cases the accountant will be able to recommend an attorney who is familiar with the accountant's recommendations and have a symbiotic relationship that will help you avoid conflicting messages between the two professionals.

Capital Building Tools

One of the most important tools is accurate financial data. If your business has been in existence for at least three full years, ask your accountant or bookkeeper to collect your financial information for this period. Now add up the gross revenues and divide by three and you will identify the average earnings for the past three years. If the revenues have steadily increased over the past three years, depict this on a chart as in Figure 6–1.

This type of graphical data provides potential funders with a clear picture of the financial health of your organization.

You are beginning to build a case that will help others understand why it is logical to invest in your event organization. There are a variety of sources you may turn to in search of starting capital or growth capital for your event organization. Remember, whether you

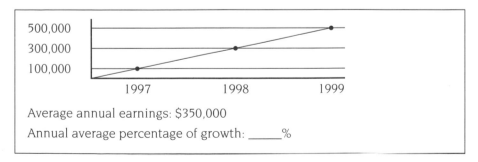

Average annual earnings: $350,000

Annual average percentage of growth: _____%

Figure 6–1   Gross Revenue 1997–1999

are an entrepreneur or an entrepreneurial employee, there will come a time when you will need to identify funding sources. The entrepreneurial employee may need seed money to fund a new division or project. The classic entrepreneur typically will need funding to start their business and may at some period in the business life cycle require assistance to expand in order to prevent decline.

The very first step in obtaining financing or capital for a new event business investment is to carefully analyze your need for money. This can be done through cash flow projections as well as identifying the actual amount of start-up cash that will be required to fund your business. Cash flow is literally the organization's ability to take in enough cash to meet its financial obligations within a specified period of time. Cash may be defined as unearned income, advances/deposits, or other sources needed to meet current obligations.

Some organizations may post a one-year financial loss yet still maintain their operations due to positive cash flow. This loss is due the organization budgeting for an excess (positive yield of revenue over expense) and not meeting this financial target. However, because of the positive cash flow, the organization can maintain their operations and will adjust their future budget to correct their financial performance. Using Figure 6–2, you can determine how much capital is needed from outside financing to start up your business.

This valuable tool will assist you in projecting throughout the crucial first year of your event business what cash will be needed from outside sources to ensure your survival and simultaneously bring you peace of mind in knowing what to expect as the months unfold before you. Remember, the goal is to make sure that you have plenty of month left at the end of your bank account!

Once you have completed the cash flow worksheet you have identified how much funding you are going to need until the business is self-sufficient (break even). To further validate this, you must complete the Break-Even/Bottom-Up Analysis as shown in Figure 6–3. This exercise will allow you to determine how much revenue will be required to break even.

The data from the Break Even/Bottom Up Analysis and the Cash Flow Worksheet will provide you with essential information that must be included with your financial statements. The complete business plan will not only include the names and backgrounds of the principals in the venture, but will also portray your ability to successfully financially manage the venture. Make certain you include in your business plan any data that will help make your case for the probable success of your business venture. Examples of this type of information are shown in Figure 6–4.

Matching the Financing Source to Your Need

Start-ups versus mature businesses often have significantly different financing needs. Event organizations may have short-term or long-term needs simultaneously. You may, for example, need to purchase a piece of equipment to fulfill an upcoming event or you may need to identify the capital to purchase a new building to grow your business. Finally, you must determine whether your business is a low-growth versus a high-growth business. Your ability to repay your loan will be seriously affected by the speed of growth of your business.

Regardless of whether you are an entrepreneur or entrepreneurial employee, you must identify the most realistic funding options for your business activity. There are essentially four categories

 Family Financing

"Dad, I'm spending over $500 per month on photo copies and this does not count my time in walking to and from the local copy store. I am asking for a loan to purchase a used copier. Can you help?" The wise father-in-law asked lots of questions. "First, what are you copying? How do you know that owning is less expensive than leasing? Have you compared the costs? What type of machine do you need? How much do you want to borrow and how long will you take to repay it?" In 1977, Joe Goldblatt's father-in-law provided the first loan to assist The Wonder Company, Inc. in solving a short-term business problem. Regardless of the immediacy of the business need, the smart lender and savvy events businessperson will carefully analyze the pros and cons of making this investment and assuming this liability. And by the way, the loan for $500 was repaid with interest to the lender within one year. Thanks Dad!

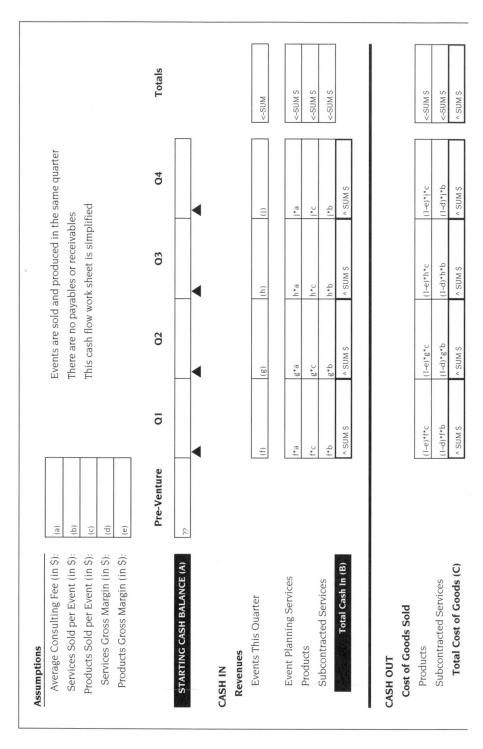

Assumptions

Average Consulting Fee (in $):	(a)
Services Sold per Event (in $):	(b)
Products Sold per Event (in $):	(c)
Services Gross Margin (in $):	(d)
Products Gross Margin (in $):	(e)

Events are sold and produced in the same quarter

There are no payables or receivables

This cash flow work sheet is simplified

	Pre-Venture	Q1	Q2	Q3	Q4	Totals
STARTING CASH BALANCE (A)	??	◄	◄	◄	◄	

CASH IN

Revenues

	Q1	Q2	Q3	Q4	Totals
Events This Quarter	(f)	(g)	(h)	(i)	<-SUM
Event Planning Services	f*a	g*a	h*a	j*a	<-SUM $
Products	f*c	g*c	h*c	j*c	<-SUM $
Subcontracted Services	f*b	g*b	h*b	j*b	<-SUM $
Total Cash In (B)	^ SUM $	^ SUM $	^ SUM $	^ SUM $	

CASH OUT

Cost of Goods Sold

	Q1	Q2	Q3	Q4	Totals
Products	(1-e)*f*c	(1-e)*g*c	(1-e)*h*c	(1-e)*j*c	<-SUM $
Subcontracted Services	(1-d)*f*b	(1-d)*g*b	(1-d)*h*b	(1-d)*j*b	<-SUM $
Total Cost of Goods (C)	^ SUM $	^ SUM $	^ SUM $	^ SUM $	^ SUM $

Start-Up (Capital) Expenditures

Improve Space	<–SUM $
Equipment	<–SUM $
Stationery	<–SUM $
Membership Dues	<–SUM $
Office Furniture	<–SUM $
Advertising	<–SUM $
Total Start-Up (D)	^ SUM $

Operating Expenses

Advertising Expense	<–SUM $			
Office/Wages/Payroll Expenses	<–SUM $			
Event Labor	<–SUM $			
Rent Expenses	<–SUM $			
Utilities	<–SUM $			
Telephone Expense	<–SUM $			
Miscellaneous Office Expense	<–SUM $			
Professional Services Expense	<–SUM $			
Total Operating Expenses (E)	^ SUM $	^ SUM $	^ SUM $	^ SUM $

Total Cash Out (=F)	= D	= C + E	= C + E	= C + E	= C + E
ENDING CASH BALANCE	= A + B – F	= A + B – F	= A + B – F	= A + B – F	= A + B – F

Figure 6–2 Cash Flow Worksheet for Exceptional Events Inc.

Assumptions

Avg. Event Management Fee	(a)
Avg. Services Sold per Event	(b)
Services Sold Margin	(c)

Avg. Revenue per Event: (d): a + b

Variable Costs

Services Purchased	(1-c)*b	per event
Event Labor		per event
Telephone		per event
Postage & Delivery		per event

Total Variable Costs: (e): ^ SUM

BREAK-EVEN

Gross Margin/Contribution Margin
(Avg. Revenue less Variable Costs)

d-e   or (d-e)/d

Profit Level Desired (Break-even)
Fixed Costs (from Left)

$ –

f

Gross Profit Required to Break even
Divide by Contribution (from Above)

(g): ^ SUM

d-e

Events Required to Break even
Multiply by Average Revenue

(h): g/(d-e)

d

Revenue Required to Break even

h*d

Fixed Costs

Advertising Expenses

Office Wages/Payroll Expenses

Rent Expense

Utilities

Base Telephone Expense

Miscellaneous Office Expense

Professional Services Expense

Total Fixed Costs:

(f): ^ SUM

BOTTOM-UP

Gross Margin/Contribution Margin

(Avg. Revenue less Variable Costs)

$d - e$

or $(d-e)/d$

Profit Level Desired (Break-even)

Fixed Costs (from Left)

f

Gross Profit Required to Break even

Divide by Contribution (from Above)

(g): ^ SUM

$d - e$

Events Required to Break even

Multiply by Average Revenue

(h): $g/(d-e)$

d

Revenue Required for $ Profit

$h \cdot d$

Figure 6–3 Break-Even/Bottom-Up Analysis for Exceptional Events, Inc.

---

1. Competitive analysis of similar organizations
2. Guarantees or letters of support from prospective clients/customers
3. Guarantees from vendors/suppliers
4. Personal financial history (include federal tax returns for the past three years)
5. Financial forecast based on the information gleaned from the Cash Flow Worksheet and the Break-Even/Bottom-Up Analysis

---

Figure 6–4   Financial Information to Include in the Business Plan

of financial assistance that are available to event entrepreneurs. They include:

- Guerilla financing
- Bank loans
- Outside equity investment
- Special programs and grants

The following specific sources of funding may provide you with the capital to not only get started but also to fuel your growth at a critical period.

Guerilla Financing

Self-Funding

Using your personal resources may be risky. After all, if the business does not succeed, how will you repay your own personal loan? How will this affect your personal lifestyle? What are the tax implications of personally investing in your business venture? If you decide to self-fund your business venture, make certain that you carefully document every step of the transaction.

One of the most overlooked areas of starting one's own event business is the concept of "sweat equity." Most entrepreneurs are willing to work long hours and defer compensation until such time as the business can afford to repay them and continue providing a regular (or semi-regular) paycheck. It is essential that you document the amount of time and the value of this time, as it must be listed within the financial reports of your business. Work as hard and long as you like, however, make certain you are keeping track of the value of your time so that at some future point you may be repaid in full for your early contributions.

Personal Funds

These funds may include savings, the sale of stocks and/or bonds, or any other liquid asset. Once again, be very careful about loaning your business money as it may reduce your personal lifestyle as well as create difficult interpersonal relationships with your spouse or partner if you are not able to repay the loan in a timely manner. If you decide to use personal funds, contact a certified public accountant and create an actual loan instrument to document this transaction. There may be a number of parties (your partners or investors) who become responsible for this loan and therefore it is essential to put this important information in writing and make certain all responsible parties execute it.

Credit Cards

Many successful events business entrepreneurs used their credit card accounts to fund the start-up of their businesses. Once again, this must be carefully evaluated, as today's average rate of interest is 18 percent, more than double current prevailing bank rates. Credit card capital should be reserved for very short-term loans that may be easily and quickly repaid to avoid exorbitant interest payments.

Barter

Often in the early stages of a business operation you may be able to trade services with your suppliers to reduce your costs. For example, when one special events company required additional funding for advertising, the owner traded his editorial skills by writing articles for a trade publication in return for display advertising space to promote his new firm. This in fact produced an added benefit in that the event entrepreneur had two appearances each month in the same publication. When you agree to barter services it is important that you use a written contract listing the fair market value of these services, as there may be tax liabilities at the end of the fiscal year.

Suppliers/Customers

Some of the most successful businesses in the world literally begin with complete financing from their vendors and customers. This option is only realistic if you have a previous positive track record with vendors and customers. Many times entrepreneurial employees who decide to become full-fledged entrepreneurs will use this source of funding because they have spent numerous years earning the trust and respect of suppliers and customers while in the employ of others.

Suppliers may provide you with extremely favorable terms to ease your cash flow during the start-up period of your business. Simultaneously, clients may provide you with a retainer or advance deposit to provide the funding essential to cover your fixed overhead and maintain your cash flow.

Whole Life Insurance

Life insurance policies build equity, albeit slowly, and may be used to provide financing. Some policies will allow you to borrow against the cash value of the policy. Check with your insurance broker to determine if these options are available to you.

 The Value of Value

The event management consultant began calling prospective clients and inquiring if they would be interested in retaining his services as he launched his independent event management firm. " I am limiting my practice to those firms that I believe will be compatible with one another and allow me to achieve an economy of scale by leveraging some costs between various clients. By doing this I am able to offer you a 15% discount on my fixed retainer. The $3,000 monthly retainer is available for a limited time at the cost of $2,550, which represents an annual saving to your firm of $5,400. To qualify you simply need to confirm you will retain my services for a period of one year. At the end of the year you have no further obligation or you may renew for additional years." The first association executive who received the offer called his board chairman and was instructed to immediately sign the contract for not one but 2 years.

Friends and Family

As Joe Goldblatt learned over 20 years ago, sometimes the first choice in seeking a lender is the most obvious: a friend or family member. Although friends and family members may or may not be willing to provide financing, you must consider all aspects of this relationship. Benjamin Franklin may have been referring to friends and family when he wrote, "Never a borrower or a lender be," yet many times a borrowing–lending relationship conducted in a formal contractual manner can be a pleasant and positive experience. Approach this transaction in a strictly business, nonemotional framework and set firm terms for repayment including penalties for lateness.

Bank Loans

Home Equity Loans

How much equity do you have in your home? What terms will your mortgage company provide if you decide to use some of this equity to start or stimulate the growth of your event business? The mortgage rate, depending on the terms, may be significantly more attractive than other forms of financing such as credit cards. This self-funding option must be carefully documented in writing to ensure proper financial disclosures and provide security for repayment.

Small Business Administration (SBA) Loan Guarantee Program

The Small Business Administration (SBA) guarantees loans in various amounts for businesses (including minority owned) that meet specific criteria set by this agency. Businesses owned by women are considered within the minority category. The SBA also offers a wide variety of educational programs for entrepreneurs. For more information about these services, contact the SBA at their Washington, D.C. district office: (202) 606-4000. They also provide significant information about their extensive services at their web address **www.sbaonline.sba.gov**.

Outside Equity Investment

Angels

The classic definition of an "angel" is a wealthy individual or organization that provides much-needed financial support due to their personal, philanthropic, or emotional investment in your project. You may seek angels to help you underwrite a community service type of event such as a fundraiser for a medical charity or other benevolent cause. And don't forget the wisdom of the legendary bank robber, Willie Sutton. When asked by television's Johnny Carson why he only robbed banks, Willie winked and said, "Well, that's where they keep the money!" Local banks can become angels by providing financing for a project they strongly believe in and reduce or waive the interest charges. But in most cases, banks don't waive the interest charges. That's why it's so important to shop around; go to the bank with which your company maintains its checking account to leverage the best deal.

Special Programs and Grants

Grants

Whether you are seeking an internal grant from another business unit such as a university facilitating fund, a private individual, or a private foundation, the grantor will evaluate three important criteria before seriously considering providing funding for your event or initiative. First, the grantor will want to ensure that your project matches the guidelines established by the grant-making body. For example, the grant may be available only for projects that meet certain educational, philanthropic, or community service requirements.

Second, the grantor will consider the capability of the potential grant recipient. Previous grants, successful completion of projects facilitated by grants, and the overall character/reputation of the potential grant recipient will be carefully scrutinized.

Third and finally, the grantor must be assured that the potential recipient will provide a comprehensive report of how the grant was used to ensure that the goals and objectives were accomplished as proposed in the initial grant request. Therefore, listing the deliverables of the project is very important in convincing the grantor that you or your organization will comprehensively evaluate the impact of the gift. Remember—individuals or organizations that provide gifts are different from lenders. They are essentially investors who are seeking a return on their investment through the deliverables of your project or event activity.

Typical Event Grants

Rarely are grants given for developing a new event. However, in many cases grants are available for expanding or re-engineering an existing event that has reached the mature level and needs to grow in order to sustain itself. Grants are often given for projects within specific events such as developing a community outreach, education, or social service program through an existing event. Grants are awarded on the local, regional, state, provincial, and federal levels. One of the best sources for identifying potential grantors is The Foundation Center located in a number of major cities in the United States.

Overcoming Credit Obstacles/Maintaining Good Credit

Before applying for a loan, check your own credit history. You can request a copy of your credit report by contacting TRW or other credit agencies. Use your credit report as an opportunity to thoroughly evaluate and analyze how a lender may view your creditworthiness. Specifically, check for errors and seek to correct them. You may ask for a review of your credit report and may provide collateral material (information supplied by the businesses with whom you are doing business) to improve your credit report.

To determine your creditworthiness, a lender will typically examine three important factors. First, they will want to know about your character, then they must determine if you have any assets you can offer to guarantee that the loan will be repaid, and finally they will want to know whether you are able to maintain a good credit record. Each of these important factors will contribute significantly to whether or not you receive the loan as well as the final terms by which you must abide in repaying the debt.

Character

A famous Hollywood actress was once asked to define "class." She replied that although no one can really define it, everyone knows it when they see it. Similarly, character is that elusive quality that we recognize but may find difficult to accurately quantify. In the eyes of the lender, character represents stability, trustworthiness, and most of all integrity. To determine character, the lender may require professional and personal references who are familiar with your financial history and are able to provide a positive reference based on their knowledge of your past history.

Collateral

Although you may not have sufficient cash to guarantee repayment of your loan, you may have other assets such as real estate, stocks, bonds, or even inventory that will satisfy the lender's need for securing your loan. Securing your loan literally means guaranteeing that you will be able to repay this loan regardless of the future outcome of the event business. In most cases it is dangerous to personally guarantee your event business loan, although some individuals have no other choice but to use their personal assets as collateral. Make certain you check with your accountant to determine the best course of action prior to executing any loan documents.

Maintaining Good Credit

Your ability to maintain a good credit record is one of the most important tools for future growth. A good credit history simply and accu-

 Crash!

When the stock market crashed in 1987, Joe Goldblatt faced a difficult decision. Suddenly his major clients were calling and canceling all events for the next quarter. Goldblatt had to decide how his business would survive in the face of these major losses. The first step was to thoroughly review the situation from a financial as well as an operational perspective. With few liquid assets, he knew that he would have to take some dramatic short-term steps to maintain his operations. Because of the economic crisis on Wall Street and

(Continues)

his lack of financial resources, it was highly unlikely that a lender would provide him with a short-term loan. Therefore, the next step was to assemble his staff and explain the current situation. He described the general economic condition and then described how this was affecting his business.

Next, he announced that his sales force would no longer receive a salary but would instead be compensated through a commission structure. He then invited each salesperson to meet with him individually and discuss his or her concerns. Although morale was low, the salespeople soon realized it would be unwise to try to find other employment, as the entire corporate world was frozen whilst they waited for signs of improvement from Wall Street.

Once Goldblatt was confident his internal staff was apprised of the serious financial situation, he needed to turn his attention to the external environment. For nearly 15 years his vendors, mostly small businesses, had extended him credit and he had faithfully paid all bills according to the terms specified. In fact, when occasionally his payables exceeded his receivables, he deferred his own compensation to ensure that his vendors, or his "partners," as he called them, were paid on time.

One by one he began the process of calling his loyal vendors and explaining that due to unforeseen circumstances his firm would not be able to honor his obligations within the time period that was agreed. He offered, however, to pay whatever he could as soon as possible.

To his surprise, by the second call he realized his gesture was unnecessary. The first vendor and also the second replied, "For over a decade you have paid your bills in a timely manner. Your reputation is above reproach. We know you will work with us to settle this account. Good luck." With a full heart and new confidence he turned to his staff and announced, "Let's get back to work, others are depending on us."

Because of the severe U.S. financial crisis, in actuality Goldblatt's vendors had little other recourse, as most of their customers were unable to pay them on time. However, due to his credit history, Goldblatt did not have the additional burden of worrying about his suppliers cutting him off or delaying their services until he could become current with his payments.

And this goodwill was the result of 15 years of excellent credit.

1. Establish reasonable terms for payment (typically, net 30 days).
2. Vigilantly collect all receivables.
3. Immediately notify vendors if there is a delay in meeting the agreed upon terms.
4. Negotiate new terms for payment.
5. Maintain open and frequent communications with your vendors.

Figure 6–5   Five Ways to Protect your Good Name

rately reflects that you are worthy of future investment by lenders, suppliers, and others because you have behaved in a financially responsible manner over a period of time. The story on pages 152–153 best illustrates how important it is to maintain a good credit history.

Yes, paying your bills on time is one way to build good credit. However, in Figure 6–5 you will find other tips for establishing and maintaining good credit.

A wise businessman once told me that if you want to be a debtor, only borrow a little money; however, if you want to become a partner, borrow a lot of money. In the 1980s, many aggressive businesspeople chose the latter approach to finding capital, and when their businesses crashed, their partners collapsed with them. When assembling financial partners it is essential that the event entrepreneur identify individuals or organizations that understand the vagaries and often-erratic cycles of this industry. To seek financial support from those with whom you wish to maintain long-term relationships, this comprehension and understanding of this unique industry or group of industries is extremely important. Without this initial understanding, the borrower and the lender are doomed from the beginning of the transaction.

Reasons for Growth

Event management entrepreneurs and entrepreneurial employees have numerous reasons for seeking capital for growth. One reason may be the need to expand operations in order to handle increased demand, another may be the need to develop new product lines to attract new markets, and still another may be the need to improve quality. Finding capital to solve these short- and long-term business challenges requires individual strategies in order to be successful.

Figure 6–6 provides specific examples of how to find appropriate funding to help your organization grow in both the short term and long term.

Arie de Geus, author of *The Living Company* and a senior staff member at Shell Oil, dared to ask the question, "What do we do after there is no more oil?" To answer this question, de Geus and his colleagues studied 40 companies older than Shell and eventually examined 27 in detail. In each case, the team focused on investigating how these companies managed to survive. Four significant findings were gleaned from this research.

The first characteristic they uncovered was sensitivity, or the ability to identify trends in the changing external environment as well as a willingness to learn and change. The second was the ability to clearly understand the identity of your organization through a commitment to specific values. These values must be shared with everyone in the organization to build a sense of cohesive community.

Third, they found that it is important to create an atmosphere of openness that encourages, indeed, welcomes new ideas. Although new ideas are welcomed, the values and mutual trust among the members of the organization must be maintained.

Finally, and perhaps most importantly, they determined that conservative financing ultimately governed the growth and evolution for long-term benefits. These benefits may include cash profits as well as re-investment in the organization. Interestingly, de Geus

Need	Short-Term Source	Long-Term Source
1. Increase inventory	Vendor credit	Bank
2. Renovation, construction	Personal funds	SBA; Bank
3. Marketing expansion	Vendor credit	Bank; Private investors
4. Staff expansion	Personal funds	Private investors
5. New project development	Personal funds	Equity partners; grants

Figure 6–6   When It Is Time to Grow: Sources of Funding

found that these four unique characteristics were evident in all organizations regardless of the type of business they conducted.

The overarching finding of this study was that each organization *did not have* a paramount concern for maximizing profits above all other considerations. The author states that "these executives know only too well that short-term profitability is no guide to future performance." He believes that the key to long-term success is not physical assets but instead people.

Similarly, Hal Rosenbluth, the owner of Rosenbluth Travel, maintains that "the customer comes second." Rosenbluth so strongly advocates this principle that he has written a bestselling book of the same title incorporating this philosophy as its title. According to Rosenbluth, serving the internal customer is even more important that satisfying the external customer. If the internal customer is not secure and content, Rosenbluth believes and de Geus has proven, the company may not survive during tough times.

Therefore, it is important to remember that before identifying capital, the event entrepreneur must carefully refocus his or her lenses and see their organization as one whose greatest asset is not a fast infusion of cash but instead a long-term investment in people. Investing in people is often not capital intensive. It may involve simple but heartfelt recognition or it may require a major distribution of profits as a reward; however, by focusing on people the event entrepreneur is building his or her capital internally. This internal development results in a trained, experienced, and loyal team that will sustain the event organization far longer than an injection of cash.

When you must identify funding, do so. However, remember, the organizations that not only survive but also thrive are those whose sensitivity, identity, and tolerance factors are carefully maintained and well aligned like the lenses in your telescope. Identifying capital may ultimately be the easy result of this careful and consistent alignment.

The View From Here

1. Maintain careful records to be able to show potential funders your financial track record over a three-year period.
2. Use the cash flow worksheet to be able to project your need for capital.

3. Use economic forecasting models to identify future macro economic trends within the event industry.

4. Identify sources of collateral to provide guarantees for lenders.

5. List all potential funders and rate their likelihood for providing you with the capital you need at the terms you require.

6. Compare and contrast funding sources to identify the most flexible and best terms.

7. Pay your bills on time. Set realistic payment terms with lenders, vendors, and others and then keep them. Establish and maintain good credit.

8. Cultivate an event organization that is sensitive, has a strong identity, and tolerates and embraces new ideas while maintaining an atmosphere of values and mutual trust.

9. Be conservative in your financing.

10. The acquisition of capital and later wealth is the natural outgrowth of event organizations who align sensitivity, values, and focus on their greatest asset: their people.

Tools of the Trade

Butler, Timothy and James Waldrop, *Discovering Your Career in Business*. Reading, Mass.: Addison Wesley, 1997.

De Geus, Arie. *The Living Company: Habits for Survival in a Turbulent Business Environment*. Cambridge, Mass.: Harvard Business School Press, 1997.

Rosenbluth, Hal. *The Customer Comes Second and Other Secrets of Exceptional Service*. New York: William Morrow and Company, 1993.

Breaking New Ground

To identify new sources of capital, explore the following activities:

1. Complete the cash flow worksheet in Figure 6–2.

2. Contact potential funders such as the Small Business Administration, your local bank, and potential investors such as family and friends. Compare the terms between each funding option.

3. Visit or contact The Foundation Center and identify ten or more potential grantors who could provide the funds your require for your event organization.

4. Carefully review your need for capital and determine how you could find alternative ways to improve quality and sustain your event organization without assuming debt.

5. Compare the infusion of new capital with the focus on sensitivity, identity, and tolerance and determine how the acquisition of capital and ultimately wealth can become a natural progression from these three characteristics.

CHAPTER 7

Monitoring Success

Step Seven: *Continually monitor the performance of your special events business and the growth of your career.*

Too often the term "monitoring" is a daunting connotation, especially for small-business people. The term often conveys singular images of costly and time-consuming surveys, statistics, and highly quantifiable empirical studies. In fact, nothing could be further from the truth.

For the purposes of this book, the term monitoring will be used interchangeably with the words query or explore. In order to succeed in the modern special events industry, you must continually ask the right questions and explore every potential option. Therefore, research may be conducted to find the first job, the next job, to buy or sell a special events business, to determine demand for new product, to evaluate service and operations, or for dozens of other purposes. In the important seventh step, you will learn how to easily, efficiently, and inexpensively conduct the type of research that will help you make informed decisions.

Today, more than ever, information is power. Among the fastest growing programs in schools and universities is information technology (IT). The systematic and efficient collection and processing of data can save you time and money. Most importantly, the proper use of information technology can help you beat your competition by finding the answer faster, and providing better service to your customers will further ensure they become your clients for life.

The model in Figure 7–1 depicts the six major reasons individuals in the special events industry conduct research. Although there are innumerable other reasons, the majority of individuals in this young

---

1. Career Development
- Career exploration
- Job searches
- Salary/benefits comparisons
- Organizational culture and reputation

2. Buying/Selling a Special Events Business
- Determining business value for sale or purchase
- Determining industry demand for services and products

3. Evaluating Service/Operations Gaps
- Employee training and delivery issues
- Customer perceptions
- The gap between customer perceptions and service delivery

4. Risk Management Issues
- Safety
- Security
- Insurance

5. Fiscal Performance
- Profit/loss records
- Consistency of percentage of return on event
- Stability of fiscal administration and performance

6. Market Research
- Competitor behavior
- Client purchase behavior
- Market size and penetration
- Potential clients

Figure 7–1   Six Reasons for Monitoring Your Special Events Business and Career

industry will at one time or another conduct research in one of these areas to find the information they need to make informed decisions.

Career Development

The easiest and fastest way to search for career opportunities is using the Internet. For example, using search engines such as CareerMosaic (*www.careermosaic*) will provide hundreds of hot links to jobs in the field of special events. By reviewing these jobs you can begin to explore the landscape and determine whether you have the experience, skills, and credentials to match the jobs that are listed. This may help you further adjust your lenses to improve your chances of finding the right job within your area of interest.

Job searches are also made easier today due to the fast growth of the Internet. Only a few years ago, according to the American Society of Association Executives (ASAE), a small percentage of trade and professional organizations had web pages. Today upwards of 80 percent of all associations have their own home pages and many contain links to career opportunities and specific jobs.

In 1998, according to the U.S. Department of Labor, unemployment stood at less than 5 percent. In fact, this reflects *full employment* in the United States. Therefore, employers were aggressively seeking event professionals to fill jobs in the expanding special events industry. One way they were conducting this aggressive search for new candidates was through their association's career opportunities web page.

The Internet can at first glance appear to be filled with jobs that have little to do with your career interest. Therefore, the first step is to narrow your search to help you find the specific organizations and jobs you are most interested in and that fit your long-term career goals.

To do this, first identify the industry segment (such as associations or hotels) in which you would like to focus your job search. Next, using the Internet search engines, begin to identify the home pages of the major organizations within this segment. Finally, search within each organization to identify where they post individual job announcements.

You may also wish to "go global" by contacting the U.S. Department of Labor home page (*www.dol.gov*) and identify specific salary and benefit trends within various industries. The U.S. Department of

Labor home page is quite extensive and provides reports on a wide variety of subjects to help you determine where you fit careerwise within the large economy.

Since finding the right job in special events is part persistence and part timing, it is worthwhile for you to carefully define your career objectives. Professional career counselors working with students earning the Master's of Business Administration degree at The George Washington University state that four decisions often influence job choice. Figure 7–2 lists these critical decision points.

You will note that in Figure 7–2, the culture of the event organization is the first consideration. If you had the choice of accepting a

---

First: The culture of the organization

- Nurturing
- Training
- Recognition and reward
- Potential for advancement
- Potential to move to another organization

Second: The opportunity to use my skills and experience to do the job I am prepared to do

- The ability to *do what I was trained to do*
- A clear connection between training/experience and application
- Coaching, mentoring to help me improve my skills

Third: Geographic location

- Weather?
- Topography? (Mountains, ocean, desert)
- Commuting distance from home to office
- Type of commute (car, carpool, public transportation)
- Cultural amenities (music, dance, art)
- Educational resources (schools of higher education)

Last: Compensation

- Salary
- Benefits
- Pay for performance incentives

Figure 7–2   Decisions Influencing Special Events Job Choice

job within a special events organization at $45,000 where you will satisfy items 1–3 *or* a $50,000 job at another organization where there is no positive correlation with these attributes, most individuals would accept the first offer. Culture, work compatibility, and geography today are more important collectively than compensation is as an individual factor. This is important information for special events employers as they are critical considerations when attracting top talent to work within their organization.

In addition to the Internet, most colleges and universities maintain extensive career services programs. Therefore, if you are a college student or a professional, you may wish to use these services to help accelerate your chances of finding the right job. In most cases, career services are only available to full-time or part-time students. However, many colleges and universities also provide services for alumni. Some organizations, such as The George Washington University School of Business and Public Management F. David Fowler Career Center, offer an electronic list server entitled *Job Forum*. This service automatically forwards job listings into each student or alumnus e-mail box on a daily basis. By subscribing to Job Forum, individuals can receive leads on jobs that are being recruited directly through their alma mater. Often the recruiters are alumni of the University and this provides job seekers with an additional connection to the prospective employer.

Organizing the special events job search using research methods involves first defining the industry segment, culture, tasks, geographic location, and compensation requirements. Next, your research must focus on specific industry organizations and referral agencies (Internet as well as institutions such as colleges and universities) where you will find job openings. Finally, you must use research methods to pursue the job opening. Creating a computer database (contacts) of available jobs and then systematically contacting the employers may provide you with an added advantage over other job seekers who only randomly or sporadically search for a job in the special events field.

Research in the area of career development provides you with tools to identify potential jobs and a system for helping you secure the one that is best for you. If you are a special events employer, using the Internet to research different industry organizations will assist you in developing compensation packages and benchmarking your salary and benefits against other organizations of similar size and scope. Furthermore, you may use these same search engines to advertise your job in a highly targeted marketplace.

Buying/Selling a Special Events Business

How do you determine the feasibility of buying or selling a special events business? Because special events is a very new field, the standard evaluation tools used in other service industries are not currently in place in this field. Therefore, special events entrepreneurs must often extrapolate formulas that are used by other similar industries.

For example, in a typical service business three factors are used to evaluate the value of the seller. The first factor is consistent profitability over a period of three consecutive years. Second is the value of current contracts (and future ones-receivables), and third, is "reputation" or "good name" value. The final criterion is difficult to quantify but is often as important as the first two if the business is highly focused on personal service (as are most special events businesses).

To use research to determine if the business you wish to sell or purchase scores highly in each of these three areas, you may wish to show due diligence by examining the financial records (usually under the supervision of a Certified Public Accountant), reviewing and validating current and future contracts, and interviewing current clients and vendors to determine the perception of the organization. Using the Internet, public library microfilm, and local newspaper microfilm records can provide easy access to the public perception of the business you are positioning for sale or wish to purchase at some future date.

When seeking a business to purchase (which is often easier and more successful than starting your own business), you must first focus your search. Industry publications (many of which are on-line) may provide classified listings such as "Business for Sale." However, many prospective buyers contact professional business brokers and ask them to conduct research to identify a special events business that would be a good future investment. While business brokers may be found in the Yellow Pages of most cities, it is best to get a referral from your accountant or attorney.

Buying or selling a business is somewhat similar to buying or selling real estate. The broker will ask you to sign an agreement giving him or her the exclusive right to market your business or seek one for you to buy. Typically these agreements are limited to three months and then may be renewed. During this period the business broker will market your special events business or identify prospective events businesses for you to buy.

Financial terms with business brokers vary; however, typically, the broker will receive between 10 and 15 percent of the gross selling price of the business and the seller (just as in real estate) pays. However, these terms are very flexible and may be negotiated, for example, with the buyer paying some of the broker's expenses or commissions.

Figure 7–3 describes the major steps that are usually followed in buying or selling a special events business.

If you are an individual business owner whose sweat equity and daily involvement are critical to the business's success, in most cases the purchaser will want you to agree to continue for one or two years in a consulting or employment relationship. This will require a separate contract (employee or consulting agreement).

Keep in mind that businesses that are for sale may not be healthy. In some cases the owner wishes to retire or in others some catastrophic event (sickness, divorce) has forced the sale of the business or the business is languishing and losing under the current ownership. Regardless of the motivation for selling the business, the purchaser must conduct a thorough due diligence. Similarly, the seller would be wise, despite his or her circumstances, to take time to research the viability of the buyer.

In the example on page 166, the over-anxious seller failed to practice due diligence and thoroughly investigate the buyer. The buyer did not have the business acumen or experience to ensure the future growth of the business. Furthermore, the business was purchased at the height of the U.S. recession of 1990 and this downturn in the economy dramatically affected the future revenues of the business.

---

1. Use research to determine the type of business you are selling or interested in buying.
2. Benchmark your business against others of similar size and scope.
3. Identify, through research, the best method for buying or selling the business (self, broker, attorney, accountant).
4. Evaluate the business you are interested in selling or buying by conducting due diligence (research).
5. Extend an offer to purchase/sell contingent on verification of due diligence (research steps).
6. Establish the terms for sale/purchase of the special events business and close the sale.

Figure 7–3 The Process for Buying and Selling a Special Events Business

"You Can Have Your Business Back"

This special events entrepreneur had long dreamed of selling his firm. The sale would be the capstone of a ten-year period of growth. A business broker was identified and the business was advertised. Three prospective buyers inquired and two actually conducted due diligence to determine the viability of purchasing the business. One of the two purchasers submitted a preliminary bid and soon a final offer was tendered. The terms required the buyer to provide 10 percent of the purchase price as a deposit and the balance would be paid as a balloon payment at the end of two years. The purchaser also accepted all of the current liabilities. The seller accepted the offer and subsequently signed an employment agreement to work for the purchaser for a period of two years. The first year following the purchase appeared to be a success for both buyer and seller. The purchaser continued to expand the business and the seller enjoyed not having the responsibility of managing the day-to-day operations as well as eliminating the risk of operating a business. However, on Thanksgiving eve at the end of the first year, things began to change.

The seller tried to make a long-distance phone call from the office and was told that due to nonpayment the call could not be connected. Minutes later the purchaser entered his office and explained that due to cash flow problems he was unable to issue the seller's bi-weekly paycheck.

Within days, the business corporation was shut down and the seller was in a lawyer's office asking for advice. Because the business was a corporation (see Chapter 6), the seller could not pierce the corporate veil and collect any past due monies from the individual who had purchased the business. The seller in fact never received the balance payment and was instead offered by the purchaser to ""take the business back."

Both the lack of business acumen of the purchaser and the struggling economy were predictable threats. The seller, anxious to sell, overlooked these important factors and ultimately suffered not only the loss of his investment but also the mental and emotional trials that accompany a financial setback of this type.

Whether you are buying or selling a special events business, thorough research can reduce your risk of failure. Do not be too anxious to buy or sell; instead, carefully look at the possibility as the potential to learn more about special events businesses through the research phase. Whether you achieve your goal of buying or selling is not nearly as valuable as what you will learn through research. In fact, the mega-business mergers that have failed to be consummated have, according to the principals involved, revealed critical information about the strategic business environment. In most cases, the mergers were between arch competitors and the resulting knowledge gave one or both firms a strategic advantage.

The U.S. Department of Commerce (*www.doc.gov*) can provide you with important information ranging from minority businesses to economic development issues that will assist you in assessing the environment nationally and globally for selling your event business. The data offered through the U.S. Department of Commerce can provide you with significant information to help you determine the demand and supply factors driving the U.S. economy as well as industry segments such as hospitality, tourism, and recreation that are related to the special events field. This knowledge can become a golden opportunity for you to lay the foundation for the future sale or purchase of a special events business.

Evaluating Service/Operations Gaps

In *Delivering Quality Service* (1990), the authors state, "Service quality is a central issue in America today. In a recent Gallup survey, executives ranked the improvement of service and tangible product quality as the single most critical challenge facing U.S. business." Now, nearly 10 years later, the term service may be easily compared to winning. Paraphrasing the legendary football coach Vince Lombardi, service isn't everything, it's the *only* thing!

The authors of *Delivering Service Quality* developed an assessment tool entitled *SERVQUAL*. Five distinct dimensions of service are evaluated through SERVQUAL.

Tangibles	Appearance of physical facilities, personnel
Reliability	Consistent performance, dependability
Responsiveness	Ability to help individuals promptly

Assurance   The knowledge and courtesy of the
                  employees, their ability to project trust and
                  confidence

Empathy   The sense that the employee and the
                  organization care about their customers

These five dimensions are extremely important in the special events industry. For example, as the customer enters the party rental showroom, the physical facilities (tangibles), delivery time punctuality (reliability), quick response (responsiveness), product knowledge (assurance), and sensitivity (empathy) to the customer's needs, wants, and desires ultimately determine the overall perceived value of the rental or purchase. This perceived value ultimately determines the price. The price determines profits and profits determine growth. Therefore, quality service is directly related to future growth.

The model in Figure 7–4 shows how important quality service is to the special events organization.

Some event organizations survey their guests before and after the event (pre and post) to identify expectations and then determine if the final perception was equal to or greater than the initial level of expectation. The entertainment firm may use the survey shown in

---

"SPECIAL EVENT" = HIGH CUSTOMER EXPECTATIONS

EVENT ORGANIZATION IMPLEMENTS SERVICE QUALITY STANDARDS:

INTRODUCTION

MINIMUM STANDARDS

TRAINING

MEASUREMENT/ASSESSMENT

CUSTOMER FEEDBACK

MONITORING BY EVENT ORGANIZATION

CORRECTIVE ACTION = CUSTOMER ASSESSMENT = CORRECTIVE ACTION

Determines:

CUSTOMER SATISFACTION LEVEL

Figure 7–4   Special Events Customer Expectation-Perception Service Delivery Process

Figure 7–5 to assess how they met the event customer's expectations. Using the method shown in the figure, you can easily show your customer that you exceeded his or her expectations. This ability to consistently *exceed expectations* is absolutely essential for the special events organization. As Figure 7–4 demonstrated, the term "special events" raises high expectations among customers.

(Pre)

Circle the answer that best describes your opinion.

1. What is your expectation of prompt response to your questions and concerns?

LOW	MODERATE	NO OPINION	HIGH	EXTREMELY HIGH
1	2	3	4	5

2. What is your expectation of on-time arrival of the performers at your event?

LOW	MODERATE	NO OPINION	HIGH	EXTREMELY HIGH
1	2	3	4	5

3. What is your expectation of our on-site supervision of your entertainment?

LOW	MODERATE	NO OPINION	HIGH	EXTREMELY HIGH
1	2	3	4	5

Expectation level: 4

(Post)

4. How would you rate the promptness of our response to your questions and concerns?

LOW	MODERATE	NO OPINION	HIGH	EXTREMELY HIGH
1	2	3	4	5

5. What is your perception of on-time arrival of the performers at your event?

LOW	MODERATE	NO OPINION	HIGH	EXTREMELY HIGH
1	2	3	4	5

6. What is your perception of our on-site supervision of your entertainment?

LOW	MODERATE	NO OPINION	HIGH	EXTREMELY HIGH
1	2	3	4	5

Perception level: 5

Figure 7–5   Service Quality Assessment

Remember that all special events organizations have both internal and external customers. Therefore, another useful type of research is the focus panel. The focus panel allows the event entrepreneur to poll his or her superiors (internal customers) or clients (external customers) to determine their attitudes and opinions regarding service delivery. These sessions should last no more than one hour and should be recorded to enable you to transcribe the comments and analyze the text to identify areas of agreement as well as discordance.

Whether you use quantitative (surveys) or qualitative (focus panels) methods to measure your customers' perception of your service quality, it is absolutely essential that you *monitor* on a daily basis to determine if you are merely meeting or consistently exceeding their expectations. Using research methodology in a formal, systematic, or even informal manner can help you achieve this important goal. And remember, good service, according to experts, is the most effective way for your business organization to grow. A massive database entitled *Profit Impact of Market Strategy* (PIMS) consistently and unequivocally proved that quality service businesses could sell their products at prices that were 5–6 percent higher than their competitors. This database studies a wide variety of products to assess consumer-buying patterns. The study determined that quality service does mean future growth. Using research to identify quality gaps and assess how to close them will ultimately propel your organization's growth in the highly competitive field of special events.

Risk Management Issues

In poll after poll, Americans state that "crime" is their number one concern. In the travel industry, women tourists state that their first consideration when selecting a destination is the issue of safety and security. The special events entrepreneur often extends an invitation to his or her guests either directly or in direct connection with the sponsoring organization. This "offer" by the host and "acceptance" by the guest immediately implicates both parties. In fact, they have entered into a nonwritten but nevertheless enforceable contract. The host agrees to use his or her good judgment, experience, and training to establish a safe environment within which the event may take place. The guest is also expected to use good judgment in participating in certain activities.

Ideally, this is the way it should be. However, anyone who has read the daily newspaper or watched the evening news knows that each week people are injured at special events and in many cases *simple* research could have prevented these costly incidents.

Large event organizations and most event venues keep on file accident or incident reports. These written documents provide a chronological log of the incidents including date, time, location, parties, and nature or description of the incident. The special events entrepreneur should ask to review these reports to determine the level of threat that may be present within the event or venue.

Police departments maintain extensive crime reports and you may request to review the reports for incidents that occurred in the vicinity within which your event will be held. Criminal activity that has been reported/documented (such as robberies, muggings, and thefts) in or near your event venue will be helpful in creating a profile of the threats that may impact your event.

This early research can help you identify weaknesses as well as threats in your event operations strategy. In addition to written reports, interviews with key officials such as the director of security, local police or law enforcement officers, can help you better understand the environment in which your event will occur.

Once you have collected this data you can make an informed decision regarding how to contain, transfer (by purchasing insurance), or even remove obvious threats from your event. This research, known as risk assessment, has consistently shown that an ounce of prevention is indeed better than a pound of cure.

Fiscal Performance

Monitoring the fiscal performance of your event organization is perhaps the most critical aspect of the research process. Each day many businesses go under, often, according to Michael E. Gerber, author of *The E Myth Revisited*, due to poor financial management. An essential part of this management process is continually conducting research/ analysis to ensure that your organization is performing efficiently and profitably.

Using profit and loss reports and comparing these reports on a monthly basis can help you track your business's growth. However, these periodic reports often are reviewed too late to enable you to take immediate corrective action and prevent rapid decline. Successful special events entrepreneurs project the ROE or "Return On Event" to make certain each event program achieves the desired financial outcome and the cumulative value of all events produces the financial yield that is most desired by the event organization.

Intel Corporation in Portland, Oregon uses extensive research to create an event financial model to make certain that each event stays on budget and meets specific financial objectives. The event manager, client, and financial analyst work as a team to produce a high-quality event that produces specific deliverables (outcomes) within budget. So, what about the many inevitable changes that all events require? Once all three team members have approved the Intel event budget, changes may be made only if the client (either the internal or external customer) approves them. This written approval process ensures that the event manager will be able to later adjust his or her final budget to reflect this change and maintain his or her profit margin. If Intel Corporation, a $20 billion leader in the high-technology field, can succeed with this system as they have with so many others, perhaps all event entrepreneurs will soon recognize the importance of research, ROE, and strict accountability to meet desired financial goals.

The Networked Event Organization

In the 1970s, DrugCorp sponsored a number of studies to improve the innovation process. During this same period a small group of researchers began experimenting with a small-scale computer conferencing system. This system, initially entitled DIALOG, was highly structured. However, within a few years, this early system was replicated and expanded, enabling thousands of organizations to quickly and efficiently communicate internally. This communication often took the form of informal qualitative research as system users analyzed and evaluated the information that was being disseminated.

Shoshana Zuboff clearly defines this innovation in her book *In the Age of the Smart Machine, The Future of Work and Power* (1988), in which she states, "Technological change defines the horizon of our material world as it shapes the limiting conditions of what is possible and what is barely imaginable." Indeed, from the intranet to the Internet, the process of conducting research is faster and more robust than at any other time in history. However, this speed and size should not be confused with accuracy or depth of knowledge. This innovation must simultaneously produce more critical consumers of information to ensure that valid and reliable data are used to make important decisions.

How important is research to the future of event management? A card player in Dan Burrus's *Technotrends* (1993) states that "Military R&D helped launch the electronics, computer, and aerospace industries." Another player adds, "Well, that's history." "I hope not," adds the first player, "industries with the highest record of research development, and capital investment have been shown to be the driving force behind the growth in jobs and the standard of living." He concludes with the warning, "If we stop priming the R&D pump, we are in big trouble."

The special events field is the original marketplace of ideas. Its very existence depends upon innovation, imagination, originality, and uniqueness. These outcomes require investment and investment must be followed by research, which will ultimately produce the sound ideas upon which special events managers can make decisions that will impact their future success.

Often the cultures of research and sales can be at odds with one another. In *Corporate Cultures*, Terrence E. Deal and Allen A. Kennedy explain that "a strong R&D department can clash with the larger organization's work/play ideas but eventually provide innovations that allow the organization to succeed where it now fails." Deal and Kennedy suggest that organizations should point out how the overall culture is richer because of the strength of the research subculture.

Within every special events organization there are a myriad of subcultures ranging from research, to sales, to operations. The effective special events entrepreneur will help each culture understand the problems of the other and provide support so that research becomes the engine that drives innovation.

Market Research

The wise entrepreneur is the one who looks carefully before he or she leaps into a new market. Too often special events entrepreneurs allow their imagination to convince them that a market exists for their product, service or new business. This can be a fatal mistake, as shown in the example on the following page.

Marketing research is the systematic examination of the factors that will reduce the risk of failure and improve the likelihood of strong

Look-a-Likes Are Not-a-Like

During the Ronald Reagan presidency, professional impersonators earned tens of thousands of dollars imitating the affable Gipper for conventions and meetings. As George Bush followed him into office, Joe Goldblatt mistakenly believed that one president's success is another's gold mine with effective marketing. He auditioned dozens of George and Barbara Bush look-a-likes and even found a springer spaniel that was a dead ringer for first dog Millie. Signing the actors and dog to an exclusive contract for one year, Goldblatt set about promoting his newest attraction. Unfortunately, he failed to first conduct market research. Had he practiced basic marketing research, he would have learned that not only could he not sell George and Barbara and Millie—he couldn't give them away. It seems that this first family did not have the "humor" quotient established by the Reagans and therefore, clients were not interested in The Bushes. Goldblatt was now saddled with a one-year contract (inventory) that drained his financial resources as well as the capital required to develop and market the attraction. All of this could have been prevented with proper marketing research.

and enduring sales. This research usually is conducted with one of the following methods.

Focus panels are formal or informal interviews with a group of prospective consumers of your product. During the focus panel, the moderator may demonstrate the product or service that will be offered and seek reactions or comments from the participants. In other cases the moderator will demonstrate a wide variety of products and services (including those of competitors) and ask the participants to comment on each one as well as to compare and contrast the value of each product. The comments that are gleaned from the focus groups provide the event marketing entrepreneur with keen insights that will assist in successfully bringing the product or service to market. For example, the comments from the focus panel may help you develop a slogan or sales pitch to positively influence others to buy.

The second type of market research involves conducting written or telephonic surveys and asking event consumers to compare, contrast, and provide their opinion regarding specific products or services you may be offering. Using either a Likert (1–5) scale or Semantic Differential (opposing adjectives), the consumer can easily describe their opinion of your product or service. When designing your survey, remember the key ideas in Figure 7–6.

Survey research may be conducted by mail, in person (such as in the shopping mall by intercepting shoppers), or over the telephone. The goal is to collect the data in a uniform manner so that it is comparable and relational. Market survey research will provide you with quantifiable data that can be computed numerically to help you make precise decisions regarding market demand. Most market researchers combine focus panels and survey research to establish a hybrid methodology to provide authentic information.

---

1. Start with the end in mind. Make certain the questions you are posing will provide the data you need to make informed decisions.
2. Keep the questions brief and understandable. Ask a stranger to review the survey to make sure he or she understands each of the questions.
3. Keep the survey brief. The more questions, the less likely you will receive a complete response. Usually 10–15 questions will provide you with the information you need.
4. Include some demographic questions (gender, age, and income) to allow you to cross-tabulate and segment your market for specific targeting of your products or service.
5. Use colored paper (yellow with black ink is best) to make your survey stand out.
6. Offer a reward (enclose a dollar) or invite the respondent to include their business card if they would like to be entered in a drawing to win a prize.
7. Plan to increase the response by following up after the initial distribution of the survey. Reminder postcards, telephone calls, or in-person collection are often necessary to receive a reliable response.
8. Try to attain a minimum 40 percent response from all surveys mailed or circulated.
9. Eliminate any surveys where the response appears to be greatly inflated, as this will skew your results.
10. Report any surveys that were not completely filled out or eliminated because they were filled out improperly.

Figure 7–6   Marketing Survey Ideas

The third and final type of market research involves observation and is sometimes referred to as participant/observer research. Using this methodology the market researcher is able to carefully and systematically study the consumer to identify specific behaviors that may influence purchasing motivations. You may either train monitors to observe and note the behavior of your customers or prospective customers or informally conduct this information yourself through taking notes during your workday. Regardless of how you collect this data, it is important that you use a written instrument to note your findings. These field notes will provide you with useful information to help you determine where to place certain products in your rental store, where to locate the concession stand at your festival, and how to stop traffic in front of your fair or fete.

Using market research to refine, target, and segment your customer base will help you become a sure shot when it comes to hitting your target market. As the cost of marketing continues to escalate, it is critically important that you sharpen your vision to carefully define those products and services that will be consistently well received by your consumers. The wise marketer of *Poor Richard's Almanac* reportedly said, "An ounce of prevention is worth a pound of cure." Over 200 years later, modern event marketers should well heed the entrepreneurial Benjamin Franklin's sage advice.

Finally, one of the primary accepted definitions of a professional discipline is a body of knowledge that may be tested through empirical research. As the field of special events grows so must the research that is conducted mature to a more scientific level. To do this, the rigor must increase. In order for this to happen either members of the special events industries will anticipate future challenges and improve research efforts or they will be caught off guard and be forced to implement research to fix their course once more. Like ships at sea, the special events organizations can either sail into the horizon aimlessly or adjust their telescopes to maintain a steady course. Those who stay on course ultimately reach their destinations with fewer surprises.

The View From Here

1. Set specific research goals (career development, service quality, marketing demand, etc.).

2. Use primary (interviews, surveys, observation) and secondary (Internet, publications) research to robustly examine specific problems and opportunities.

3. Budget and encourage research and development activities within your organization.

Tools of the Trade

Burrus, Daniel. *Technotrends 24 Technologies That Will Revolutionize Our Lives*. New York: Harper Business, 1993.

Deal, Terrence E. and Allen A. Kennedy. *Corporate Cultures, The Rites and Cultures of Corporate Life*. Reading, Mass.: Addison-Wesley, 1982.

Gerber, Michael E. *The E Myth Revisited*. New York: Harper Collins, 1995.

Zeithaml, Valerie A., A. Parasuraman, and Leonard L. Berry. *Delivering Quality Service*. New York: The Free Press, Macmillan, 1990.

Zuboff, Shoshana. *In the Age of the Smart Machine, The Future of Work and Power*. New York: Basic Books, 1988.

Breaking New Ground

To improve your research practices, conduct the following activities.

1. Use the Internet to identify the career landscape for the special events job you desire.

2. Design a pre and post survey to identify the gaps between service expectation and perception.

3. Observe your prospective customers to determine their buying habits in a shopping center.

4. Conduct a telephonic survey of prospective customers to identify their preferences regarding a new service you wish to test market.

5. Ask to review the incident records for a recurring event or the police reports for the area where your event will be held. How will you use the data you have discovered to make decisions that will reduce, remove, or transfer the risks associated with your event?

CHAPTER 8

The Marketing Plan

Step Eight: *Create and execute a cost-efficient and effective marketing plan.*

Among unseasoned special events entrepreneurs, marketing is commonly considered synonymous with the act of selling. But sales only constitute one component, and if successful, a happy end result, of effectively marketing your business. A central component of every business plan, marketing is the process of identifying the wants and needs of your prospective clients and communicating that your business is uniquely qualified to provide the products or services necessary to meet them. Understanding the needs of your market as you develop your product offerings is critical to your company's survival. While it is admirable, indeed, to build the proverbial "better mousetrap," you won't sell many of them if your customers do not have a mouse problem.

In addition to direct sales, classical marketing tools include advertising, promotion, publicity, and for an increasing number of companies, special events! There is an unlimited wealth of opportunities with which to communicate to your target prospects, but even the richest and most profitable companies are extremely selective in choosing the most efficient and effective ways to market themselves. That is what has made them so rich and profitable in the first place!

179

Anything for a Buck?

Through careful market planning and the practice of effective marketing techniques, you will ensure that your two most limited resources—time and money—are spent wisely and yield the best possible results. When you are just starting out, it is very tempting to go after any kind of business seemingly within reach. After all, you have invested time and money in your venture, and the sooner that cash starts flowing in faster than it flows out, the better. In the beginning, it may be unwise to turn down work, any kind of work. If your overhead is particularly high, it may be more than expedient to consider work that you might pass up later in the life of your business. The ultimate goal of any business is to generate income for its proprietor, partners, or stockholders. If a business is not generating money for those who gave it life, it is not worthy of survival. Before constructing your marketing plan, however, it is important, to define as clearly as possible the types of clients you wish to pursue and how the types of products and services you wish to provide them helps to meet their needs.

Deviating from this plan is not unusual in the beginning. David James of Panther Management Group recalls his company's first few years: "Back then, if you asked me to describe my company in three sentences, it would have been: 'Well, we look for work. We get it. Then, we take the money and try to survive.' We would do anything to survive and make money. Literally, we would have painted some guy's office if he wanted."

The marketing plan for your company or department should be based on the financial and strategic assumptions made in the earliest stages of developing your business plan. Its preparation will also help to refine the assumptions in your business plan based on how you intend to go about executing the marketing process and creating revenues. It is wise to launch your business with a competitive market strategy grounded with the answers to the four important questions listed in Figure 8–1.

These four questions describe the complex relationship between your special events organization and the market in which it will operate, and closely correlate with the three phases of designing an effective marketing plan, as described in Figure 8–2.

1. What product or service am I demonstrably qualified to offer?
2. To whom can I sell these products or services?
3. What differentiates me from the competition?
4. How will I go about communicating with potential clients in the most convincing way possible the clear benefits of selecting my product or service over that of my competitor?

Figure 8–1   Creating a Competitive Marketing Strategy

Phase 1: Define your market

Phase 2: Craft your unique message

Phase 3: Bring the message to market

Figure 8–2   Designing Your Marketing Plan

Phase 1: *Defining Your Market*

To clearly define your market, set out to answer the first two questions: what product or service am I demonstrably qualified to offer, and to whom can I sell these products or services? Although much of the balance of this discussion will assume that you have already identified your own inventory of talents and qualifications, you will need to ensure that all of your marketing plans are consistent with what you can effectively deliver to prospective clients.

With your organization's qualifications kept in sharp focus, identify your *target market*—those clients you most wish to reach. It is essential to understand who you will be trying to serve before you can understand their wants and needs, and well before you can create the best message to reach them. Figure 8–3 lists just some of the types of special events markets in existence today, such as corporate, social, not-for-profit, entertainment, and civic event producers, specialists providing products or services to event producers, and retailers providing their products or services to either event organizers or end users. You don't have to attempt to serve just one of these markets, but it would not be wise to try to be in all of them (see Focusing Your Market Strategy). Consider how big a market, in dollars, you will be entering

Corporate Events
Customer Hospitality Events
Dealer & Sales Incentive Events
Destination & Guest Management
Grand Openings
Holiday Parties
Industrial Shows
Meetings & Conventions
New Product Introductions
Sponsorship Consultation &
Fulfillment
Team Building Events
Trade Shows
Conventions and Expositions
General Management
Opening Ceremonies
Destination Management
Tours
Spouse/Partner Programs
Hospitality and Entertainment
Awards Banquets
Social Events
Religious Celebrations
(Confirmations, Bar/Bat Mitzvahs)
Society Events
Weddings
Entertainment Events
Arena Shows
Concerts
Made-for-TV Events
Sporting Events
General Management

Halftime & Pre-Game
Ceremonies
Corporate Auxiliary Events
Civic Events
Civic Holiday Celebrations
Festivals
Parades
Not-for-profit
Cause-Related Events
Fundraising
Political Events & Rallies
Specialists
Audio/Visual
Balloons
Décor
Entertainment
Event Public Relations
Floral
Lasers
Lighting
Meeting Services
Party Rental
Pyrotechnics
Speech Writing and Coaching
TelePrompTer
Talent Agencies
Transportation
Video Production
Retail
Florists
Party Goods
Travel Services

Figure 8–3   Typical Special Events Markets

and set realistic expectations of what percentage of that available money, or *market share,* you can expect to capture. Is the market flat, increasing, or decreasing in size? How many companies are currently competing, and how well established are they? Is there something of substantive value you can offer to prospective clients that they can not?

Figure 8–4 illustrates a *market share analysis* for competing special events planners in a small U.S. city. In this hypothetical example, there is a total of $4.15 million being spent annually by clients in the market, divided between five suppliers. The budget assumptions made by the principals of Most Excellent Events suggest that they expect the company to be third in the market, with a market share of 22 percent ($900,000 of the total $4,150,000). If a new company were to enter the market, either their share would have to come at the expense of the five more established companies, or the market might have to expand to enable all six companies to survive. In other words, the total dollars being spent by the all of the companies comprising the market would have to increase to support all of the suppliers.

You need to define your market in geographic terms as well. Will you target clients or events in your immediate area, or will you cast your net nationally, or even globally? Will your local clients take you on the road with them? The size of your market universe will help you determine the best geographic strategy. If you are a laser company, you will want to look for business beyond your city of residence because it is the only way to get enough business. On the other hand, if you are a floral designer, the competition outside your market from local suppliers in those cities might be too strong, and the fees you must charge to cover travel and expenses may make you uncompetitive.

Company	Size of Market	Share of Market (%)
Most Excellent Events	$ 900,000	22
Sometimes Great Events	$ 950,000	23
Events With Style	$ 350,000	8
Spectacular Results	$ 1,500,000	36
Events For Less	$ 450,000	11
TOTAL MARKET SIZE	**$ 4,150,000**	**100**

Figure 8–4   Market Share Analysis

Regardless of your segment of the market, there are many road-blocks to developing business outside your home base. Many clients like to be able to meet with their suppliers, particularly creative suppliers, regularly and at their convenience. For these clients' projects, a hometown-based supplier would be most preferred. In other cases, clients will find it advantageous to work with special events suppliers located in, and more familiar with, the distant city hosting the event. An unfamiliar special events supplier in a city that is distant from both the client and the event site is at a competitive disadvantage from the start.

In order to succeed in the national or global marketplace, you have to convince the client that your event management prowess is not a commodity—that it is not the same regardless of what company they ultimately hire. First, you have to be convinced your products or services are unique enough to justify tearing down the geographic barrier. Then, you have to convince your potential clients. Let's say you leave your offices in Los Angeles to travel to New York City to drum up some business. Think about the 260 million people you fly over on your way to the East coast. Are you so unique that among all of those people between those two points, there is no one who can deliver what you can to the client 2,500 miles away? If so, by all means, go for it! Are there no suppliers among the 16 million people in the New York metropolitan area who could do your job? Maybe there are, but your job is to convince your prospect, of your unique-ness and more importantly, to deliver on that promise come event day.

Focusing Your Market Strategy

While critically important, simply knowing the dynamics of the market—size, growth potential, location, and the competitive environment—will not define your target market finely enough. To conserve your limited time and financial resources, it is usually wise to focus your marketing strategy on segments of the marketplace in which you will have the greatest success in generating revenue. This does not infer that you should turn down potentially profitable work on which you can deliver exceptional results but which falls outside the self-defined boundaries of your target market. This strategic focus-ing process only seeks to increase your chances of success by ensuring that the messages you create, and the media through which you speak, are best targeted to those clients most likely to choose your company's products or services.

Special events companies can define and pursue their markets based on four key strategies—the shotgun approach, the rifle shot approach, the niche approach, and the preferred/exclusive provider approach—and some combine various aspects of each into the unique strategy that best suits their particular business.

The Shotgun Approach

In the events industry, businesses that use the shotgun strategy market themselves as providing "any and all kinds of events products or services for any and all kinds of events or any and all kinds of clients." If there is a piece of special events work out there, the shotgun strategist wants to have it. While this type of strategy may allow you to adapt to any identified client need, it is also the one which poses the most difficulties in targeting, reaching, and effectively identifying the unique wants and needs of specific clients. When you fire your marketing shotgun, you will scatter your effort over a wide area with less precision. You may or may not hit your target straight on, wasting a large percentage of the total effort in the process. With limited start-up capital and staff, most new businesses can not afford to waste their time or financial resources.

By contrast, the rifle shot and niche strategies, which will be discussed shortly, hone in on a specific target and/or offer a more defined product or service. When these strategists take careful aim, they are more likely to hit the target with a lot less wasted effort.

Note how every step in the development of your marketing plan continually questions and re-questions the essence of your overall business plan. As you develop your marketing strategy, re-examine the underpinnings of your business plan—both your strategic and financial assumptions—to ensure that all three are still compatible. Do not be surprised if the development of a sound marketing plan necessitates frequent readjustments of some of the most basic assumptions of your overall business plan. These adjustments are normal and healthy parts of the planning process.

The siren song of the vast multi-billion-dollar market of client corporations who should all be devoting their special events budgets to you is alluring to be sure. The simple fact is it is extremely difficult to attempt to be all things to all people and still maintain consistently high standards of quality. The failure of many start-up businesses can be traced to an unfocused marketing approach. Think of your market as a farm, and you as the farmer. Each type of crop (type of prospective client) requires different care, and each is harvested (marketed to) differently. There is nothing wrong with planting more than one type of crop. In fact, it is wise because it offers protection against species-specific diseases (economic downturns in your various clients' industries) that could wipe out your farm. However, on a small farm, you would not attempt to plant more than a few different species. As a farmer with a small—or no—staff beyond yourself, you could not keep up with all of the species-specific maintenance required.

The essence of the shotgun approach in the event business is going after whatever work you can dream up as you think of it. This is like planting different crops on the same field. Imagine the difficulty in farming a field where in the same row, you have carrots, wheat, corn, and onions. Not only is market maintenance impossible, harvesting your crops (marketing to clients and booking projects) would be incredibly difficult. The shotgun approach in its purest form as applied to the event business could result in a Dust Bowl for your business. Because the very definition of the special events business is so very broad, in our industry the shotgun strategy is frequently doomed to failure. So, too, bringing your message to market in shotgun fashion ensures a great deal of wasted money and activity.

The Rifle Shot Approach

Now, let's say you grow only corn. In this one-crop shop, you may become the world's leading corn specialist, your opinion and expertise sought out the world over. But, what happens when the corn harvest is poor? Or, demand drops? Or, disease or insects invade your field? The corn can be wiped out, and until a new crop can be planted, grown, and sown, you are without income.

Rifle shot companies have abounded among marketing agencies for many years. Advertising firms may specialize in automotive advertising, pharmaceutical advertising, or public service advertising. Public relations firms might specialize in entertainment, politics, or packaged goods. Sometimes firms differentiate themselves from one another by the type of client they typically work for, or the size of their accounts. But, long term, the successful agency diversifies its client base to at least some degree, the better to weather economic downturns in one or more of their clients' industries.

Successful event companies exhibit behavior similar to their elder cousins in the marketing family. They also typically specialize in the types of clients they service—corporations, civic organizations, municipalities—the types of services they offer, and/or the types of events with which they are associated.

Entrepreneurs employing the rifle shot approach focus on a small number of specific targets in the market. In so doing, they use their capital and staff more efficiently, and hopefully more effectively, than organizations employing a shotgun marketing strategy. However, in this relatively new and burgeoning industry, competition is brisk even among those companies employing a rifle shot strategy. For this reason, many entrepreneurs enter the marketplace with a highly specialized, even more finely targeted strategy—the niche approach.

The Niche Approach

If you are the only company offering a particular service or product for specialized use or to specialized clients, you are a niche marketer. A niche only stays a niche as long as only you and perhaps a very limited number of other competitors are in it. Adopting a niche strategy is risky, but potentially most lucrative. While you may be the only supplier in your niche, you have to have performed sufficient due diligence to ensure that it is a product that clients want or need. It could well be that the reason your new product or service idea does not yet exist is because it is a solution to which there is no problem, and therefore, for which there is no market. It is essential that you perform whatever research is necessary, formal or informal, to determine that your new product will meet a need, or solve a client's challenge in some new and exciting way.

Let us assume, however, that your idea is one that your research suggests can provide a new resource which prospective clients will find very attractive. The more attractive and potentially lucrative your market niche is, the more likely that new competitors will target your company as one to challenge for available dollars. When adopting a niche strategy, your marketing plan should anticipate competition sooner or later. Occasionally, this competition will come from larger, well-established companies with greater resources who will come a-farming in the fields you have spent time, money, and sweat fertilizing. Unless you plan for this eventuality, these larger, more highly capitalized companies can wage battles to drive you out of business.

Special events niche businesses that manufacture new and innovative products that would be initially unobtainable elsewhere would be wise to protect their company's future growth by pursuing a patent. This federal protection encourages innovation by ensuring that companies investing in the successful development of a new product will be able to protect their new ideas from copycat marketers, recoup their investments, and prosper from their own ingenuity. If you suspect that your new product is unique and meets an unfulfilled need in the marketplace, consult a patent lawyer on how to proceed. Expect the successful patenting process to take a year or more, and include your attorney's legal fees in your budget.

In cases where special events entrepreneurs can not obtain a patent, niche strategies tend to work best when you can find a market with low overhead and limited enough application where it is just plain unattractive for a competitor to share the available market with you. Some examples of successful niche marketers in the event industry include:

- *Sculptchair (Scottsdale, Arizona).* Founded by Mitchell Kelldorf, Sculptchair is a supplier of patented, stretch-to-fit chair covers and accent bands. Available in a large variety of colors and prints, these covers provide a custom fit to any standard banquet, stacking, or folding chair (see Figure 8–5). Event planners, hotels, and casinos regularly use Sculptchair covers to achieve dramatic effects in both large and small spaces. Functional chairs are transformed into artistic props for weddings, excitement-builders for conventions, and imaginative decorative elements for theme parties. Several factors have contributed to Sculptchair's thriving success within the narrow niche of chair covers. First, creative marketing entices potential users with the product's visual-impact possibilities. Second, fair rental and purchasing pricing offers a low-risk expenditure to the client. And finally, the product's patent protects Sculptchair's investment while enabling them to educate the industry and potential clients about their product, discouraging competitors from cannibalizing the narrow niche.

- *Argonne Productions (Atlanta, Georgia).* Argonne is led by Emmy Award–winning parade producer Don Whiteley. Don's experience in parade management is vast and storied, but his business began when he was offered the position of parade director for the "Salute 2 America Parade," produced by WSB-TV in Atlanta, Georgia. In 1986, Don formed Argonne to develop and manage the parade staged for the celebration of the Coca-Cola Centennial, and has since

Figure 8–5 Wedding photo courtesy of Sculptchair/Allen Creative. Copyright © Lee Gordon.

managed such nationally significant events as the "We The People 200" Parade, the Presidential Bicentennial Procession, the Operation Welcome Home Ticker Tape Parade, and London's acclaimed Christmas Parade. Don now employs a staff of four full time, and hundreds at parade time, but his product is himself—expertise in parade production and operations borne of decades of experience. There are others like him in cities across the country, but few who cut as wide a swath across the globe.

• *Scott Givens (Santa Monica, California).* Scott Givens unwittingly entered the special events industry as an engineering student at Purdue University. A gregarious sophomore involved in a multitude of student activities, Scott was determined to add excitement to the lifeless student audience attending the weekly football games by creating a "card section." He and some fellow students recruited 600 participants to sit in the stands behind the school band, and to hold up cards that together combined to form giant whimsical messages (e.g., "Hi, Mom! Send Money!"). Scott designed a new message each week on a sheet of graph paper. Since then, his computer-generated, large-format card stunts have become famous, having been featured at the

Super Bowl, Goodwill Games, the U.S. Olympic Festival, and approximately 100 other events. Using his core business of large-format visual effects as a springboard, Scott now also produces entire entertainment events across North America and Australia. "Making the transition is really hard, but it's important to me to be able to find new ways to apply my creativity. I'll always be available to the industry as the "card guy," but my long-term goal is to continue to expand my role as a producer."

• *JRP Group (Toronto, Ontario).* The three partners that comprise JRP Group—Jim Palmer, Richard Baker, and Paul Palmer—specialize in producing on-ice hockey skills competitions. The two Palmer Brothers are best known in Canada as the creators of "Showdown," a 24-episode per season made-for-television ice hockey skills competition featured on the Canadian Broadcasting Corporation's long-running "Hockey Night in Canada" program in the 1970s. JRP Group developed the NHL SuperSkills competition for the 1990 NHL All-Star Weekend in Pittsburgh, which has since become an annual fan favorite. The response to the event has been so strong that JRP has also produced similar competitions for all National Hockey League teams, as well as for dozens of minor hockey leagues and junior hockey organizations throughout North America.

When you write a business plan for a niche company, remember that the key to growth is market expansion. Ask yourself how many other applications exist for your product or service, but be careful that you are not expanding the market so far or so fast as to attract the competition. A prudent niche marketer will always have a plan for where to take his or her product next once the niche starts to mature.

Exclusive and Preferred Suppliers

As an entrepreneurial employee, look at what kinds of other businesses your existing client base utilizes as a result of their relationship with you. If you are a hotel or convention center manager whose clients frequently employ the services of an outside audio-visual company, consider the feasibility of adding that service to your own portfolio to capture more of the client's revenues. You may decide to create an internal resource, enter into a joint venture with an existing entity, or select a vendor who is exclusive to your facility. As a special events entrepreneur, you can work this logic in reverse to identify what kinds of venues you frequently interact with directly or indirectly, and determine whether a mutually beneficial supplier relationship is advantageous.

For an entrepreneur, securing an exclusive supplier relationship is like money in the bank. It's one-stop shopping for the client, and you are guaranteed an income from your partner's business. Your costs-of-goods-sold are low, typically only the pre-agreed percentage of sales due back to your partner in the form of commission. Of course, providing quality service is essential to remain the exclusive supplier when contract renewal time arrives. If you are an event venue, the quality of the vendor you select to be "an exclusive" must be carefully considered. Clients will be forced to consider the quality and cost-efficiency of your exclusive suppliers as a key decision point on whether or not they will hire *you*—particularly if there is heavy competition in your segment of the business. A convention facility in New England, as an example, maintains an exclusive relationship with a decorating company. On one hand, this enables the decorator to charge higher rates in the absence of competition and provides the convention center with a lucrative source of revenues that they may not have otherwise earned. On the flip side, it makes the venue less attractive to those with limited budgets, or those who have the option of going to other facilities where decorating companies must compete with one another for the business.

If as an event supplier you can not entice a venue to provide you with an exclusive relationship, try to become a "preferred supplier." Preferred supplier contract terms vary widely; however, the basic concept is that a venue will recommend your company or service to those clients who may be in the market. The venue has an incentive to "sell" your company because you will pay them a commission. However, the client is not obligated to use you, so you will have to budget dollars for sales—you may have to pitch the business brought to you by the venue, competing with others in the marketplace. Commissions paid by "preferred suppliers" to their partners are typically lower than exclusives.

If you are pitching yourself to a venue or other partner as an exclusive or preferred supplier, be prepared for the fight of your life. But, if you can pull it off, it will pay handsome dividends. To be appealing to your potential partner, you will have to provide first-class product or service—your partner's reputation will be based on your ability to deliver. You will have to demonstrate your consistency and trustworthiness on this. Exclusive suppliers can expect to pay their partners a percentage of the gross revenues derived from their activities in their host's home. Try to keep the percentage low, perhaps on a sliding scale based on volume. This will keep your prices attractive and/or preserve more revenues for yourself, while providing your partner with a strong economic incentive to sell your company. On a final note, if you do develop an exclusive or preferred relationship, do not count on it for 100 percent of your business. Because contracts expire, relationships change, and venues can suffer catastrophic losses due to acts of God, be sure to develop enough outside work to sustain your company should the relationship come to a sudden end.

Unless you have a niche opportunity that you are willing to research and are relatively certain you can develop without better-capitalized investors invading your small market, a modified rifle shot approach provides the lowest risk. A modified strategy is suggested because at first, pursuing too finely defined a target may not provide enough "hits" to sustain a new business. Sometimes it is best to initially target two or three different but related markets, but to start with the markets you know well. Once you have started to service the markets you are already familiar with, you can use new cash to build your marketing activities among new or related markets, and broaden the range of products and services you offer.

Phase Two: Crafting Your Unique Message

Once you have defined your market in economic and geographic terms, and have further defined your strategy on the segments of the market on which you will concentrate your efforts, you must next determine how your organization or product uniquely relates to your prospective target clients. If you have done a complete job of defining your market and how your organization relates to it, you will be able to summarize the results of Phase One with a single sentence. As an example: "Applying 25 years of combined experience, *Props R Us* will supply the best value in high-quality decorative props to hotel and off-premises catering companies in the Dallas-Ft. Worth Metroplex, with the goal of capturing 20 percent of the estimated $2.5 million in expenditures in the market within three years."

This statement goes back to the most basic and important question: "What product or service am I demonstrably qualified to offer?" If you believed that you could achieve greatness through sheer willpower alone, you would not have purchased this book. Though self-confidence is an admirable and necessary trait in an entrepreneur, it takes more than a dream and determination to build a successful business. It also takes expertise and experience. You may dream of being the best goaltender the hockey world has ever seen, but if you can't stop a puck better than your competitor, your career will be a short one. Start with a realistic goal based on realistic expectations. Simply put, identify a product, service, or segment of the market in which you have demonstrable qualifications, but keep in mind that your competition could make similar—or even superior—claims.

To put yourself at a competitive advantage, you have to position your organization so prospective clients will perceive your organization as the best choice for the product they need, or the work they need performed. That is why it is wise to consider the second question while crafting your message—*what differentiates me from the competition?*

Once you have identified the product or service you will offer based on your demonstrable expertise and experience, consider what sets you apart from the competition. Before designing your advertising, writing your press releases, or even submitting a client proposal, make a list of all of your organization's positive qualities that can help result in a positive outcome—a new piece of business (see Figure 8–6).

Many of the items on the list would certainly appear on any list created by your competitors, and in some cases may compare favorably to yours. But, it's the combination of strengths and how well they relate to the wants and needs of your clients that often determines the likelihood of being selected.

If you have ever interviewed job applicants, you can easily put yourself in the shoes of a potential client. When you ask job candidates to identify their greatest personal strength, most answer: "I am very

---

1. Principals have a combined total of 25 years of corporate and entertainment event experience.

2. Fortune 500 clients include Intl. Widgets, Federated CelFone, Copyclear Copiers, and TruTuf Lawn Tractors.

3. Our warehouse of over 1500 customizable prop elements is one of the largest in the area.

4. Winner of five *Special Events Magazine* Gala Awards.

5. A company technician will be present during each client's event to ensure smooth operation and top-quality presentation.

6. Our unique buy-back option on custom-made props can increase the impact of a client's events, while actually saving them money.

Figure 8–6   "Props R Us" Competitive Qualities

organized." While an essential and admirable trait, it is hardly unique. Since there is no way to distinguish job candidates based on this universal claim, you are unlikely to hire someone based on this single characteristic. Decide what characteristics of your organization are the most attractive to your potential universe of clients before you commit yourself to a message, and emphasize those you feel will most influence them to choose you over your competitors.

If you can not identify benefits unique to doing business with you, don't panic. Your product or service may be excellent, but not unique. You should then attempt to develop unique benefits, and later how you will communicate them to potential clients, as keystones of your marketing plan.

When designing these unique benefits, remember that the most successful marketers do not sell benefits—they sell solutions! When comparing their qualities against the competition, the principals of Props R Us determined that while they were supremely confident in their capabilities, there was nothing that set them uniquely apart from their competition. To achieve uniqueness, they studied the buying habits of their clients and identified a unique, new competitive feature. Custom-made props are typically more expensive than stock items. To encourage demanding clients looking for better-quality props to consider higher-margin, custom-built pieces, Props R Us developed a new competitive quality:

Props R Us determined that most clients have neither the space nor desire to keep custom-made props after use. Therefore, when quoting on custom-made pieces, Props R Us decided to offer both a full-priced option for those who anticipate keeping their purchases, and a "trade-in credit" for those clients who intend to dispose of their work post-event. Props R Us bases the credit applied on the company's ability to construct the custom props such that they can be cost-effectively disassembled, refurbished, and reused as rental units.

Props R Us then crafts its message to showcase its competitive benefit as a solution: "If you buy from us, you can afford to incorporate desirable, high-impact, custom-made props into your special events budgets at little more than renting pre-made, often-seen units."

Phase 3: Bringing Your Message to Market

The operating philosophy in devising your marketing plan should always be to identify where your target prospects look for information and insight, and to get in their way. Integrate a consistent message into all of the marketing tools available, and you will be able to convert client exposure into awareness, awareness into consideration, and consideration into the ultimate goal—selection.

When selecting the tools with which to market your company, remember that you, too, are a customer. You will be marketed to by all of those companies that will be more than pleased to help you find ways to spend your marketing dollars. You have to be selective to determine the best ways to spend them, and the best ways are those that have the best chance to result in new business for your company. To exercise this selectivity, you have already identified (a) what you want to say to your prospective clients, and (b) to whom you want to say it. Now, it all comes down to how and where you will say it.

Spending on marketing is much like buying a financial instrument such as a stock, bond, or certificate of deposit. No one would hand money to a broker or bank without some level of confidence in receiving some increase in value. Likewise, the wise marketer seeks out opportunities that maximize results while minimizing costs. This relationship between costs and results is frequently referred to as "return on investment" (ROI). If a stock is costing you money instead of making you money, you get rid of it. Elements in your marketing plan should be dealt with the same way. It is important to find the right ways to increase your business, and as important to know how NOT to spend your money.

Consider your marketing focus—is it a shotgun, rifle shot, or niche approach? It is your job to put your message where your target market can see it and be captivated by it. Where are they looking? What are they reading? How can you touch them? Remember that, for the most part, your future clients are not looking for *you*. You have to be looking for them. What are the best tools to get "in their face"? There are a wide range of such tools available, including advertising, publicity, promotion, direct sales, and even special events! In each case, creativity and effective placement are of paramount importance to marketers in our creative industry. Let's explore which tools might be the best for your business.

Your Company Brochure—Your Most Important Advertising Tool

If you create no other advertising tool, spend the majority of your time and whatever you can spare financially on creating a brochure or sales kit representative of your organization's creativity, expertise, and experience. Your brochure, in whatever form it takes, is the most likely marketing tool to be compared side-by-side to that of your competitors. The company brochure can be designed for many purposes: it can serve as a direct mail piece, as a leave-behind during personal meetings, and as an accompaniment to creative or capability proposals. If you neglect your brochure, your competitors are sure to gain an advantage. The quality and staying power of their company will be judged superior to your own if their brochure is more professionally prepared and finely targeted. You would never show up to a business meeting unshaven and wearing Bermuda shorts, and expect to close a sale (unless you are in the Bermuda shorts business). Your brochure positions you and your organization as much as your wardrobe, your sales pitch, and your ideas. When it is pulled from a file cabinet or left behind after a meeting, clients will judge competing companies on the professionalism of their collateral material as much as on any other single criterion.

When ITT Corporation was first founded, it was a small telecommunications company that owned a few small telephone utilities in South America and the Caribbean. To give the impression of a large, multinational corporation, its founder established its headquarters office a thousand miles away in New York City, and named the firm International Telephone & Telegraph. The name, while completely justified by its presence in several small countries, gave customers and potential business partners the further impression that being an "international telecommunications company," it would have to be bigger than the already gigantic American Telephone & Telegraph (some even mistakenly thought it was the parent company). In 1998, the remnants of what began as a small telecommunications competitor were sold for $13.3 billion.

Most special events entrepreneurs can not start big. But, how you present your organization in printed materials, and especially through your brochure, can make you appear as big as anyone else. In general, it is wise to spend whatever you can on the development, creation, and printing of your company brochure.

Because your brochure is so important, it should be finely targeted to intrigue, excite, and inform the prospect who will be reading it. And, while its creativity should be involving enough to capture the attention and imagination of the recipient, it should require no great investment of time and energy to read on the part of the recipient.

The Creative Management Group, a full-service special events firm in New York's Buffalo-Niagara Region, created an innovative brochure design only 6 inches wide by 6 inches high. A dramatic full-color event photograph containing the single word "Excitement . . ." draws the reader into opening the flap, revealing a second photograph of the company's work, and the headline "Anything is Possible." The reader is challenged by this message to open flap after flap. *If anything is possible, what kind of possibilities does my next event have?* the brochure subtly asks. The final flap reveals CMG's list of services, types of events produced, and of course, a contact name and number.

EVENTURES, a New York City–based mega-events production company of which Frank Supovitz was a former partner, created a versatile brochure that was essentially a shell, into which single page inserts that would be most applicable to the particular prospect could be enclosed. As EVENTURES serviced a wide range of clients, from municipalities to sports organizations to corporations, a single, inflexible brochure would have been less effective, and producing a series of brochures for each type of client would have been cost-prohibitive.

As previously mentioned, while the form of your brochure should reflect your creativity, do not neglect function and ease of use at the expense of innovative design. Imaginative marketing techniques need to be designed with functionality in mind. While some may look good on paper, some may actually end up working against you. Consider how your marketing tools appear to the unfamiliar prospect or client. See Figure 8–7 for some examples of marketing efforts gone awry.

Whenever you send your brochure to a prospect, regardless of whether it was requested or unsolicited, include a brief cover letter. Although it should be impeccably composed and executed, don't spend an enormous amount of time on the cover letter, since many of them will never be read before being sent to the trash bin. If the recipient requested it be sent, be sure to say so in the very first sentence. If there is a specific reason why you have sent your brochure unsolicited, mention that instead. Briefly introduce yourself and your company, and explain in one or two paragraphs why you have sent your brochure. Then, let your brochure do all the work until you place your follow-up call.

Print Advertising

Print advertising is one of the most common tools special events marketers use to create awareness of their companies, products, and services. For a creative industry such as special events, the most effective advertising frequently is creative advertising. Since most of the work

- To add a sense of festivity to a mass mailing, a special events company sprinkled loose glitter and metallic confetti into the envelopes containing their marketing brochure. As prospects opened the envelopes, the confetti spilled over their desks, coffee, and computers.

- A resort hotel mailed their brochure in a clear plastic envelope filled with sand and metal confetti. Not wanting to spill this detritus over their desks, many prospects may have simply tossed the package into the garbage. In actuality, the mailer was a double envelope, with the sand sealed off between the outer layer and the brochure. But, you have only a few seconds to convince someone to open your envelope. Don't give them an excuse not to. In this case, many potential customers may not have taken that amount of time to figure out that the package was designed to be completely safe.

- A municipal convention and visitors bureau designed its brochure as an interactive CD-ROM, which could not be scanned by the recipient for information without first installing it on the prospect's computer in order to be read. The expensive animations and graphics were a waste for busy executives without the time or an incentive to take their computer off-line to install the CD-ROM, as well as those without CD-ROM drives on their computers.

- A sales pitch letter was rolled, tied with a mylar ribbon, and inserted into a plastic bottle along with an American flag and streamers. The recipient pulled out the cork and spent 30 seconds unsuccessfully trying to remove the letter from the bottle before he tossed it in the garbage without ever knowing who sent it.

Figure 8–7   Stupid Marketing Tricks #1: Form Over Function

product of a special events company is creative in nature, creativity in advertising—from magazine and radio ads, to brochures, flyers, and other direct marketing pieces—can serve as a clear demonstration of the innovative talents of the advertiser.

For Sculptchair's Mitchell Kelldorf, advertising is a key part of the marketing plan. Kelldorf's product—form-fitting Lycra chair covers—is well suited to print advertising because the product is so visual. The quality, versatility, and wide range of colors can be easily communicated using photographs. But Kelldorf does not stop there. One of his company's popular print advertisements adhered to the old sales adage—don't sell benefits or features, sell solutions! Beneath a full-color photograph of chairs at a gala dinner covered with Sculptchair product, the key copy points are featured in large, bold script:

> *"So Nancy said, 'Don't sit there. Those are part of the decorations.'*
> *And I said 'For cryin' out loud, Nance, those are the chairs'."*

Kelldorf's vision for possibilities, as reflected in his advertising, is actually an outgrowth of the vision that led to his company's genesis. While working on events for the high-end cosmetics industry, he noticed that clients staging dinner galas spent a great deal of money on centerpieces, props, and table linens. But, regardless of how much money was spent in decorating an event, the chairs were still just the chairs. "The more décor was added, the more skeletal the chairs looked," he recalls. He first started covering the chairs with table linens, but with so much attention paid to customized décor through the venue, the linens looked like what they were—an afterthought. Kelldorf's advertising is effective because it reflects the basic philosophies behind the founding of the company. Sculptchair's product is not positioned as a product, but as an event solution. Only after the reader's attention is grabbed by the header does the rest of the copy describe the qualities of the product:

> *". . . Sculptchair chair covers and accent bands can give your special*
> *event that extra edge that separates the good from the spectacular.*
> *They stretch to fit. And they come in a full spectrum of very hot colors*
> *and prints . . ."*

When assessing the value of placing print advertising in media such as newspapers and magazines, look at not only the quantity of their readers (circulation), but also the quality (the composition of their readership). If you are a supplier to other companies in the special events industry, you must advertise where your prospective buyers look for information or ideas, such as *Special Events, Event Solutions, Successful Meetings,* and *Lighting Dimensions,* among many others. Most magazine advertising sales departments can provide you with not only the number of readers, but also with statistical information on their readership, including their types of business (SIC codes), their purchasing and sales volumes, their business titles, and frequently, their level of purchasing and decision-making authority. Select the magazines whose readership matches up with the target market you have defined, and assess the value of advertising in their publication versus others on a cost per thousand (CPM) basis; that is, how much money an advertisement costs to reach each 1,000 prospects. Try to calculate your own CPM figure based on what percentage of a publication's readership would represent your definition of your target market. If you can afford to advertise in more than one publication, by all means, do so. If not, determining the right publication to be seen in can be based on your own CPM calculation.

And, don't overlook the least expensive and easiest form of advertising—your local business-to-business telephone directory. Ensure that, at minimum, your company is listed within your business category, and assess whether your target prospects would seek out and qualify companies like yours through the directory before you decide to strengthen your presence by buying additional exposure through display advertising.

Direct Mail Marketing

Many event companies use mailings to create initial awareness among potential clients and then follow up with qualified prospects via telephone calls and/or their brochure. Creative mailing programs can create expectations at a fraction of the cost of sending complete brochures to a mass audience:

- Exhibé, a San Diego-based marketing communications company specializing in the trade show business, sent a series of scenic postcards to qualified prospects before following up with a phone call. The cards featured scenes of Yellowstone National Park, alligators in the Everglades, and San Diego Harbor, and included simple messages from the "vacationing" partners describing their travels away from the office (see Figure 8–8). This direct marketing tool established an intimacy between the company and the recipient, and followed the same basic rule as brochure and print advertising—keep it simple, but intriguing. In addition, the great thing about postcards is they don't need to be opened, and they take next to no time investment to read.

- Caribiner, one of the world's leading business communications companies, produced a postcard featuring a one-panel cartoon evocative of the popular "The Far Side" comic strip on one side, and a handwritten personal note from the sales contact on the other, suggesting that the recipient could expect a follow-up call (see Figure 8–9).

Good to be back. Travel is great, but there's
no place like home – especially when it's
San Diego.
Let's get together to talk about a new venture
called **Exhibé** – the best thing to happen to
the trade show business in southern California.
Exhibé is a fresh, vital and cost effective
approach to the challenge of looking great in
front of your customers. **Exhibé** offers
everything you need to maximize sales
performance – direct mail, video production
– even help with your most complex marketing
and sales problem.
Call us at (619) 401-1323 to discuss creative
solutions for your individual needs.

Best regards,
Michel, Valerie, Alan, Linda & Mark

Frank Supovitz
Nat'l Hockey League
1251 Ave. of the Americas
4th floor
New York, NY 10020-1198

Figure 8–8   Courtesy of Exhibé Media Communications. Copyright 1998,
Exhibé. All rights reserved.

"It rains too much, it's too far from the beach and there are no golf courses.
I tell you, boss, Waterloo is no place to hold an important meeting."

Figure 8–9   Copyright © Caribiner International, Inc.

- EVENTURES utilized the "engagement notice" technique. When a new client executed an event contract, the company created a simple engraved card similar to a personal announcement, heralding the "engagement": *"EVENTURES is proud to announce its engagement to produce the Stanford University Centennial Gala on September 30, 1991,"* followed by the company address and telephone number. Engagement notices crossing a prospect's desk were opened because they arrived in small, undaunting envelopes that looked like RSVP's to a gala or wedding. Subsequent mailings were also likely to be opened because the prospect knew that the messages were simple, interesting, and required no great investment of time.

- Caribiner also used the engagement notice technique after its successful management of the Hong Kong Handover Ceremonies, creating a powerful, handsome marketing keepsake piece that looked so much like an invitation to an event of historic proportions that it would be difficult for a recipient to discard (see Figure 8–10).

- The Wonder Company, Inc. used a quarterly newsletter filled with inexpensive ideas for producing special events on a shoestring budget.

Figure 8–10   Copyright © Caribiner International, Inc.

In designing and executing their products and projects, successful special events professionals pay attention to every detail, and spend hours researching the best solutions for their clients. Your marketing tools should reflect the same level of knowledge and exacting quality.

A letter addressed to the NHL's Frank Supovitz from a special events organizer seeking new clients that boasted of their attention to detail opened with the salutation "Dear Bob."

An envelope addressed to the same NHL executive contained a letter addressed to the NFL, and vice versa.

Business ethics are discussed more fully in Chapter 10. Suffice it to say truth in marketing goes a long way. A falsehood or half-truth can go even further, but often in the opposite direction.

A special events company pitching a professional sports organization claimed they had organized a large national touring event the recipient knew had been managed by someone else. It turned out the company's principal had been hired out as a freelancer to handle operations in one local market. While they might have been otherwise qualified to manage the prospect's events, their misrepresentation cost them nothing more than a cursory look.

It is a small world, and an even smaller industry. Among the client companies listed by a special events freelancer was one at which the recipient worked previously. During the follow-up phone call, the freelancer unknowingly claimed to have worked for the listed client at the same time as the prospective employer who had never heard of her.

In addition to your own database of contacts, you may want to broaden the reach of your direct mail campaign by utilizing a rented mailing list. Shop for mailing lists just like you shop for print advertising opportunities. You can usually rent lists from the same trade publications you advertise in, or select from specific lists that match up with your target market from a commercial mailing service. In most cases, you can increase the effectiveness of a list by asking the rental company to customize the contacts to your preferences—companies within a certain geographic location only, executives of certain titles or professions, or by other demographic or psychographic characteristics as you define them. Lists usually rent for between $75 and $150 per thousand names. Because most services are reluctant to allow you to see the mailing labels yourself for fear of piracy (i.e., you are renting names, not buying them), you usually have to hire a mailing service to apply the labels and postage and bring the mail to the post office.

It is most helpful to gauge the effectiveness of your direct mail campaign by encouraging the recipient to respond for either a brochure, additional information, a call from a sales representative, or for a premium item. Studies conducted by the Direct Marketing Association suggest that you can greatly increase the number of responses by including a postage-paid business reply card or envelope. If you are mailing nationally, including a toll-free "800" or "888" number or an e-mail address can also enhance your results.

The Internet

The Internet is in its most formative years as a marketing tool, which is why advertising on it is relatively inexpensive today. For prospective clients, it is also the least intrusive way to gain additional information and sample a supplier's creativity without the fear of being subjected to the "hard sell."

If you establish a company web site, be sure to include its address, or URL, on every marketing communication you issue—from your brochure to print advertising, direct marketing, even your business card. Casually interested prospects can then visit your company in the anonymity of cyberspace, explore your products, services, and past work at their leisure, and request additional information or initiate contact only if they choose.

Like print advertising and direct marketing, enter the world of marketing on the web only if you have the resources to ensure that your site will reflect your company's creativity and professionalism. There are many Internet producers who will develop your site for a fee. Develop your site with an eye toward linking to other sites that will drive business to you. You can purchase or trade for an advertisement on another web site that serves as a hyperlink—a button that effortlessly brings the cyberspace traveler to your site from another and vice versa—for relatively little money.

It should be kept in mind, however, that the Internet has not yet matured as a reference tool. A 1998 search on the C/Net browser turned up 5.96 million different listings for "special events suppliers." The same search using Alta Vista resulted in 1.85 million. It is highly unlikely that any prospect looking for a special events supplier will rummage through that many selections to find your company. While there are some remarkable special events resource databases on which you may consider listing (see Figure 8–11), the question of whether your target market is using them to search for companies like yours is up to you to answer.

Up Close and Personal

Today's bookstore business sections are filled with volumes of outstanding books on salesmanship and effective sales techniques, a small number of which are referenced at the end of this chapter. It is highly recommended that every entrepreneur and entrepreneurial employee read and periodically review the latest sales literature available to continually sharpen and re-sharpen their person-to-person marketing skills.

Remember that no matter how large an organization becomes, the successful chief executive is frequently the best salesperson in the office, the leader who arrives on the scene to "close the deal" after the groundwork is laid. When ultimately hiring a dedicated salesperson, most successful chief executives would search for someone with "a lot of contacts." As the leader in your organization, building your own database of contacts is essential to expanding your business. The more you know about your prospects, both professionally and personally, the more likely you will be able to sense their wants and needs, and propose correct, competitive, and effective solutions to meet them.

A successful salesperson will use a spreadsheet, database program, or even an index card file to compile information on their con-

---

http://www.nscee.edu/unlv/Tourism/suppliers.html

http://www.eventideas.com

http://www.specialevents.com

http://www.macgrafx.com/events/business.html

http://www.event-solutions.com

http://www.eventsource.com

Figure 8–11   Internet Advertising Opportunities for Special Events Organizations with Web Sites

tacts. They will organize this data so they can access it at a moment's notice should a prospect call. The sales professional will rate them on the likelihood and desirability of their business. They take mental notes relative to a prospect's personal likes and dislikes, values and lifestyles, interests and hobbies, without seeming to pry. During meetings at the client's office, they take note of family pictures, art, bric-a-brac. On sales calls, they keep chitchat to a minimum, but add just enough personal insight to reinforce connection with the client. If there's a magazine article they think a prospect would find intriguing, they'll clip it and send them a copy. The successful salesperson looks for personal commonality—if both they and the prospect collect model trains, and there's a train show in town, they'll send tickets, or invite them along. But, they try to remain genuine. Because they respect their client's intelligence and perceptiveness, they know that feigning interest in a client's hobby, lifestyle, or values is risky, and will probably result in the client attributing their insincerity to everything else they say.

Whether you are starting small, or will have a dedicated sales force by the time you open your doors, today's special events marketplace demands that *everyone* in your organization—from the receptionist to the CFO to the top dog—be a salesperson. Your employees should appreciate that fact because they are paid with money, and that money comes from sales. Therefore, sales must be every employee's primary objective.

Because every employee is, tacitly or overtly, a salesperson, every employee should be prepared to represent your company to potential clients. They may meet them at a seminar, on an airplane, on the telephone, on line at the movies, or at the neighborhood barbershop. Give them the tools to represent your business to that potential cash resource by communicating your organization's goals and objectives, and the types of clients and projects you are seeking.

Once you have qualified a prospect, communicate regularly, frequently, and time-efficiently. Respect the value of their time as you would value your own. Don't call them "just to check in." Everybody else is doing that, so the likelihood of getting a piece of business by calling to engage in meaningless chitchat is not only wasteful, but also potentially annoying to the client. Remember to set yourself apart from the competition with every call—have something meaningful to ask or say with every contact. How many times have you made or received some version of the following call?

Checking with Interest

A NHL special events employee opened a checking account at a major New York bank. After the customer service representative mentioned that the bank vice president was a big hockey fan, the events staffer brought an upcoming project to his attention. This initially casual conversation resulted in a meeting between the bank and the league's marketing departments, and led to a significant commitment on the part of the bank to sponsor a NHL event that met both of their needs.

Ineffective: The "Just Checking In" Call

Caller: Hello, Frank. It's Joe Jones from Most Excellent Events. Just calling to say "hi," and see if you've got anything coming up we can help you with.

Prospect: Hi, and no, there's nothing going on right now.

Caller: Okay, well, keep us in mind. I'll be back in touch in a few weeks.

Prospect: (Trying to be polite) Okay, fine.

While there are literally hundreds of variants on the theme, the following two calls illustrate how you can draw a prospective client into further involvement. That involvement can evolve into a relationship, and from the relationship, perhaps a sale will be made.

Effective: The "Personal Interests" Call

Caller: Hello, Frank. It's Joe Jones from Most Excellent Events. The reason I'm calling is to let you know we've just added CelPhone as a client. We're working on the product introduction on their new digital networking service, and I was really impressed with it. I remember that you really liked that cell phone you had just bought. Have you heard of this digital system?

Prospect: Yes. I saw it at the Electronics Show. It's going to be the next big thing in office productivity.

Caller: We were impressed, too. And, we were really
            honored to get the account. It's a big, publicly visible
            introduction, and it's great that a company like
            CelPhone trusts us with it. If you have some time
            next Wednesday, I can arrange for a press pass for
            you. It's at the Windsor Hotel.

Prospect: That's nice of you, but I'm busy on Wednesday.

Caller: Of course, but I hope you'll think of us, too, when
            you do your next product introduction.

Prospect: We don't have anything coming up that's quite so
            amazing or publicly visible.

Caller: I understand. But we started out small with
            CelPhone, just planning small executive retreats for
            them.

Prospect: Really? We've got something like that coming up in
            August. Maybe there's something there for you.

Caller: I'll be in your neighborhood tomorrow. Is there a
            convenient time for us to meet? I'll bring one of
            those new phones for you to see . . .

Effective: The "Investigative" Call

Caller: Hello, Matthew. This is Ethan Jacobs from Incredible
            Events. We just produced an event for Tough Sell
            Realty at the newly restored Catherine Theatre. Have
            you been there since they reopened?

Prospect: No, but I've heard great things about it.

Caller: If you have the time, maybe we can meet down there
            and I could show you what we did for Tough Sell.
            Both the client and the venue were pretty excited
            about it.

Prospect: I'd like to see the theatre, actually. Set up a tour with
            my assistant.

These special-events-business-specific examples are just a small
sampling of the kinds of effective general sales techniques that are
available in books devoted to the subject. Finding new ways to get past
the resistance of a prospective client is key to winning new sales.
Rehearse your calls as fastidiously as you would rehearse an event!

Think about how you want your audience to respond before you step onto the telephonic stage. Then, go do the show, and make some sales!

But, you have to develop these contacts before you can wage a *first-contact campaign*—the process of researching, developing, and qualifying leads, and ultimately contacting them with the objective of arranging a personal meeting or further interaction. A multitude of resources are available to you with a little effort and detective work. Search both local and national daily newspapers every day for the latest information on the companies, individuals, and events you most want to attract as clients. Try to determine which newspapers, magazines, and trade print publications your target clients read, and subscribe to as many as you can. Make a list of all of the companies in your market area that stage the types of special events in which you specialize. If you don't know whether a specific company stages special events, start with these types of businesses that frequently do:

- Companies that depend on a large network of dealers, agents, wholesalers, or sales representatives often stage new product launches, sales meetings, and sales incentive events to communicate with their field force (e.g., insurance, real estate, office equipment, automobiles)
- Companies in highly competitive and rapidly evolving industries, where frequent new product launches targeted to specialized audiences are the key to competitive survival (e.g., pharmaceuticals, computers, packaged food)
- Companies that are approaching major corporate or product milestones (e.g., 10th, 25th, 50th, 75th, 100th anniversaries)

As previously discussed, most clients will choose to work with companies that are in either the same geographic location as their headquarters office, or in the market in which their special event will take place. If you are a company that relies on in-bound (out-of-town) business, become a member of your local Convention & Visitors Bureau (CVB). Most CVBs maintain a database of major groups coming to their city, from hotel block bookings or convention center holds, along with contact names and numbers. Be sure you are on the list to receive this information if it is available to members.

If your client base will be primarily local to your own headquarters offices, review the membership roster of your local Chamber of Commerce for likely candidates. Call the target company's public relations department for information on the types of special events the firm stages, and which departments or individuals within the company are responsible for them.

Attend trade events in which your target prospects participate, and take particular note of the list of speakers. Many will be leaders in their field, and potential clients. Network with other special events professionals in your area, particularly if your clients are not the end-user, but rather other companies in the special events field. Take the opportunity to "press the flesh" at industry seminars, workshops, conventions, and meetings, and turn introductions into relationships, and relationships into sales!

The First-Contact Campaign

It is surprising that the same special events entrepreneurs who painstakingly plan and rehearse their client's projects often do not plan their first-contact campaign to the same exacting standards. The concept of "first impressions are lasting impressions" is never more applicable than as applied to the first conversation between the special events entrepreneur and their target prospect. Recognize that your future client is probably extremely busy, so that any telephone time you get with them is precious, and should be used effectively.

Use the following guidelines to help you plan and conduct a successful first-contact call:

1. If possible, send a brief cover letter and brochure, or recent news release, to the prospect a few days before you call.
2. Do your homework in advance. Remember that your prospect's time is valuable. Don't waste it by asking them for information that is easily attainable elsewhere. Sound as knowledgeable as you can about their special events needs.
3. Introduce yourself and your company. If you have not already done so through other research, confirm that you are talking to the correct person at the company. If not, find out who would be the best person to speak with.
4. Don't use familiar names until invited to do so.
5. If appropriate, tell them how you learned of them or their company. If you saw a quote from, or read about, the contact, be sure to mention it. People enjoy knowing that their opinions are read. If another individual referred you, either from inside or outside their company, be sure to mention their name.

6. You probably won't get the job over the telephone, so don't risk seeming overly aggressive by asking for it. Your objective is to get a meeting to determine how best to match your company's products or services to the client's wants and needs.

7. Try to get the information you need without asking "yes" or "no" questions. An unfortunately placed "no" can quickly put an end to your call.

8. Find out if the prospect uses an events company for their projects and if they are happy with them.

9. Never denigrate a competitor. It could imply that you do not trust the client's judgment on selecting them in the first place. Resist the temptation to join in if they mention a bad experience.

10. Refer to events and clients in your portfolio that the prospect can relate to.

Many of these guidelines can be seen in action in the hypothetical call presented in Figure 8–12, in which the sales associate for a special events company specializing in corporate events proposes solutions to a client's problems.

Jill Hayley:	Good afternoon, Mr. Gallagher. My name is Jill Hayley from Most Excellent Events. I sent you a copy of our brochure after I read your interview in the *Bay Area Business Journal* on Monday, and I was very impressed with the company's expanded marketing plans.
Mr. Gallagher:	Thanks. What can I do for you?
Jill Hayley:	I wanted to contact you because Most Excellent Events just produced a product launch for Bay Leaf Coffee's new line of herbal teas, which they felt was a very powerful and successful program for them. You may have read about it in the same issue of the *Business Journal* that you were featured in.

Figure 8–12   Sample Introductory Call

Mr. Gallagher:	I can't honestly say I remember.
Jill Hayley:	I know you are probably very busy, but if you can spare 20 minutes sometime later this week, I can share with you some of the reasons why companies like Bay Leaf and WorksRight Copiers look to us year after year to create and manage their special events.
Mr. Gallagher:	I'm sure that you do great work, but we already have a special events company that we have worked with for years, and we're very happy with them.
Jill Hayley:	That's terrific, Mr. Gallagher. You probably work with a great special events company.
Mr. Gallagher:	We do—Incredible Events. We really enjoy working with them, and don't see any reason for that to change.
Jill Hayley:	I'm sure they must do wonderful work for you. But, as your marketing plans expand, you may find that no special events company—not even Incredible Events—would be able to handle the workload. When the number of projects becomes too great, or come one on top of the other, and you feel that the addition of a new project might jeopardize the others, we would be ready and able to help out on as large or small a basis as you see fit.
Mr. Gallagher:	Well, I have been a bit concerned about next April. It's going to be a difficult period—a new product launch with a series of consumer promotions, as well as conducting sales meetings in six regions, and an executive retreat right on top of that.
Jill Hayley:	We first got started with Bay Leaf by managing their executive sales retreat, and they were so happy with our work that we've been able to handle a lot more for them since then. I'd like to show you some of our corporate work when I come by. I promise to be out of your office in less than 20 minutes. And, I'll bring along some samples of Bay Leaf's new herbal teas and coffee for your office. Would Thursday or Friday be better for you?
Mr. Gallagher:	Friday morning, about 10 o'clock.
Jill Hayley:	Thank you, Mr. Gallagher. I look forward to seeing you then.
Mr. Gallagher:	Call me Jim.

Figure **8–12** Continued

The Impenetrable Wall?

As anyone who has ever made a cold call will tell you, it is frequently difficult to reach the contact directly. Unsolicited sales calls—even ones like yours—are the primary reason why most busy executives have a receptionist, secretary, or assistant to screen their calls. To increase your odds of success, therefore, the best time to place your call is when the assistant is not there—between 8:30 A.M. and 9:00 A.M. (just before the assistant arrives), 12:00 noon to 2:00 P.M. (when they are most likely to be at lunch), or between 5:30 P.M. and 6:30 P.M. (after they have most likely left for the day). There is no guarantee you will get through, however. Don't be surprised if your contact has a battery of others who pick up the calls when the assistant is not available.

Because your prospective client evaluates his or her assistant's effectiveness based on how well they screen out undesirable calls, it would not be unusual for you to have trouble speaking directly to the contact at first. Like your prospective client, their assistant's time is limited. Many, particularly those desirous of advancement at some future time, are at least generally aware of how their supervisor conducts their business. If the assistant does not connect you to the boss, try to engage them in the same type of first-contact call as you would have had if you had been put through. In many cases, this will make the assistant feel valued and respected, and could provide you with valuable information not attainable elsewhere. If, in the process, they seem too busy to complete the call, or their telephone keeps ringing in the background, ask for a good time to call *them* back. They will tell you if the questions you are asking are out of their league. Finally, ask the assistant for the meeting, inviting them, as well. Let them tell you if their presence is unnecessary.

Your relationship with the contact's assistant can not be overstated. After all, they know that if you do ultimately win their company as a client, you will be working with them on a regular basis as well. Making them feel respected will only help your sales efforts.

Your Best Work Is Your Best Sales Tool

One of the best ways to demonstrate the quality of your work to a potential client is to actually invite them to experience a project firsthand. When negotiating your contracts, try to include the client's permission to invite a limited number, perhaps 3 or 4, potential clients from noncompetitive companies to attend as your guest—and at your expense. Or, if the event is so exclusive as to prohibit this, perhaps you can arrange for them to see the event site just before show time, during setup, or for a rehearsal. If a picture is worth a thousand words, just imagine the impact of immersing your prospective clients in your work live and in-person. When they do arrive, be sure to greet them, then unless they request otherwise, leave them alone to enjoy your work without intrusion.

If your projects are too inconveniently timed or located to enable your target prospects to attend, send them a souvenir or premium item commemorating the event, a selection of colorful photographs, or perhaps a short, professionally edited videotape. Either live or in recorded fashion, it is your obligation to transport your future clients to your events, or to expose them to your best products.

As the marketplace becomes more competitive, the use of video-taped sales reels has become more prevalent. Some special events companies create an annual reel with selections from several of their most highly effective projects. Others edit short highlight packages of individual events. If you have the money, the most effective method is to create short, 30–45-second highlight segments for each event you feel best represents your firm. Then, edit together the segments most applicable to a prospective client on a single customized reel no more than $2\frac{1}{2}$–3 minutes in length.

From the recipient's point of view, sales reels take very little time to review, and can be scanned in fast-forward mode to enable them to find what they believe to be intriguing or applicable to their business. Keep these characteristics in mind when designing your sales video. Keep the length short—no more than 3 minutes—have it professionally and briskly edited, and use exciting music and images with greatest impact. Remember that you are not making *Ben Hur*. If you haven't said convincingly what you wanted to say in the first 3 minutes, the chances that a prospect will watch any longer are slim. And, don't forget the tendency for the viewer to zap through your video in fast-forward mode. Upbeat music, quick cutting and well-photographed images will help to fight this tendency.

CD-ROMs

As interesting and creative a medium as they are, CD-ROMs are not yet effective marketing tools for the mass market. Some special events companies and venues have designed elaborate CD-ROM "brochures" incorporating graphics, video footage, animations, and even games to send to prospective clients, either as stand-alone pieces or accompanying their printed collateral. This approach can be particularly effective for companies that specialize in hi-tech segments of the industry, and those marketing to technically oriented clients. The disadvantage, however, is that CD-ROMs require so much time to load, install, and manipulate before the recipient actually gets to the message you want them to see, that many won't even try. Remember, whether it's your brochure, video, sales letters, or advertisements, be as creative as possible, but make it easy for the reader to see your message clearly, and be able to scan your materials for information of interest to increase the chance that they will ultimately pick up the phone.

Publicity

Publicity, the placement of information about your company or event project in objective media such as newspapers, magazines, radio, and television, is far more believable than advertising. Even the most unsophisticated client knows that advertising is created, placed, and paid for by the company seeking to make a sale, and is therefore suspect and biased toward driving sales. Objective journalists with no stake in whether the reader patronizes a company or purchases a product being written about, on the other hand, create the articles and stories encountered in the media. While objective reporting is extremely valuable and worth pursuing, it is also the hardest and potentially the most time-consuming marketing tool to exploit.

As you develop new events, products, and solutions, share the news with your colleagues and potential clients. If an event you are involved with is newsworthy in itself, participate in your client's publicity campaign. Become a sincere spokesperson for the event, by providing your local newspaper with a behind-the-scenes preview of upcoming plans at your office. Invite your local radio stations and television outlets to the event site during installation or rehearsals. This kind of publicity creates awareness for your business, as well as the events themselves. It is, of course, essential that your client approves of this effort, but except in the cases of internally directed corporate events and private social events, most projects—from public celebrations to sporting events to new product introductions to fundraising and consciousness-raising events—will benefit from the exposure.

Some special events companies that can afford it will hire a public relations agency or consultant who comes armed with the special relationships that facilitate reaching the editors most likely to assign a reporter to cover your events. Most firms, however, can not afford the fees and expenses of retaining professional public relations counsel. Luckily, as the special events industry is frequently responsible for highly visible work product, piercing the hard shell of the media is often not as difficult as it would be for most other businesses. Much like contacting prospective clients, make sure that you are respectful of the editors' time and their constant bombardment from all of the other businesses seeking free exposure. Make sure each of your press releases contain a "hook"—something objectively interesting, intriguing, or newsworthy to capture the reader's imagination—when you make this first contact.

Many editors and writers will be easier to reach after sending a pitch letter or news release that excites them. If you can not tell your story through an exciting release with a powerful lead paragraph, chances are a writer who will be less familiar with your event and industry will not be able to either. Craft your release so you could imagine it being used verbatim as a news item. Write a headline and subhead that tell the entire story in summary form. Keep the release clear, concise, and devoid of obvious puffery. Limit its length to a page, if possible, and to no more than two pages.

If you are undertaking a publicity campaign without the benefit of an agency or consultant, follow the procedures and guidelines below to help you plan and conduct a successful first-contact call to the media:

1. Compile a list of the appropriate story or assignment editors (e.g., business, entertainment, social, city desk editors) in the applicable city's newspaper, magazine, radio, and television media to whom you wish to send your release. Ensure that all names and addresses are current.

2. Remember that news has to be new. Date the release, and mail, fax, or messenger it to every contact on your list on the same day.

3. Be sure that every word in the release is used and spelled correctly, and that the body copy is grammatically correct.

4. Include brief but meaningful quotes from the highest-ranking client and company officials available. Remember that quotes should highlight why your "news" is exciting and worthy of coverage.

5. Always include a company contact name and number at the end of the release.

Sample News Release Headline and Lead Paragraph:

New Holographic Projection Technology Puts the Audience in the Action

Revolutionary Entertainment Process to Be Seen in Chicago for the First Time

The motion picture screen no longer imprisons movies. Animated characters can now walk among us as holographic projections you can interact with, yet pass your hand right through. This new technology, the shape of things to come in the entertainment industry in future decades, will be seen for the first time in Chicago at a major corporate event for the Grocer's Pizza Convention, produced by local special events company, *More Better Events* . . .

When the event itself is not the "hook," try to identify business or human interest stories that can be derived from each project, your company's competitive qualities, or the reputation of your principals.

Sample News Release Headlines and Subheads:

Brooklyn Confetti Maker Dumps on the Big Parade

Two Tons of Colorful Recycled and Water Soluble Paper to Add to Spectacle With No Impact on the Environment

Cooking Up a Storm for the Green & Grey Game

Leading Washington-based Special Events Company Selected to Manage First Major Bowl Game Hospitality Event Outside Beltway

New City-Wide Festival to Debut in Spring

Special Events Company Marks a Quarter-Century of Helping Boston Celebrate with Its Most Ambitious Project to Date

6. Remember that generating media interest is also a sales process. Follow up with the entire list of media contacts to offer further information and interview opportunities no less than two days, and no more than five days, after sending.

7. Make your first effort your best. If the release results in no media interest, do not rewrite and resend it. But, you may recontact

those media who indicated some level of interest and have not yet filed a story.

8. If your release results in a story, send a brief thank you note to the editor and writer, with an inexpensive premium item or event souvenir as a small token of appreciation.

Beyond the exhausting, but potentially worthwhile, exercise of attempting to place stories in the media, you can increase exposure for your company by positioning yourself as an expert in your field. Offer to write a magazine article relating to your area of expertise for a trade or general interest publication, or to serve as a speaker at an upcoming convention or trade event.

Needful Things

Many special events concerns use premium items to reinforce or maintain top-of-the-mind awareness for their companies. Like many other marketing tools, the best kinds of premium items do not have to be expensive, but should express your firm's creativity. The best giveaways will serve as useful reminders of your business. If you own a party supply store catering to the private consumer, kitchen magnets may be just the thing—they tend to support children's photos, and children have birthdays, and birthdays mean parties. If you sell to commercial businesses, conversation pieces that sit on a desk, bookshelf, or credenza are especially effective because they provide constant, attractive reminders of your company. Credit card calculators, picture frames, and desk clocks are popular, but in every case ensure that the quality of the item is reflective of the quality of your company. Items that look cheap, break, or wear out easily speak ill of your company's demand for quality. Don't be afraid to look for ideas beyond the standard items in marketing premium catalogs. A lighting company might send important clients and contacts desktop reading lamps that look like small theatrical lighting instruments, or an audio company might send a custom-made CD of popular or holiday music.

Some premium items don't have to be expensive or permanent to make an everlasting impression. New York City-based destination management company Empire Force Events provides current and prospective clients with a box of taxicab-shaped "animal crackers" as one of their welcome gifts. They also provide a box of these complimentary "traffic treats" to all of their clients' guests on every destination management program.

The Proposal: Your Marketing Plan's Grand Finale

The proposal you ultimate present to your client is perhaps the most important part of your marketing campaign for new business. All of the time, energy, and money you have spent on marketing have been invested to get you to this point. Because the stakes are at their highest, it is essential that you have all of the information you need to make your proposal the most effective marketing tool in your arsenal.

To ensure that your presentation will meet the wants and needs of your prospective client, be sure you have answers to these questions:

1. What are your clients' objectives for their event? Afterwards, how will they measure its success in meeting these objectives?
2. Is the client selling, positioning, or entertaining, or all three?
3. Who will make up the audience (e.g., position or profession, income level, educational background, cultural background, previous attendance at similar events, expectations)?
4. How does the client want the attendees to feel, and what action do they want them to take after the event?
5. What budget range are they considering? What does the budget include?
6. What has the client liked about events they have staged in the past? What have they disliked?
7. What does the client look for in a special events company, and what do they expect of it?
8. How many other companies are submitting proposals? Are any of them already favored to get the project? If so, why is the client putting the event out to bid?
9. What does the client want included in the proposal (e.g., corporate capabilities, creative treatment, cost estimate, and illustrations)? When do they want it? How many copies?
10. How will the client evaluate the proposal? What are the most important elements of a successful bid?
11. Who will be making the final decision on selecting a special events company?

Once you have created the proposal you feel best meets the wants and needs of your prospective client, insist upon presenting it in person, particularly if you have never done business with the client in the past. As the special events industry is a "people business," to be most effective, send nothing by mail or messenger ahead of time. The client will not be hiring your proposal; they will be hiring you. While we live in a highly literate society, nothing puts a concept across like a live human being. No proposal can answer questions as they occur, respond to objections as they arise, or explore unwritten alternatives during its presentation. Do everything in your power to get yourself and your ideas in front of the decision maker, and win them over with your style, intelligence, and articulate manner.

Of course, you never want to go overboard in your presentation. Too much of a good thing can sometimes backfire, as occurs in the following examples.

• In 1989, Radio City Music Hall Productions presented its beautifully bound and professionally written 50-page proposal to produce the 200th Anniversary of George Washington's Inauguration to the chairman of the New York City Commission on the Bicentennial, the senior partner of a highly respected New York law firm. Scanning the prodigious document's elaborate overview, creative treatments, illustrations, and company background information during the presentation, the chairman cut the meeting short and instructed the special events team to "go back and boil this down to a few pages of bullet points. There is no way I'm ever going to have time to read this thing." Hundreds of dollars and countless man-hours were wasted on producing a proposal that overdelivered to the extreme simply because the client was never asked what they would look for in a proposal. The company was lucky—on the force of their reputation and similar work on past projects, they were given a chance to re-present, and ended up winning the business.

• Another special events company who was asked to present a corporate capabilities proposal to produce segments of the NHL All-Star Weekend was not so lucky. A formal "Request for Proposal" outlined the criteria by which interested special events companies would be considered for the job, and clearly instructed companies not to provide creative treatments, which would only be developed in conjunction with the client after the project was awarded. One company's presentation was halted in progress when it became apparent that the majority of their proposal dealt with the creative approach to the event, and not their ability to manage the project, as requested. The company was not considered for the project due to their inability to follow the client's instructions.

Demonstrate your ability to understand the prospect's wants and needs by designing an on-target, competitively priced proposal that delivers precisely what the client is looking for, and you will greatly increase your chance of capturing the client's business. Only then will every step in the marketing process, from basic research to advertising, publicity, promotion, and direct sales have been worth every penny!

The View From Here

1. Marketing is more than just selling. It is the process of identifying the wants and needs of your clients, and communicating your unique qualifications to provide the products or services necessary to meet them.

2. Useful marketing tools include advertising, publicity, promotion, direct sales, and special events.

3. Your marketing strategy should be based on an assessment of your qualifications, the differentiating characteristics that separate you from your competition, the nature of your target market, and how you will go about communicating with them effectively.

4. Design your marketing plan in three phases: define your market, craft your unique message, and bring the message to market.

5. Respect the time of your target prospects by making all of your marketing communications brief, easy to understand, convenient, and intriguing.

6. Remember that your proposals are also marketing tools. Be sure that they address and satisfy the wants and needs of the prospective client.

Tools of the Trade

Beckwith, Harry. *Selling the Invisible: A Field Guide to Modern Marketing*. New York: Warner Books, 1997.

Crandall, Rick. *1001 Ways to Market Your Services (Even If You Hate To Sell)*. Lincolnwood, Ill.: Contemporary Books, 1998.

Debelak, Don. *Marketing Magic*. Holbrook, Mass.: Adams Media Corp., 1994.

Hopkins, Tom. *How to Master the Art of Selling*. New York: Warner Books, 1982.

Breaking New Ground

1. What kinds of events companies would be well suited to pursuing a shotgun marketing strategy? A rifle shot strategy? A niche strategy?

2. Write a press release for a fictional special events company's new project or product.

3. Role-play a first contact call with a resistant potential client.

4. What would you do if you were invited to submit a proposal for a client's event, for which the budget is clearly insufficient, making it impossible for your organization to meet their expectations?

5. You learn from a client that a competitor has cast aspersions on your organization. How do you respond?

CHAPTER 9

Finding and Keeping Great People

Step Nine: *Identify, recruit, select, train, and reward valuable associates.*

A successful special event is like a symphony, a melding of harmonic parts working together to render a perfect and emotional sensory experience. As both the composer of the symphony and the conductor of your orchestra, you will need to create the score and ensure that all of the musicians play to the same tempo. The management and operation of your special events business should feel symphonic, but without proper and vigilant management of your human resources, it can take on discordant tones, and not only affect your own business environment, but also the end result of your clients' special events.

As any conductor will tell you, the composition of his or her orchestra is every bit as important as the composition they are playing. So, too, the quality of your special events projects is wholly dependent upon the quality of the members of your special events team. This chapter will help you select the best players for your special events, keep them playing harmoniously, and if necessary, reassign, release, or replace the ones playing in the wrong ensemble.

As you develop your business plan and indirect expense budget, you will need to analyze the number and types of employees you will require, as well as how you will compensate them in the form of wages and benefits. Because revenues for most special events companies are project-dependent, and the flow of work and cash is frequently irregular, many keep their indirect expenses manageable by hiring as few permanent employees as possible. When the work flow requires it, these companies will employ additional full- or part-time temporary staff, freelancers, interns, and even volunteers to help develop, manage, and execute their special events. Regardless of the type of strategy you use, always strive to attract the best staff you possibly can. Clients gauge the service and competence of a special events company by the employees that represent them, and whether the staff is paid or unpaid, permanent or project-specific is immaterial to their impressions. The people-oriented quality of the special events business does not end at pre-event marketing, it just begins there. You must ensure that every member of your ensemble is studiously evaluated, painstakingly selected, and considered to be among the best at what they do. How every one of them performs their jobs and represents you will play a role in the client's future decisions to select your company again, or look elsewhere. Invest your time and money in attracting the very best.

The Employer–Employee Partnership

Many employers are of the attitude that they are doing their employees a great personal favor simply by hiring them, and feel that their commitment to their staff ends with a weekly paycheck. The wise event manager realizes that a good employer–employee relationship is actually a partnership. The employer is buying the time and expertise of an employee, and therefore has the right to expect the loyalty of his staff. At the same time, the employee is providing services that the employer is essentially reselling to his clients at a profit, and may therefore be considered one of the products of the company. As a result, the employee has the right to expect a fair wage, good working conditions, and the respect of their employer. Low morale and high rates of turnover can be expected in workplaces where this mutual respect is lacking.

Many special events employers also fail to recognize that they are competing for a relatively small work force of skilled and experienced professionals, and more vigorously so in times of low unemployment. In a creative field such as special events, clients value the relationships they build with their suppliers, so when a key employee departs for greener pastures, there is always the risk of the client taking their business to the new employer. To those clients who stay, a high turnover rate suggests that the company might be unstable and financially unsound, and that it might be worthwhile to look at alternatives in the short term.

Therefore, it can actually be a competitive advantage not only to hire the best employees available, but also to retain them as long as you can. This would suggest paying competitive wages, providing a safe, fun, and attractive workplace, and offering whatever benefits are within the financial ability of the company to provide. In many jurisdictions, there is no legal obligation to provide employee benefits such as medical or life insurance, a pension plan, revenue sharing, or any other "perk," although doing so would certainly make you a more competitive employer. And, not offering medical insurance might actually increase your payroll costs, as in-demand employees would have to pay high rates to purchase coverage on an individual basis, and expect the employer to recompense them in the form of a higher salary.

Reading the Score

Unlike most of the component parts of your special events business discussed in this book, there exist a wide range of federal, state, provincial, and municipal statutes that dictate policies and procedures relative to how an employer may hire, compensate, manage, and terminate employees. While this chapter will outline some of the general legal definitions and obligations governing your staff, it should not be considered legal advice. You should also consult with your attorney to ensure you operate in compliance with all regulations. General information on employment labor and workplace standards, including a highly recommended *Small Business Handbook,* can be accessed through the U.S. Department of Labor's web site at *www.dol.gov*. Your state department of labor (e.g., *www.labor.state.ny.us* in New York) can also provide you with employment data and important regulatory information.

Employees versus Independent Contractors

Among the most misunderstood concepts in the special events business is how the law defines employees versus "independent contractors," as defined by the U.S. Department of Labor and Internal Revenue Service. Understanding this distinction is essential, as there are different laws governing the compensation and tax treatment of independent contractors. *Running afoul of the law can subject your organization to substantial federal and state penalties, as well as possible civil action.*

In our industry, most organizations try to operate with a minimum of permanent staff to keep indirect, or overhead, costs at a minimum. They hire only the people they need every day, all year long, to operate their business, which may include bookkeepers and accountants, marketing and sales staff, and receptionists and secretaries. In some cases, the roster of permanent staff may begin and end with the principals themselves.

Staff for individual events often includes temporary specialists, or freelancers, and workers. Many companies assume that just because freelancers are being hired on a temporary, single-project basis, they are independent contractors and not subject to the same regulatory requirements as a permanent employee, such as unemployment insurance and payroll taxes. In fact, depending upon how you define the relationship between your company and these individuals, freelancers are most often considered temporary employees in the eyes of the government. Because the distinction between employees and independent contractors is so hazy, it is often tested in the courts. Since your business relies on your availability to produce events, and not on defending yourself in the courtroom, it is highly recommended that you seek legal counsel before retaining event staff as freelancers that fall close to this hazy line.

For the purposes of payment of taxes and compliance with regulatory requirements, the New York State Department of Labor will define you as an employer "if you control what will be done and how it will be done." To the government, other litmus tests for an employer–employee relationship include:

- Requiring the full-time services of the worker
- Stipulating hours of work and prior permission for absences
- Requiring attendance at meetings and/or training sessions

- Requiring oral or written reports
- Defining their work as integral to the conduct of the company's business operation

Treatment of employees is subject to the terms of the Fair Labor Standards Act of 1938, which established standards regarding a minimum wage, overtime pay, recordkeeping requirements, and child labor practices. The basic provisions of the Act permit the employment of some individuals at wage rates below the statutory minimum wage under certain conditions, including vocational education students, full-time students, and those whose "productive capacity is impaired by a physical or mental disability."

When a special events company hires a freelancer as an independent contractor, the relationship is not subject to the rules of the Fair Labor Standards Act; neither is the company responsible for withholding income taxes, remitting payroll taxes, nor being subject to a former contractor's claim for unemployment benefits. For this reason, federal, state, and provincial governments have begun to crack down on the practice of hiring temporary employees as independent contractors when the relationship is not totally in compliance with the conventional definition.

The Department of Labor defines an independent contractor as "an independent business which performs services for other businesses as an established part of its own business activities." While there is no published rule beyond this definition as of this writing, there are several conditions that test whether an independent contractor relationship is indeed valid, and if they are not met, will send up red flags to the IRS, as described in Figure 9–1.

One of the ironies of the special events industry is that the companies with which you compete for business have equal access to the same group of freelancers you do. Therefore, you will be competing with them not only for a piece of business, but for the potentially unique services of a freelancer. Frequently, the talented individual you had mentally selected to fulfill a role on a particular project will be faced with a choice of assignments between two companies, or may already be committed to another company during the period you need them. Companies that invest in the best pay competitively, and treat their freelancers with respect so that if they have to choose between two offers of similar levels of compensation, they will choose to work with you. If you make working on your project torturous,

- A contract should exist between your company and the independent contractor clearly outlining the scope of the work and the total dollar value of the contract, as well as any other negotiated deal points. The contract should specifically define the worker as an independent contractor.
- The independent contractor provides a skilled service that is not part of the day-to-day operation of the company.
- There is a specific end date for completion of the contractor's project.
- Contractors are not paid an hourly wage or weekly salary, but on a completed project basis. There may, however, be "progress payments" to the contractor, that is, a schedule of payments to be made before the completion of the project.
- Contractors are not included in any employee benefit plans.
- Employees of the company do not directly supervise contractors. Only their final work product is subject to the company's review or approval. In the strictest view of the law, while the employer has the right to inspect the final product, the freelancer is contracted to deliver a finished piece of work, and is in complete control of how that work will be completed.
- Contractors carry independent insurance. Within your contract, the contractor should be required to provide the company with evidence of general liability coverage, naming your firm as an additional insured.
- Contractors should provide their own equipment and supplies. If your company provides the contractor with equipment (e.g., access to computers, copiers, fax machines, telephones) or supplies, be sure that your contract defines this as an arrangement of convenience, and not an entitlement of employment with the company.
- A contractor has the right to hire and fire additional employees at their own expense to assist them in completing their project. These assistants would be employees of the contractor, not of the special events company, and therefore not subject to the company's approval.
- Independent contractors have their own business cards.
- Contractors have the freedom to provide services concurrently for other businesses, whether competitive or noncompetitive to the company.

Figure 9–1   The Independent Contractor Test

you will quickly find yourself short of the freelancers you want and having to settle for second- or third-best. As a result, your events also run the risk of being second- or third-best.

Casting the Best Players

Many special events companies will spend a greater percentage of their annual operating budgets on personnel than in any other area, perhaps more than in all other areas combined. Referring back to Figure 5–1, the master indirect expense budget for Most Excellent Events anticipated *more than 60 percent of its total annual operating expenses would be devoted to salaries and benefits.* The U.S. Department of Labor estimates that the cost of replacing the wrong employee for any given job can be as much as 30 percent of the replacement's annual salary. Since most special events companies' operating budgets run close to margin, it is essential to hire right, and to do it the first time.

You have already hired your first employee—you! During the process of developing your business plan and budget, you evaluated your strengths and weaknesses, and identified the types of individuals you will need to compensate for the latter. Create a job title and job description for each of the permanent and temporary positions you wish to fill before you begin your search. This will help you focus on the skills and characteristics you need in the person who fills the position and will assist you in the search for the right employee. It will also help keep the winning candidate focused on what will be expected of them. Figure 9–2 provides an example of a job description for the position of marketing director.

Creating job descriptions will also help you to avoid a common tactical mistake. Sometimes, in your professional travels, you encounter someone you really want to have join your company. If the job description fits, by all means have them try it on. But, many times, while the prospective employee may be wonderful in many ways, they do not supplement the weaknesses you identified in yourself as the principal, nor possess the essential characteristics required to fulfill the job as defined. In fact, if they possess many of the same weaknesses as you do, you may be creating more of a problem than you are solving if you were to hire that individual. Don't fit the job to the person. Fit the person to the job!

Job Title: Director of Marketing

Reports To: President/Creative Director

Position Overview: An upper-level management position with the prime responsibility for the development of new business, and the maintenance and expansion of the company's existing client base.

Position Responsibilities:

1. Achieve gross sales of $500,000 in the first year, with the objective of increasing first year's sales by 50 percent during the succeeding two years.

2. Develop and manage the company's marketing budget.

3. Create and manage effective and cost-efficient advertising, publicity, and promotional campaigns to support the company's sales objectives.

4. Work with the president/creative director on the development of winning creative and corporate capabilities proposals to prospective clients.

Education and Experience Required:

1. Minimum of a B.A. in Marketing or Business Administration

2. Minimum 5 years of business-to-business marketing experience with a proven track record relative to the successful development of new business.

Figure 9–2   Sample Job Description

Four Sources for Finding the Best Players

Now, it's time to search for your dream candidate. Looking to your competitors as a source of talent could be risky and open both you and your prospective employee to a host of problems. An employee already ensconced in a competitor company may require more money—maybe 25 percent or more of their current earnings—to even consider the job. Depending upon the job and the employee, the competitor could also take legal action to prohibit the employee from taking the job, arguing that they possess potentially damaging trade secrets such as contact names and phone numbers. Or, they may invoke a "noncompete" clause in their employment agreement. Also consider that bringing a competitor's employee into your office could expose them to information and insights that could be damaging to you should they not ultimately take the job.

But, if you are looking for specialized experience, you may have no logical choice but to first consider your competitors' employees. In these cases, it is wise to use a search firm—sometimes known as a "headhunter"—to ferret out the most serious contenders without tipping your own hand. A headhunter will typically investigate a prospective employee's interest without identifying your company's name. They will also conduct the first interview to determine whether it is worth your time to consider the candidate. Because headhunters are not inexpensive (they may charge the employer a fee representing as much as 100 percent of the successful candidate's first year salary) it is recommended that they be used only for the most high-level and important permanent positions.

A second method of attracting attention to your organization's job opportunities is to advertise in your local newspaper or in trade publications specializing in your segment of the special events industry. Your newspaper will produce the best results for non-industry-specific jobs such as receptionists, secretaries, bookkeepers, and other low-level staff positions, while the trades will serve you better for positions that require applicants with more specialized backgrounds. Searching for the right candidates for your job opportunity can be a particularly time-consuming exercise. To keep this important activity from diverting more time than is necessary from the essential responsibility of developing new business and producing projects for their clients, some special events entrepreneurs will place "blind ads," containing a very brief summary of the position's job description. A blind ad does not identify the name or telephone number of the company, but provides a brief description of the job and requisite skills or experience and encourages applicants to respond to a post office box or newspaper box number by mail (see Figure 9–3). While this lengthens

---

DIRECTOR OF MARKETING, SPECIAL EVENTS

Leading producer of special events in New York City seeks proven marketing professional to expand business. Create and manage all aspects of marketing campaigns and participate in the development of winning client presentations. Minimum 5 years of business-to-business marketing experience. Salary plus incentives commensurate with experience and performance. Respond to Job Search, P.O. Box 555, Empire City Station, NY, NY 10000.

Figure 9–3   Sample Blind Employment Advertisement

the process of receiving responses by a few days, the resumes you receive can be reviewed at your convenience. Without having to respond to every telephone call from interested parties who may or may not be qualified for the job, you can devote more time to servicing your clients.

As a third option, if you can spare the expense, you can save even more time by using a reputable local employment agency, particularly for jobs that do not require an extensive background in the special events industry. The employment agency will have a large number of potential candidates for entry-level jobs and can send you a number of pre-screened resumes upon your request for your review. In the event that an agency does not have any candidates suitable for your position, they will undertake to create effective advertising for you. For their time and expertise, you can expect to pay an employment agency in the area of 20–25 percent of the employee's first-year salary for successful placements, although this figure is negotiable. In addition, many will guarantee the suitability of candidates placed through their agency by not charging you for new hires that do not stay with the company for at least 3 months.

Finally, there is a rapidly developing network of higher education programs specializing or offering continuing education units in event management. These schools are an excellent source of both new and experienced talent, as well as interns—as discussed later in this chapter.

The Audition—Interviewing Prospective Players

A resume, regardless of how you come to receive it, will provide you with a screening mechanism that will help you to narrow the field to a handful of potential candidates worthy of a first interview. Your mission is to try to determine the candidate's ability to perform in the position defined by your job description. Determine in advance by what minimum characteristics their ability may be assessed—their knowledge base, experience, and your perception of their ability to perform within the work environment. When you interview a candidate, keep these objectives at the forefront of every meeting to help keep you focused and avoid the legal minefield that rightfully guards against discriminatory hiring practices.

The first two factors—expertise and experience—are usually outlined in the applicant's resume. An interview provides you with an opportunity to explore more of the details of an applicant's experiences, and enables them to describe in their own words the challenges they have faced and the solutions they applied to deal with them. These insights can help you to evaluate the veracity of their claims of expertise. During the interview, be a better listener than a speaker. Allowing the candidate to speak more than you do allows you to assess their abilities far beyond the words on the printed page, and will help you to evaluate the third factor—their ability to perform within the work environment. Welcome them to share their feelings on the value of their past experiences, their relationships with their past employers, and their expectations and aspirations for the future.

There are some "red flags" to watch for during the interviewing process, possible portents of things to come. Remember your first interview, and how important it was to present a positive picture of your employability. Consider how important the interview might really be to an applicant in the following situations:

- The candidate arrives late or in inappropriate attire
- The candidate appears ambivalent about the opportunity
- The resume and cover letter are untidy, ill-composed, and contain typos or misspellings
- The candidate answers questions in "yes" or "no" fashion with a minimum of elaboration
- The candidate expresses a view that your opportunity is a trial to see if they like the job, your company or the industry

In response to past abuses, the U.S. government enacted a range of regulatory legislation designed to protect the rights of aspiring employees, including the Americans with Disabilities Act (ADA) and the 1991 Civil Rights Act. The Equal Employment Opportunity Commission (EEOC) has issued guidelines which, to the entrepreneur exercising common sense and good judgment, should not interfere with hiring procedures. These "rules of the road" have been established to ensure equality of opportunity, that everyone who applies for a job with your company be treated with fairness, and without regard to their race, color, religion, sex, or national origin.

Often, interview questions that might be deemed inappropriate in a court of law should a candidate file a suit are asked without malice or intention to conflict with EEOC guidelines. According to the Bureau of Business Practice (BBP)/Prentice Hall *Personnel and Human Resources Guide,* an objective, job-related approach to interviewing is recommended to avoid any appearance of impropriety, as described in Figure 9–4.

- Explain the essential functions of the job and ask the candidate whether they can perform those functions. Focus on abilities, not disabilities or limitations.

- If not already apparent from the resume, ask the applicant what academic, business, or social experience they possess that would make them most suitable for the position. Asking about what school an applicant went to, to what social organizations they belong, or where they were brought up, could be misconstrued as having cultural overtones, and should be avoided.

- Let the applicant know if the position requires lengthy hours and 6- or 7-day weeks, or frequent travel requiring overnight stays, and ask if they would be able to fulfill these obligations. It is not appropriate to ask what personal commitments might preclude the applicant from working under these conditions.

Figure 9–4   The Job-Related Interview Approach

As potential partners, it is important that both the company and prospective employee describe their expectations of one another, even at this early stage. Ask the applicant what they hope to get out of the job and where they expect to be one, three, and five years later. Be sure to represent yourself honestly in responding to their aspirations relative to your anticipated ability to meet their career goals. Describe what you believe the least attractive parts of the job will be, and gauge their response. Now is the time to measure their resilience and flexibility, their willingness to do what it takes to get to the next plateau in their career.

Regardless of the suitability of an applicant, or the speed with which you must fill a position, make no commitment regarding the likelihood of their being offered the job during the interview. Give yourself the flexibility of interviewing additional candidates, as well as allowing yourself the time to gather additional information about the applicant before an offer is made.

Verifying and Confirming

Imagine a well-dressed person greeting you on the street with an engaging smile, and saying: "If you give me $36,000, I can double your money in just one year!" How likely is it that you would give them the money? Very unlikely, we hope, because although they may appear well groomed, articulate, and remind you of your great uncle Charlie, you really wouldn't know anything about them. Your job applicant is essentially the same—you will be paying them thousands of dollars over the course of the year with the intent that they will help your business succeed and grow. If you don't check them out completely, you may be putting your money at as great a risk as the victim of the sidewalk con game.

After an applicant you are seriously considering leaves your office, initiate a comprehensive reference check. It is very easy for anyone to deceitfully falsify their resume, misrepresenting their educational background, job experience, or other applicable data that might figure prominently in your decision to hire. Trustworthiness is essential and you must use every effort to ensure this trait is strong and present in any prospect prior to tendering a job offer. Therefore, it is highly recommended that you investigate the candidate's background to ensure that their education and experience are as they advertised. If the candidate did not supply a list of references in advance, request one during the interview. Remain cognizant of the fact that these references are provided by the prospective employee, and are more likely to provide prejudicially positive results. Contact some of the candidate's past employers who are not listed as references. Ask the applicant if their current employer can be contacted for a reference. Frequently, you can not contact the employer without putting the applicant's current job in jeopardy, but on occasion, they will be quite aware, and supportive, of the job search.

When contacting references, stay away from the same questions you avoided during the interviewing process. Practice good listening techniques during your reference check, and let them talk as freely as they desire with a minimum of prompting. But, be sure to investigate the following:

- Confirm the applicant's past job titles, key responsibilities, dates of service, and if possible, level of compensation.
- Describe the position the applicant is being considered for. Ask about similar responsibilities under their past employers, and how well they were performed.
- Did the former employee demonstrate an ability to work well with others?
- What would the former employer identify as the applicant's greatest strengths and weaknesses?
- Did the former employee leave the company on their own volition?

- Would the former employer hire them again?
- Does the former employer recommend the hire of the applicant?

You may encounter a former employer who refuses to give a reference or feedback of any kind. When you do, it is possible that the employer is unable to comment due to pending litigation involving the applicant or with another former employee which makes such feedback inadvisable. It may also indicate a negative working experience with the applicant, with the lack of response serving as a prudent defense mechanism against possible future legal action, such as a defamation of character suit. In such cases, you may be unable to draw any concrete conclusions, but you should at least be able to confirm the applicant's term of employment, job titles, and job descriptions to ensure they are in agreement with their representations.

Only after conducting personal interviews, undertaking and analyzing reference checks, and assessing whether the candidate has the necessary qualifications to perform the job, would it be wise to consider making an offer.

The Offer and Acceptance

Think hard and long before making your offer to a prospective employee. An ill-chosen employee can be as costly as an ill-chosen mate, both emotionally and financially. When you are sure they are "the one," call the candidate and begin the negotiation regarding salary, start dates, and other details of employment. When you have settled on a compensation package, start date, and other job-related parameters, put the offer in writing.

In most cases, if a prospect requests an employment agreement, it is wise to resist. Like many other industries, special events businesses need to remain flexible due to the uncertainties of the market. The only advantage you enjoy by having a written employment agreement is prohibiting the employee from suddenly moving to your competitor, but one who is clever and determined enough can circumvent even this. On the flip side, a written agreement locks you into retaining the employee for the length of the term. Although you may have the ability of terminating the contract due to poor performance, breach, or conduct unbecoming an employee in your organization, the courts frequently favor the employee in disputed matters. You may be able to reach an amicable parting of the ways by "buying out" the contract during a time of financial stress, but terminated employees are just as likely not to be amicable. Finally, entering into an employment agreement subjects you to the possibility of having to renegotiate its terms from top to bottom upon its expiration.

If you treat your employees as true partners, there will be fewer staff looking for work elsewhere, and less of a need for a contract. There are, however, reasonable safeguards you can employ to protect your investment in an employee working without a contract. If the employee will be exposed to trade secrets or other confidential information in the course of their employment, you can ask them to sign a confidentiality or trade secret agreement, prohibiting them from sharing this information with any outside party, including competitors. This agreement can be signed as a pre-condition of employment, but should be discussed with the applicant either before, or coincident with, an offer of employment (see Figure 9–5).

In consideration of my position and employment with Most Excellent Events (the "Company"), or its subsidiaries or affiliates, I agree to keep confidential, and not divulge to others, during the course of my employment, secret and confidential information and data regarding the business of the Company, its customers, products and services, methods, systems, business plans or marketing methods and strategies, costs, or other confidential, secret or proprietary information. Further, I agree to keep confidential the secret and proprietary information of the Company's customers, clients, and vendors. In the event that my employment with the Company terminates, I agree not to divulge or use such confidential information and to return promptly to the Company all documents, and other materials owned by the Company.

In addition, it is understood that while employed by the Company, I will promptly disclose to it and assign to it my interest in any creative concepts, scripts, designs, inventions, and other intellectual properties made or conceived by me, either alone or jointly with others, which arises out of my employment and thereafter the connection with any controversy or legal proceeding relating to such creative concepts, scripts, designs, inventions, and other intellectual properties and in obtaining domestic and foreign patent, trademark, copyright, or other protection covering the same.

Date: _____ Signature: _____

*(Used by permission. Copyright Proskauer Rose LLP, 1998.)

Figure 9–5   Sample Confidentiality, Patent and Trade Secret Agreement

Another form of protection for the entrepreneur involves having the new employee sign a *covenant not to compete*. This document is an agreement on the part of the employee not to use the training and experience gained from their employment with you to engage in direct competition with your company after voluntary or involuntary termination. The enforceability of a "covenant not to compete" will be subject to different standards from state to state. However, in most cases, these agreements must include the definition of a reasonable time period (e.g., one or two years) after termination, an exact description of what activities would constitute competition, and a definition of the geographical boundaries of the restriction. Recognizing that workers in some industries, such as special events, would find future employment difficult without engaging in some form of competitive activity, some states, including California, have declared covenants not to compete unenforceable.

Keeping Your Ensemble Together

If you have spent any time in the special events business, you probably know first-hand that as exciting and exhilarating an industry as it is, it can also be exhausting. The frequently long hours and sometimes frenetic activity can quickly lead to employee burnout, particularly for those new to the field. New entrants soon discover that their choice of career is not simply a change of job, but a major change in lifestyle.

The theory behind the effective retention of good employees and freelancers is not unlike general marketing theory—identify the employee's wants and needs, and do your best to fill them. Most employees want to be motivated, and their sources of motivation may include to varying degrees compensation, career development, recognition by their superiors, peers, and the industry, a particular kind of work environment, and self-fulfillment, among others. But, no matter how fulfilling a job is, no matter how wonderful the work environment, compensation is still the most important motivator to most people.

For the purposes of compensation, there are two classifications of employees defined by the Fair Labor Standards Act, a law which regulates employment practices for companies with an annual dollar volume of business of $500,000 or more. *Nonexempt employees* are those who, by virtue of their job descriptions, are not considered part of management, and who may be paid hourly or weekly. Their nonexempt status refers to the legal requirement to pay them overtime wages at one and one-half times their regular rates of pay for hours worked in excess of a 40-hour week. *Exempt employees,* defined by the Act as executive, administrative, and professional employees (i.e., management), are not entitled to overtime pay regardless of the number of hours worked. Be sure your job candidates understand and acknowledge whether the position they are being considered for entitles them to overtime pay.

Profit-Sharing

Because of the cyclical nature of the special events business, some firms pay permanent employees a relatively modest base salary with profit-sharing bonuses based on the company's annual performance. This pay structure enables the entrepreneur to maintain a predictable weekly payroll, and provides an effective incentive to permanent employees to help generate revenues and keep expenses, direct and indirect, at a minimum. If you have five permanent employees, you can easily explain the need to practice fiscal responsibility directly where it hits home the most: *"For every dollar we spend over what we should, it could cost you 20 cents personally."* If you have a real profit-sharing structure, you will be amazed at how much more efficiently money will be spent—20 cents at a time!

It is not uncommon to compensate senior employees with some form of equity in your firm to keep your payroll costs manageable in the first, most financially risky, years. You can use the offer of equity to attract better talent for less money, employees who will view your operation as an investment in their own future and work harder than most to fulfill your long-term vision. Other companies offer a limited number of employees the ability to purchase equity positions in the organization to raise additional capital (check with your attorney for legal requirements). Entrepreneurs who want to use the equity as a tool to improve productivity, performance, or financial health, without losing control over their company, would be wise to ensure that they never distribute more than 49 percent of the total equity in their company across all of their employees.

If you are the sole proprietor or stockholder, you have total flexibility in how, or even if, you will share profits at year's end. Once you have taken on true partners through the offer and distribution of equity, you have an obligation to distribute profits in proportion to each equity partner's interest in the company. That does not mean you have to distribute all profits. It would be wise to retain some or all earnings in any given year to provide a cash reserve against future financial stress, and/or to recover any start-up capital you, and other capital partners, originally invested in starting the company. There is no rule of thumb for how much of your annual earnings should be retained, but it would be a lofty aim to have as much as a year's worth of operating capital available when times are good. After that, you may want to distribute profits to yourself, your equity partners, and partner-employees first, leaving some bonus money available for distribution to your other permanent employees as you see fit. Again due to the irregularity of most special events firms' workloads, it is highly recommended that profit-sharing and bonuses be distributed on an annual basis, rather than on a project-to-project basis or any more frequently during the year.

Sales Incentives

As mentioned in Chapter 5, you can reward your sales staff with commissions or incentive bonuses based on their gross sales volume. This provides sales managers with an incentive to close sales and keeps them focused on maintaining or exceeding expected sales levels. You should design your commission structure based on the employee's base salary (e.g., the higher the base salary, the lower the commission rate), your expected gross sales target, and perhaps the value of each contract. If your objective is to exceed your annual financial goal, set a higher commission rate for sales in excess of the target to provide a powerful incentive to exceed expectations. You can also offer noncommissioned employees the ability to earn bonuses for bringing new clients and projects to the company. Figure 9–6 provides two examples of possible sales commission formulas, although you can certainly customize your own incentive scheme to fit your business.

Successful Special Events Start with Teamwork

Working on special events is like living in a goldfish bowl. Your special events team knows that if something goes wrong, there is every likelihood that the audience, participants, and sponsors will know. The ever-present pressure to perform flawlessly, and for annual projects,

---

Commission Structure Example 1: *Fixed Base Salary + 5% of gross sales over* $500,000

Computation of Annual Earnings on $750,000 in gross sales:

Base:	$40,000
Commission (5% of $250,000):	$12,500
Total Earnings:	$52,500

Commission Structure Example 2: *Draw Against Commission + Pre-Defined Scaled Percentage*

Computation of Annual Earnings on $900,000 in gross sales:

Draw Against Commission	$30,000
(At a 5% commission rate, the minimum sales volume required to repay the draw would be $600,000)	
5% commission on sales between $600,001–$850,000	$12,500
7.5% commission on sales between $850,001–$1,000,000	$3,750
Total Earnings:	$46,250

Figure 9–6   Sample Event Sales Commission Formulas

better than the year before, sometimes transcends the size of the paycheck. Establishing and nurturing an environment where everyone working on a project is functioning like a team—where everyone succeeds or fails together—is essential to both staging great events and keeping your team together to produce greater successes with each project.

A $50,000 sports car can boast a powerful engine, superior handling, and superb body detailing, but a loose clamp holding the exhaust system to the undercarriage can cause this mechanical marvel to screech to a halt. A top-notch event can be similarly undermined. The best work of the world's leading designers, producers, and engineers can amount to disaster if one coordinator fails to deliver a featured performer to the right place at the right time. The special events team is only as strong as its weakest member.

To build an effective team, start by drafting the right players for the job. Then, be a tough coach and an enthusiastic cheerleader. Provide decisive and definitive direction so that every player understands the goals and objectives of the company or project, while keeping spirits high. Lead by example—the special events team will take on the persona of the coach. A positive and fun work atmosphere depends on the coach/cheerleader setting the tone.

Create an organizational structure for your company, department, or event production team that clearly outlines lines and areas of responsibility for every member. Try to avoid having any member report to more than one supervisor. Provide this information in the form of an organization chart or in writing. You can also add structure to your organization by creating a policy and procedures manual that outlines what you expect of employees, as well as benefits and codes of conduct. It can also help to protect you against litigious former employees terminated for cause. Creating a manual is neither time-consuming nor expensive if you use one of the computer-generated programs now available, such as *Employee Manual Maker* by Jian.

Communicate with your team regularly on their performance. Set aside time with your permanent staff for formal evaluation on a regular basis, at least annually, and more often if you are able. Using their job description as a guide, rate their performance and capabilities. In between evaluations, provide frequent feedback. If a team member is performing well, tell them often enough to keep their energy at a peak, but not so often as to sound insincere. If a team member is performing below expectations, challenge and encourage the employee to improve with more immediacy. And, if the employee does not show signs of improvement, take the steps necessary to replace them to avoid the risk of having their attitude or performance infect the rest of the team.

Lead by listening. Encourage each member of your team to approach you with questions, concerns, suggestions, and comments on an as-needed basis, and when possible demonstrate your responsiveness with action. Being a good listener is essential, but unless your employees get the sense that you act on their concerns, they will surely stop talking. Regard the suggestions of the most junior employee on staff with the same importance as the most senior, and recognize improvements born of their recommendations with a memo and express verbal approval in front of their peers.

Try to set aside some time and money to treat your event team to a post-event "wrap" party. Invite everyone involved—permanent staff, freelancers, independent contractors, and perhaps key vendors—to celebrate another job well done. If you can make working on your projects fun and eventful experiences in themselves, your permanent employees will stay longer, and your freelancers will re-join your family again and again. A week after the project, convene a postmortem of the event that gives every member of the team the ability to analyze successes, identify shortcomings, and propose new approaches for future events.

Employee Problems and Conflict Resolution

If you have chosen your team well, recruiting a "problem employee" will be a rare occurrence, but employee problems are a daily reality to most companies. If, for whatever reason, you discover that you have selected someone clearly ill equipped to do the job for which you have hired him or her, react quickly and decisively. Many of these revelations will surface within the first few days and weeks of employment, and when they do, meet privately with the employee to re-assert your expectations. Clearly identify steps for improvement, and set a time frame (a probationary period) in which you expect to see results. During this time period, provide feedback to the employee—positive or negative—as to whether they are headed in the right direction. You should see a sense of urgency on the part of the employee to correct their under-performance, and in most cases you will. If you do not see a commitment to improve, and more importantly, if you do not see results by the end of the time frame you have defined, make the difficult decision to begin the process of terminating the new employee.

In some instances, it will take longer for evidence to present itself that the employee is simply the wrong person for the job. This is particularly true of salespeople who consistently under-deliver or event staff who are incapable of providing the quality of service you and your clients demand. In the case of a permanent employee you feel is unable to meet the demands of an event just around the corner, try to move them to a less critical function. Then, either divide up their responsibilities among other members of your event team, or retain a freelancer or independent contractor to tide you through the event. Take the time to explain to the employee why you have taken this action, and that you expect them to prove their worth to the company and project by executing their revised duties with the highest degree of professionalism and quality. Once you inform them that you have initiated their probationary period, the problem employee will either resign from the company, or commit him- or herself to making a sincere attempt at improving their performance. If they do the former, you have not only saved yourself poorly invested money, but also the time it would have taken to discover that they would not have altered their performance anyway.

Doing your homework during the hiring process is a critical element in ensuring that your employee problems do not stem from problem employees. The issues that you face as a manager can grow exponentially as you build your company or event team. Busy special events entrepreneurs must make time to build strong, positive relationships among their team members, but as any manager will attest, there will always be conflicts of personality or understanding. The first signs of these kinds of problems are usually subtle, and because they usually do not begin by overtly affecting job performance, you may become aware of them long after they begin developing.

When you encounter problems with employees, the first question to be asked is if the problems are a result of poor communication or leadership from above. Satisfy yourself that this is not the case by meeting with the employees and encouraging them to identify any problems they may be encountering at work that might affect their job performance. You might discover that their poor job performance results from poor relationships with fellow team members, or feelings of confusion or frustration born of a perception of poor direction or communication from above. Ask them to candidly elaborate upon these frustrations, and when they have finished speaking, commit to continually trying to build good team performance and fostering good communication. This acknowledges that you accept your responsibility to be a good manager, but does not accept or assign blame. Explain to the employee that since your objective is to establish a good working partnership with each employee, it is important that they communicate with you as well as you communicate with them. Point out that if internal frustrations affect their ability to perform to your level of expectation, then it is their responsibility to approach you with their points of view *before* it affects their performance.

Other frequent sources of employee dissatisfaction include compensation, the pace of career advancement, and the rate of growth in responsibilities. If there are performance reasons why the employee is not growing, and you have not already addressed the subject, this is an excellent time to clear the air. Most frequently, it is simply a matter of the economics of the company that impedes the progress of ambitious and talented special events professionals. In these cases, honesty is again the best policy. If you value the employee, share your dreams and aspirations for the company, and describe your visions for their participation in helping to realize these dreams.

It is important to note that there are situations that can not be considered when evaluating an employee's performance. Respecting the protected expression of legal rights, an employer is not permitted to judge an employee based on complaints lodged with the company or a governmental agency about sexual or racial harassment, potentially discriminatory hiring or employment practices, or questioning the legality of company or employee actions (i.e., "whistle-blowing"). Neither can an employee be discharged or subject to disciplinary action for filing a complaint with the Occupational Safety and Health Administration (OSHA), or refusing to follow management's instructions due to a concern for their safety and the safety of others.

Whether or not the employee identifies an internal obstacle to their fulfilling their end of the partnership, clearly identify the reasons for your dissatisfaction with their performance and your expectations for the future. There are some situations in which no matter how well you compensate, coach, and cheer a particular employee, they will never live up to your expectations, nor will you ever live up to theirs. Sometimes, as hard as it might be to undertake extreme action, termination of the employee is the only solution.

Termination

No one should take the termination of an employee lightly. Termination can be devastating to a human being on just about every level— financially, emotionally, and psychologically. On your side of the ledger, you will have to invest the time, energy, and money to engage in another search for the right employee, and not the least of considerations; your employment insurance tax rate could be subject to increase.

On the other hand, you are spending your company's money to remunerate an employee for providing a quality of service you expected upon their hire. In return, you have every right to evaluate whether you are receiving the return on this investment to which you are entitled. The level of quality your employees convey to your clients reflects upon your overall operation, and could well affect the likelihood of future work.

One of the reasons you want to be sure to have given underperforming employees a chance to improve is to reduce the chance of a wrongful termination suit. It is essential that when you meet with employees to identify areas of weakness, expectations, and a time frame for improvement, you follow up with a memo to both the employee and your file. Any additional thoughts you share with the employee during the term of their probationary period should also be articulated in writing. This paper trail will make it difficult for the employee to assert that they were unaware of your dissatisfaction, or that they were not afforded the opportunity to respond.

Prepare to break the news to the employee by reviewing their file to satisfy yourself that you have given them every chance to bring their work up to expectation. Jot down an outline of speaking points you will use during your last meeting with them to ensure you do not fail to cover every important detail. Be sure that your reasons for termination are consistent with past practice, that is, there are no similarly under-performing employees being given preferential treatment.

There are occasions when termination is not a result of under-performance, but of financial stress on the company, or a single, grievous, and unprofessional act on the part of the employee. In the case of the latter, such as inappropriate rudeness to a client, the release of confidential information, a work-related physical altercation, gross insubordination, or criminal activity, your action should be swift and definitive. Immediately suspend the employee without pay, and schedule a meeting once tempers have cooled.

Whether you are forced by an employee's inappropriate action, by their inability to perform or improve, or a financial crisis at the company, follow these guidelines when meeting with the employee:

- Document all discussions and actions in writing.
- Maintain a calm, professional demeanor.
- State clearly and concisely why you are exercising your option to terminate their relationship with the company.
- Make no superfluous comments regarding their job or them personally, that does not relate to the direct cause of termination, as these are the most likely to do damage in the event of a lawsuit.
- Outline your plan for severance benefits, such as severance pay, health insurance coverage, or outplacement counseling, if any. If you do offer post-employment benefits of any kind, ensure that the employee signs a separation agreement that offers these concessions in return for releasing the company, and its principals and stockholders, from possible legal action stemming from the termination.

- Be sure to recover company property such as keys, access and identification cards, and equipment such as laptop computers. Withhold the former employee's final paycheck or severance benefits until all property has been returned.
- Schedule an exit interview during which the employee can articulate their comments on the company and their experience while employed there, as well as to provide you with important additional feedback without the confusion of inflamed emotions.
- The exit interview would also be a good time for the employee to return to remove their personal effects from the premises. It is recommended that the employee be asked to leave the building soon after being terminated until the exit interview to avoid potential sabotage, such as erasing computer files or removing proprietary information or other company property.

Working with Freelancers

As awareness of today's special events industry continues to grow in the general business marketplace, it has become a powerful attractant for young professionals looking for a more exciting, creative alternative to their current positions. As your business's reputation grows along with it, you will find more and more potential employees and contractors seeking you out. Freelancers expand their network of possible employers by attending trade events and meetings in search of companies just like yours. Meeting them in these casual surroundings can provide you, a prospective employer, with a great deal of insight into their suitability for your business or an upcoming project.

Freelancers can be retained either as employees or independent contractors. Contractors function essentially as vendors, so you have far less control over their work product. A freelancer retained as a temporary employee can be monitored much more closely, and can be devoted exclusively to your project if you define their responsibilities as such. Freelance employees are subject to the same policies and procedures as any other paid staff member, and may be hired, evaluated, and terminated in the same way.

As previously discussed, freelancers and independent contractors are free to work for any number of companies during the course of the year. When you have a temporary position available, it is neither unusual, nor a breach of business etiquette, to contact one of your competitors for a referral. Nor should you hesitate to recommend a trusted freelancer or contractor to a competitor when they call you for the same. After all, just because you did not hire the freelancer full-time because you had no need or ability to pay them year-round, does not mean that the freelancer does not have a need for money year-round. Keeping freelancers working and happy is good for your business, because it enables these talented individuals to stay in the industry, making them more likely to be available to you when you do need them.

As freelance employees frequently specialize in a particular area of special events management, they are particularly valuable for the management of event-specific functions not required year-round by the company, such as transportation systems, guest management, and show production, among many others. A freelancer can also be used to fill in for a permanent employee on leave, for a special internal project, or to temporarily replace a terminated employee. And, when you are looking for someone to fill a newly available permanent position, your pool of trusted freelancers should be the first place you look for proven winners with a minimum of recruitment expense.

Interns

Tracking right alongside the explosive growth of the special events industry is an explosion of interest in the pursuit of jobs from undergraduate and graduate students, as well as professionals from other industries looking to shift to an exciting new career. On the industry's side, there is an ever-present need for intelligent, creative, and resourceful event team members whose event experience might be slim to nonexistent, but whose talents can be applied to a project with a minimum of training, and at a minimum of cost.

One way of obtaining the manpower you need to produce an event is by recruiting and/or hiring interns. An internship program is a mutually beneficial relationship, where the employer provides experience and training to a temporary employee in return for college credit and/or a small cash stipend. The hiring of interns is subject to the same regulatory requirements as the hiring of any company employee, although the level of compensation is usually very low, and employee benefits usually are absent. Therefore, you should exercise just as much caution in interviewing and selecting interns as you would in hiring a full-time employee.

An outstanding method for identifying worthy intern candidates is through colleges and universities requiring students to complete a minimum number of internship, or practicum, hours. Check whether colleges and universities in your area offer students credit for internships in your industry before you have a direct need for interns. Schools with special events and sports management programs, such as The George Washington University and New York University, are excellent resources. Other departments, such as theater, tourism management, and business administration, may also provide qualified intern candidates, depending upon the nature of your projects. However, if an intern is not providing their services in return for college credit, they must be paid the applicable minimum wage, as well as overtime benefits.

Internships are training programs, not temporary clerical agencies. You will be doing a great disservice to the school, the student, and the future of the special events industry if you entrap an intern into a purely secretarial function. If students do not gain valuable experience in the course of their internship with a special events company, the university would not be obligated to honor subsequent requests for interns. This practice also establishes a reputation for the company among the students, which could make it more difficult to attract qualified employees from among graduates in the future.

Internships are also a great way to "try out" possible future candidates for freelance and full-time jobs. There is no better way to expand your list of potential superstars to consider for future opportunities than by observing how an intern performs in the real-life laboratory of special events.

Volunteers

The practice of using volunteers in nonsupervisory roles is commonplace in the production of civic celebrations, sports events, fundraisers, festivals, parades, and political events, and to a lesser extent in corporate events. Volunteers are eager to help their communities, their sports teams, causes they believe in, even their employers. They are frequently used as talent hosts, parade marshals, greeters, information representatives, production assistants, and clerical support for a wide range of special events.

Pam Cheriton, a freelance special events professional now living in Sanibel Island, Florida, has developed a specialty in the area of the creation and management of volunteer programs for such volunteer-intense projects as the NHL FANtasy and Major League Baseball's FanFest. Pam notes that even though the use of volunteers in the production and management of events is not new, more organizers use them poorly than wisely.

She first started working with volunteers while serving as a floor manager at a large festival. "I had 150 volunteers assigned to my area, and no one arrived knowing what they were supposed to do. Because they were poorly selected and poorly informed, they didn't know what kinds of responsibilities they would have during the event. Many were disappointed once they got there, and decided not to come back the second day."

Applying her theatrical training, Pam likens the selection of volunteers to the casting of a show. To begin collecting potential volunteers for the "audition," she goes to friendly sources—fan clubs, sponsors, and convention and visitor bureaus, among others. Where a large number of volunteers are required, newspaper, radio, and local television advertising is particularly effective. Interested parties are invited to fill out an application noting their areas of interest and hours of availability, and attend a mandatory Volunteer Interest Meeting. Because the event organizer is responsible for the actions of the volunteer, no one is selected sight unseen, even though it would be far quicker, easier, and less costly.

As with regular employees, the goals and objectives of the event should be made known to all at the meeting. Pam begins the agenda with an icebreaker, a short and entertaining skit to set a fun tone for the evening, as well as for the volunteer program at-large. Then, senior event officials welcome the group and describe the event accompanied by multimedia graphics and video. When it's Pam's turn, though, the meeting is all hers. Although her theatrical training was designed to place her in the wings, she is truly a presence on-stage, and her highly contagious enthusiasm infuses the potential volunteers with a sense that working on this event will be fun! In the midst of all of the flag-waving, Pam sets the rules of engagement for the audience.

"Paint as much of a picture of what you expect as possible. You don't want any surprises or disappointment," she advises. Tell them all about the rewarding experience they will enjoy, but also about their responsibilities in helping to make the event a success. "And, don't forget to tell them about the perks, like costuming they get to keep (e.g., t-shirts, caps, etc.) and the gifts they will receive after fulfilling all of their shifts."

Next, the volunteers are broken up into smaller groups, by area of interest or assignment. At this point, staff members in charge of each area have the opportunity to meet briefly with each prospect to identify their special skills and suitability for the job on their applications. Just as is the case when hiring an employee, it is improper to deny anyone the right to participate as a volunteer based on race, sex, or physical challenges. For the physically challenged, however, it is important to place them in a role that makes both them and you feel comfortable and appreciated.

Each applicant is told that their interest and generosity of spirit is appreciated, and that because of the limited number of opportunities available, volunteers available for the most days and hours required will be given preference. Each is provided with a date by which they should hear from the organizer by mail, and that if they do not receive a letter, they will not be required.

After the meeting, Pam slots applicants into jobs based on their availability, feedback on the quality of their brief interaction with the staff at the interest meeting, and their stated areas of interest and experience. An orientation meeting is scheduled just prior to the event, during which each volunteer receives their job description in writing, credentials, uniform, and on-site training for their assignments. Any additional "perks" are distributed immediately after the event is completed to encourage the volunteer to return for their subsequent shifts.

The care and feeding of volunteers puts them somewhere between staff and guests. In a sense, they *are* guests, since they are giving of their time and have the purest of interests in seeing the event succeed. "The first hours of an event are essential," says Pam, "because they will determine whether the volunteer will stay with the program for the length of their assignment." If they see confusion, in-fighting, or experience unpleasantness from the staff, they are sure to jump ship. During this period, you and your company are on probation. Keep them challenged and busy by resisting the temptation to overstaff with an abundance of free labor, but do not require more of them than you would of a staff member. Rotate them to different functions and areas of the event, if possible, and be sure to give them plenty of breaks. Feed them, if your budget allows.

If you make them feel appreciated and respected, volunteers will work tirelessly for you. For that, you will owe them a debt of gratitude, and the best way to express it is to say it personally. Pam and her event clients host a post-event party for their volunteer staff, where each receives a memento of the program as a small token of appreciation. "You want them to leave the event with a sense of pride and accomplishment, feeling good about the experience and you!"

Isn't that the way you want *everyone* in your orchestra to feel? Whether first violin, second percussion, or the electrician who checks the music stand lights, every member of the ensemble—whether in a performing or supporting role—is critical to your success as conductor. When you can get everyone playing with synchronous and harmonious perfection, you can indeed make beautiful music together.

The View From Here

1. An effective employer–employee relationship is a partnership in which the employee provides their talents and experience to the employer, who provides compensation and opportunity for career growth.

2. Special events companies depend on well-functioning, talented staff to provide high levels of service to their clients. It is essential to select the best employees possible, and to work proactively to ensure that they work together as a team.

3. Special events organizations utilize a combination of permanent staff, freelancers, contractors, interns, and volunteers to run their businesses and produce work for their clients.

4. The processes of hiring and firing, as well as the continuing employment of both permanent and temporary staff, are heavily regulated by both federal and local governments. It is essential to be familiar with the laws that define your responsibilities as an employer.

5. One of the most misunderstood concepts in the special events business is how to classify and compensate temporary event staff, or freelancers. Evaluate the benefits, risks, and responsibilities of retaining freelancers as either independent contractors or temporary employees.

Tools of the Trade

Adams, Bob and Peter Veruki. *Streetwise™ Hiring Top Performers.* Holbrook, Mass.: Adams Media Corporation, 1996.

Lusky, Paul M. *Slam the Door on Employee Lawsuits*. Franklin Lakes, N.J.: Career Press, 1998.

Whitmore, John. *Coaching for Performance*. London, UK: Nicholas Brealey Publishing, Ltd., 1996.

Willingham, Ron. *The People Principle*. New York: St. Martin's Press, 1997.

Breaking New Ground

1. Role-play an interview between a special events entrepreneur and a prospective sales employee.

2. What kinds of life experiences might help to prepare a potential intern candidate for an assignment with a special events business?

3. What are the potential risks of hiring a highly recommended candidate for a sales position who insists on a high-base salary in lieu of a generous commission incentive plan? What possible reasons might they have for their position?

4. What would you do when after promoting a previously well functioning employee, it becomes apparent that they cannot fulfill the objectives of their new position?

CHAPTER 10

Achieving Success

Step Ten: *Produce greatness: create the recipe for enduring success.*

This book has prepared you for the pursuit or expansion of a profitable career in the exciting world of special events either as an entrepreneur or as an entrepreneurial employee in an existing organization. Perhaps you are already an industry leader with highly regarded creative talents. Blend that creativity with equal parts of a well-reasoned, comprehensive strategic business plan and a marketing strategy with realistic, achievable goals, and you have the recipe for enduring success.

Like any recipe, results vary from chef to chef. But, the first attribute that all great chefs share is a drive to achieve perfection. As is true of the culinary arts, there is no substitute for quality ingredients, masterful preparation, and impeccable presentation to achieve greatness in your special events. Good enough is never good enough. Insist upon every event living up not only to your client's standards, but also to your own. Instill this sense of pride and priority in every staff member and every vendor, and give every client the impression that their project is the most important you have ever worked on.

While you may accept the dictum that you can never truly attain perfection, you will never be able to produce greatness without working tirelessly to push the edge of the envelope with every event. There will always be obstacles along the way—difficult clients, burned-out, bickering employees, or ambivalent external forces—but it is essential to keep your eye on the prize, the best produced, financially responsible, most on-target event you can. Because more than strategic planning, and more than marketing, your special events are by far the very best investments you can make to capture more business for your organization.

Take "Yes" for an Answer!

Producing greatness frequently involves achieving an end result everyone thought could not be done. Recognize that sometimes the naysayers are right, but only when such projects or portions thereof are either completely out of human control, or would be better left undone for reasons of safety, legality, or ethics. You can not cause the sun to shine for your parade or festival. But, if such factors are not a concern, and you are convinced that a perceived impossibility can yield greatness, go for it and apply the same creativity to your pursuit of the impossible as you would to designing your special event.

 Stopping Traffic

A series of public celebrations were planned for the grand opening of Toronto's Hockey Hall of Fame in June 1993, from dedication ceremonies to private receptions to large-scale public events. The proposed finale event was envisioned as a noontime public procession of 90 Hall of Famers ending at the new facility, followed by the world's largest "face-off" at Front and Yonge Streets directly outside. The intersection, a heavily traveled confluence of two thoroughfares under the administration of two different government agencies, had never been closed during a workweek. Resistance to the closure by both agencies was resolved after the Mayor, the Metro Chairman, and the Governor-General of Canada were invited, and agreed to participate in the procession and face-off. The photograph of all 90 honored members holding their hockey sticks at the ready in front of this spectacular building appeared in newspapers across the continent, providing instant recognition for the spectacular new facility.

Learn to take the word "can't" out of your lexicon, and you will be surprised how many great ideas can become great events. Endure the blank stares when you propose the things that can't be done to those you will need to help you accomplish them by turning "can't" into "how *can* this get done?" And, if you run into the final wall of opposition, settle at worst for "not for now" instead of "no."

Clients hire event specialists based on relationships and talents. Frequently, risk-averse clients unfamiliar with the industry will first come into contact with individual event specialists employed by a medium- to large-sized company, taking some degree of comfort in the perceived stability a more highly capitalized supplier. Soon, a client realizes that it is people who manage and execute events, not organizations. After all, whose vision realized *Star Wars,* George Lucas or 20th Century Fox?

Regardless of how you first met them, clients will come back to you if they trust you. They will trust you if you have consistently demonstrated an ability to meet their objectives creatively, manage their budgets cost-effectively, and apply a strict code of ethics to your business dealings with them, as well as with others. Embracing a personal and professional code of ethics is an excellent place to start, but exhibiting a sense of respect for your clients, suppliers, co-workers, staff, and all event stakeholders is essential to developing a key ingredient for your successful recipe—a spotless reputation. Honesty and integrity are not just doing the right thing. To your clients, these qualities add unparalleled value to your relationships.

You are also known by the company you keep. Every industry must be represented by honest, responsible, and ethical businesspeople. And, every industry also has its share of cads, the unscrupulous, and the mean-spirited. Surround yourself with staff, suppliers, partners, clients, and others who share your high standards and strong values.

You expect your clients to stick to their end of the bargain—you expect them to pay you on time, to provide the financial resources as defined by your contracts, and you expect them to provide you with excellent referrals to other prospective clients. In return, they expect you to live by your agreements—they expect you to apply their money wisely and cost-effectively to increase the production value of their projects, to represent their company as though you were an employee yourself, and even to return those unexpended funds to which they are entitled, if your agreement so specifies.

Some people may "do the right thing" because they believe it to result in an exalted form of existence. Some prefer using guilt and trepidation as motivators, mindful of the fact that what goes around comes around. A constant theme in this book has been the truism that the event business is built upon and maintained by positive interpersonal relationships. A top executive in a major professional sports organization began in the special events business by delivering interoffice mail, and 20 years later now hires some of those same people as suppliers. Had his formative experience with those event professionals been negative, it would be highly unlikely that he would ever consider hiring them today. Remember that as you ascend the business ladder to ever-greater achievement, you will meet the same people on the way down that you did going up.

You Can Take This to the Bank

Reputations follow you in any business. Guard yours as though it were moral currency. Associate with the unsavory, and the aroma rubs off on you. While moral currency won't pay the bills, in the long run it has everything to do with how likely you will be able to generate monetary currency. Think of your reputation as a series of "trust accounts" opened by everyone with whom you do business. Your stakeholders—your clients, bosses, suppliers, staff, and even your competitors—have the exclusive right to make both deposits and withdrawals.

You encourage deposits in these trust accounts every time you demonstrate your trustworthiness to the account holder. This trustworthiness can be expressed in many forms—your competency, your creativity, your ability to achieve the client's objectives, your ability to complete your assignments on budget, your payment histories, and of course, the reliability of your word. The more consistently you demonstrate success against all of these benchmarks, the greater the account balance you will accrue over time.

All of these same account holders have the exclusive right to exact withdrawals from time to time. And, when a withdrawal is deemed necessary, it typically is of greater impact than any one deposit. There is no event professional who has not been surprised with an over-budget project on occasion. Bring your client an over-budget event, and he or she will surely make a hefty withdrawal. If the size of your trust account is vast enough, it won't bankrupt your relationship. But, regardless of your track record, bring enough over-budget projects to your boss, and you will soon find your account bankrupt, and your flow of deposits—including those of the financial variety—cut off.

You can not proactively manage withdrawals. Only your account holders can determine the size they wish to make, or whether any other positive factor might offset some of the damage. To some account holders, over-achievement of their objectives can reduce the withdrawal for being over-budget. An increased volume of business can counteract withdrawals for slow payment to suppliers. Or, a reduced balance on your final bill might attenuate some failure to meet a client's objectives. But, a withdrawal for unethical behavior results in a closed account every time.

While you have no power over withdrawals from your own accounts, you have ultimate power over everyone else's. Employees who consistently under-perform can affect your own reputation, as can suppliers who provide work late or of inferior quality, or co-workers upon whom you rely to get the job done. Evaluate the relationship, its value to your organization, and whether the disappointments can be resolved. Then, make your withdrawal, and if the relationship proves bankrupt, invest your trust somewhere else. Sometimes, although it is hard to do, you have to release an employee, seek a new vendor, and even walk away from future work brought to you by a client who behaves in bad faith, pays unreasonably late, or who has refused payment to which you were clearly entitled.

The balance in your reputation's trust account, and whether it is increasing or decreasing, establishes a credit history accessible by prospective clients and future employers. Much as a financial lender will contact a credit bureau such as TRW or Equifax to determine your creditworthiness and the likelihood you will repay your debts, potential clients can call Dun & Bradstreet for a "D&B" report and past clients for referrals. If you have left a trail of bankrupt trust accounts, prospective clients will be reticent to open one with you no matter how clever your market strategies, and no matter how creative and on-target your proposals. In the long run, moral bankruptcy will surely beget financial bankruptcy.

The story is similar for entrepreneurial employees. To a prospective employer, the reputations of the companies you carry on your resume will reflect upon your desirability as an employee. If the companies for which you worked are perceived as unreliable, untrustworthy, or laggards in your industry, so will you be. Employers frequently look to aggressive and successful competitors to recruit new talent. Even though their corporate mission might include putting those competitors out of business, they respect the achievements of a worthy opponent.

Organizations, like individuals, maintain a series of trust accounts among a broad range of competitors, employees, suppliers, marketing partners, and even the media. As an employee, you participate in a form of profit sharing—your trust account is inextricably linked to the reputation of the corporation for which you work. If you are a respected member of a respected company, your trust account is filled beyond the level you could achieve alone. But, if that company is determined by prospective employers to have a low balance, your marketability will be greatly diminished.

The Importance of Being Earnest

Earlier in this book, you met Don Whiteley of Argonne Productions, a niche special events organization specializing in the production and management of parades worldwide. During a routine medical exam in 1997, Don was diagnosed with cancer and began undergoing a physically debilitating program of chemotherapy. Don's stellar reputation for excellence, honesty, and partnership, which he applies to every new project, client, and supplier, had imbued his trust accounts with great riches among a vast network of colleagues throughout the industry. During his travails, too weakened to work, many of these same colleagues sacrificed their own vacations and personal time to complete Don's projects and meet his production obligations. Don has since returned to work in good health, and today owes his friends a great debt in preserving his business—only they were too glad to do it.

Consider your position in the special events industry. Do you have colleagues who would do the same for you? Would you do the same for them?

In your first eighteen months of operation, your careful and meticulous investment in moral currency pays great dividends in the form of a seemingly continuous stream of business. Your loyal clients have stuck with you through thick and thin, and they have made new deposits in your trust account because you have executed your responsibilities on time, on-target, and on budget. But, now their projects are over, and you suddenly realize you need more that just those clients whose trust helped to get you started. So busy were you producing all those events that there was no time to cultivate new, prospective clients. It takes time to develop those new prospects, close business, sign contracts, and get deposits. And, you are spending more and more money on indirect expenses all the while.

"Uh-oh! That's not how it was planned to be," you mutter to yourself in a moment of private anguish. Is your plan defective, or is the market just drying up? If it is drying up, when is it going to re-hydrate? Will the money you have made in your first 18 months last the next 18?

Have no fear! Many event entrepreneurs fall into the same trap when they first set out. They are so busy producing events that they neglect to set aside sufficient time to market themselves. So, while the first year can be good, the second year can be deadly if you did not pay adequate attention to marketing your services. If you are suffi-ciently capitalized, you may be able to afford a full-time salesperson who has the contacts and experience which may help to overcome the uneasiness and perception of risk that many potential clients feel when dealing with a start-up firm. If you are a one-person staff, you have to discipline yourself, even force yourself, to constantly market while you produce to avoid the marketing/production roller coaster described in Chapter 1.

Admittedly, we are all in this business because we want to live creative lives. We love to take a concept and add the special touches that excite, enlighten, and entertain. But, a daily focus on marketing and strategic planning is essential to make it in today's marketplace. It may not be as fun, but unless you continuously analyze your com-petition and find new ways to get your product in front of the cus-tomer, you will not get the opportunity to enjoy the fun part. There is more competition than ever before, and as the industry continues to mature, the competition is getting smarter, as well. Indeed, some of your competitors are probably reading this same book. Therefore, establish your points of difference, make your plan, and get your mes-sage into the marketplace.

The Future of Event Management

The special events industry is here to stay, but now that it has legit-imized itself as a modern profession, it must also behave like one. It will contract and expand as competition reaches the saturation point.

And, as a service business, it will be subject to the economic pressures of each of its clients. The special events industry grew out of client corporations' needs to find new ways to cut through the clutter of traditional marketing techniques such as advertising, publicity, and promotion. Properly employed, special events touch the consciousness like no other marketing medium, and therein lies its strength.

But, special events are a lagging indicator, which means that after the economy takes a turn for the worse, you can be sure that the marketplace for event suppliers will not be far behind. You can not easily measure the success of an event with a "cost per thousand" analysis as is true of other marketing methods, such as advertising or publicity. And, because events can be significantly more expensive than placing a flight of radio time or a run of local print advertising, events are likely to be among the first items to be dropped from your clients' marketing plans when the economy gets tight. Diversifying your revenue streams and client base can help you survive the inevitable cyclical downturns in the economy.

Like other marketing service businesses such as advertising agencies, promotions agencies, and public relations firms, the work product of the special events industry reflects on the client, and rarely on the firm producing the event. Today, most in the audience are blithely unaware of the existence of an event industry. It is almost always the sponsor or client who takes the bows, and that is both a further strength and a weakness of your chosen profession. Ultimately, the entity spending the money will receive the recognition, and they should. That is why they spend it in the first place. As a service business, it is our job to make our clients look good. As an event business, it is incumbent upon you to elevate your organization's standing within our profession, and to elevate our profession along with it.

A group of 25 distinguished leaders in the events industry convened at the Biosphere 2 Research Center to ponder the future of event management. This group included 9 certified special events professionals and represented nearly 500 years of cumulative professional experience in the events industry. Together, this group examined the environmental, technological, and economic challenges their profession would face in the future. The result of their deliberations are shown in Figure 10–1.

Charter
Researched and Submitted by
Leaders in the Special Events Industry
Columbia University's Biosphere 2
May 3, 1998

Introduction

The event industry is one of the world's largest employers and contributes major positive economic impact. The event industry is not only our profession but also a personal mission through which we are able to make a positive contribution to the lives of millions of people. Through events, human beings, communities, and organizations mark important milestones. As event professionals we are responsible for positively impacting people and the environment in which we live. We are humbled by this responsibility and share a reverence for this mission. We give thanks for the heritage that we have received from past generations and embrace our responsibilities to present and future generations of event professionals.

The event industry stands at a defining moment. A fundamental understanding and commitment to environmental, technological, and economic challenges is needed to ensure a sustainable future for this industry and the professions it represents. Foresight and positive use of knowledge and power are the foundations for a successful future of the event industry. We must advance the event industry, finding new ways to balance self and community, diversity and unity, short-term and strategic goals by using and nurturing, preserving, and expanding.

In the midst of all of our diversity as a special events industry, we are one humanity and one family with a shared destiny. The economic, technological, and environmental challenges before us require an inclusive ethical vision. Alliances must be forged and cooperation fostered at every level, in every profession, and in every community on earth. In solidarity with one another and the community of life, we the stewards of this profession commit ourselves to action guided by the following interrelated principles.

Mission

To anticipate environmental, technological, and economic change in order to ensure a successful and enduring industry, we must:

1. **Serve** *as responsible custodians of the natural environment and educate others to understand this value and financial benefit.*

(Continued)

Figure 10–1   The Future of Event Management

2. **Improve** our technological capabilities to simultaneously reduce cost and improve quality.

3. **Establish** strong mutually beneficial strategic alliances for educational, social, and economic benefits worldwide.

Responsibility and Accountability

We believe that in order to achieve long-term sustainability for this profession, it is essential that we continually monitor, evaluate, analyze, and correct these goals as needed to ensure proper accountability.

1. **Serve as responsible custodians of the natural environment and educate others to follow our example.**

   a. Commit to be cognizant of and do well by the environment.

   b. Use pre-cycling and other pre-planning strategies to reduce negative impacts on the environment.

   c. Develop written environmental policies for our businesses, professional organizations, and industry.

   d. Continually monitor environmental changes in order to develop new strategies to lessen negative impacts.

   e. Promote positive environmental practices within our businesses and industry to encourage others and newcomers to share this responsibility.

   f. Utilize green achievements as a selling tool and positive public relations opportunity for current and future clients.

2. **Improve our technological capabilities to simultaneously reduce cost and improve quality.**

   a. Utilize technology as applicable for every facet of the event industry.

   b. Invest in the research and development of software that will improve efficiency, quality, and financial yield.

   c. Encourage the development and use of technology (i.e., World Wide Web, Internet 2) for the production and marketing of events.

   d. Reduce technological cost through cooperative agreements.

   e. Improve communication and collaboration through encouraging the use of electronic systems by internal and external publics.

   f. Provide training for ourselves and those we supervise to ensure educational parity with these emerging technologies.

Figure 10–1   (*Continued*)

3. **Establish strong beneficial global strategic alliances and cooperate with one another for mutual economic benefit.**

   a. Provide competitive compensation schemes to attract the highest qualified employees.

   b. Encourage inclusiveness among all peoples for maximum participation in and benefit from the events industry.

   c. Identify systems that determine the actual economic return on each event/investment.

   d. Balance the need for qualified employees and economic expansion, with realistic forecasting to ensure strong financial growth.

   e. Share, invest, and utilize initially quality re-usable goods, emerging technologies, and environmental awareness to reduce cost and increase financial yield.

   f. Create cooperative buying opportunities with industry partners.

   g. Seek out and encourage suppliers who use green practices.

   h. Encourage organizations to utilize events to increasingly communicate their mission or cause.

Covenant

Embracing the values in this Charter, we can grow into a sustainable profession that allows the potential of all persons to fully develop in harmony with the events industry. We must preserve a strong faith in the possibilities of the human spirit and a deep sense of belonging to the universal family of event professionals. Our best actions will embody the integration of knowledge with compassion for others.

In order to develop and implement the principles in this Charter, the members of the special events industry should adopt as a first step an integrated ethical framework for future sustainable policies. This framework should serve as an irrevocable covenant that will remove all previous and future barriers in order to achieve the principles set forth in this Charter.

Adopted by acclamation the 3rd of May, 1998 by the event industry leaders whose names appear below.

Craig Aramian

Rusty Aramian

John Baragona

Jaclyn Bernstein

(Continued)

Figure 10–1 (*Continued*)

Robert Bottoms	Jim Jones
Larry Clark	Tim Lundy, CSEP
Alice Conway, CSEP	Nancy Lynner
John Daly, CSEP	Rick Neter
Janet Elkins	David Peters
Liese Gardner	Sheri Pizitz, CSEP, CMP
Brinda Gore	Carol Ann Roe
Dr. Joe Goldblatt, CSEP	Tedd Saunders
Renee Grannis	Julia Rutherford Silvers
Dr. William Halal	Eleanor Woods, CSEP
Robert Hulsmeyer, CSEP	Dana Zita, CSEP, CMP

Figure 10–1   (*Continued*)

Staying on Top

Once you have succeeded in strengthening your standing within the industry, constant vigilance is required to stay there. To do so, you must stay abreast of the latest developments and technologies of the trade.

For example, it was not long ago that the preferred method of creating presentations for industrial events was the use of 35mm slides. Today, the simplicity of computer programs such as Microsoft Power-Point™ enables event managers to prepare elaborately designed presentations including multi-colored graphs, charts, and animated text at a mere fraction of what 35mm slides used to cost, and with the added capability of on-site editing even seconds before an event begins. If two competitors bid on a small corporate event, one recommending the use of 35mm slides, the other proposing the less expensive, more advanced alternative, which do you think would get the job? Almost every aspect of the special events industry is touched by technological innovation, and staying informed on new tools and techniques are an essential competitive requirement.

Another emerging area of opportunity is the use of the Internet as an event communication and information medium. Properly employed, the Internet provides unprecedented potential for event professionals and their clients to globalize their event marketing efforts.

The National Hockey League's All-Star fan festival, the NHL FANtasy, is a 200,000-square-foot hockey theme park which has traveled to the host city of the NHL All-Star Game since 1996. Until redesigned as a combined live and cyberevent in 1998, the FANtasy provided exposure for the League and its sponsors in only a single city. Now, fans outside of the host city can "attend" and tour the FANtasy through their personal computers, extending the event's reach from 50,000 local fans to literally millions worldwide.

There are many ways to stay on top of the newest developments in technology. Be sure to position yourself among your suppliers as a "cutting edge" organization, and ally yourself with the best, most highly regarded vendors. As new lighting technologies come to market, your lighting supplier should consider you a prime customer for the premiere of these new tools. Continually scan the trade publications and attend industry events in your segment of the business. Finally, stay on the lookout for the use of technologies in related fields such as architecture, cinema, computer technology, advertising, and publishing, among others, for potential application in the production of special events.

What makes special events as an industry so exciting is its position as much more than a marketing tool. It is a way of touching people, of motivating, of creating memories, and marking milestones. For this reason, event planners and producers are now being approached for new and exciting types of projects formerly beyond the pale of our traditional marketplace. Recently, the architect for a new entertainment center used the services of an event producer to help design the facility's entrance lobby to give it a "sense of arrival and excitement." Retail developers are retaining consultants with event backgrounds to help create spaces and programming which will help to differentiate their facilities from their competitors'. In short, there is a tremendous demand for the creativity and expertise available from our industry, both within the boundaries of traditional event management, and outside. Figure 10–2 provides a sample of growth areas for today's special events entrepreneur.

Throughout this book you have been offered a series of views on the roles of entrepreneurial techniques, skills, and opportunities within the growing special events industry. Now, it is your turn to lift your telescope, once more adjust the lenses, and focus your vision for long-term success as others have done before you.

The passion exemplified by individuals such as Jaclyn Bernstein, Rob Hulsmeyer, Mitch Kelldorf, and indeed dozens of others is inspir-

Corporate Human Resource Development Events

Regional, State, and Local Government Economic Development Events

Institutional Advancement (Museums, Higher Education) Events

Not-for-profit Educational, Trade, and Philanthropic Organization Events

Sports Organization Events

Retail Organization Events

Health and Medical Organization Events

Technology Company Events and Product Introductions

Telecommunications Company Events

Media Organization Events

Source: The George Washington University Event Management Program.

Figure 10–2   Special Events Expansion: Ten Growth Opportunities for Event Entrepreneurs

ing. These "new generation" event entrepreneurs are now leading the way as the special events industry grows in size, quality, and prominence.

Your own passion for this profession coupled with a realistic outlook and supported by unflagging persistence will serve you well in the days and years to come. In fact, true event entrepreneurs are never finished in their quest for excellence. They continually raise the bar seeking higher quality and better service for their industry. Indeed, they understand that to be successful in the long-term means never ripening, but remaining green and growing throughout their entire special events career.

 Go Write the Grandchildren

Joe Goldblatt received a telephone call from his 82-year-old father one night and was startled by his wise father's question. "What is your e-mail address?" asked the senior Goldblatt. For years, the father had not written his son, preferring instead to speak by telephone or in person. Therefore, Joe was surprised and puzzled by the request. "Why do you want to know?" he asked. Mr. Goldblatt responded: "I am going to begin writing my grandchildren." When Joe further queried his father about why he would use e-mail rather than traditional mail, his papa responded adamantly and incredulously with "E-mail is the future of communication. I want my grandchildren to hear me and to respond. Joe, there's no getting in the way of the future. You must anticipate the future and go there."

Less than a year later, after celebrating his 60th wedding anniversary with a large party attended by his children and grandchildren, Max Goldblatt sat down with his family to watch the video of the event. As the video ended, his son turned to see his father's reaction and was stunned to discover that the old man had quietly passed away.

Later, at the memorial service, the minister said that Mr. Goldblatt was continually surprising his friends and family with his many interests. Then, he revealed a secret that only Max and his wife had known. Max Goldblatt had enrolled in a senior computing course at the local community college and after a year of hard work had earned his certificate. As part of his homework, he had been instructed to use e-mail to "write your grandchildren."

Throughout Max Goldblatt's long life, he had reminded his son that to ripen or settle for the status quo was the first step toward decay. Instead, he encouraged his children and others to "stay green and growing," and often referred to hockey great Wayne Gretzky, who skated to where he thought the puck would be. So, go write your grandchildren! As a special event entrepreneur you are writing the future legacy of this industry through your enterprising efforts. Good Luck!

Goldblatt's college professor commanded that his students use e-mail to write their grandchildren. The authors of this first book on the subject of sustainable business success for event entrepreneurs similarly challenge you. Write your business plan as though you are writing a chapter in the future of the special events industry. Pick up your telescope, adjust the lenses, sharpen your pen, increase your power, and create the future of your profession through your commitment, dedication, and passion for growth in the events industry. Together we can produce enduring greatness and share this recipe with countless generations to come, as we remain green and growing in this ageless and timeless profession to which we are privileged to contribute.

Appendix

A. Sample Values, Vision, and Mission Statements

Event Management/Consulting Organization

Values: Innovation, team work, achievement, consistency, dependability, profitability.

Vision: A global enterprise that is recognized as a leader in the field of special events planning and management.

Mission: Our team is committed to the global delivery of dependable, consistently professional and innovative special events concepts and operations that enable our clients to achieve their goals while ensuring profitability to promote growth and continuous improvement for our organization and clients.

Special Events Services Firm (i.e., *lighting, audio-visual, entertainment, caterer*)

Values: Punctuality, quality service, satisfaction, zero errors, safety, added value.

Vision: An international quality service provider identified as among the top enterprises in the industry by clients and competitors.

Mission: We believe that high-quality service that has zero tolerance for errors and promotes associates who safely deliver added value will be recognized as the leader in the special events industry. To achieve these objectives we are committed to:

- Provide the highest quality of service to our clients, vendors, and colleagues
- Continually reduce operational error through consistent evaluation and correction
- Consistently identify methods for providing added value for our clients and rewarding our vendors and colleagues for innovations that promote these value-added services.

Retail Special Events Firm (*i.e., rental, party stores*)

Values: Quality products, excellent service, speed, convenience, responsiveness, variety, selection, good taste.

Vision: The "store of choice" in our market for a wide variety of high-quality, tasteful products provided in a convenient location by responsive professionals.

Mission: Our team is dedicated to providing the highest quality and greatest selection of products for our customers. Through excellent service, convenience, and responsiveness we aim to continually satisfy and anticipate the needs of our valued customers.

B. Business Plan Outline

I. Introduction
   A. Goals and objectives of the business
      1. Profitability
      2. Careful growth
      3. Diversification
      4. Franchising
II. History/Background
   A. Profiles of the principals
      1. Business or related experience
         Financials for business or similar enterprises

   2. Industry experience

      Employment history/management experience

   3. Education

      Business education

   4. References

      Customers, prospective customers, lenders, notable persons (elected officials)

III. Competitive Environment

   A. Similar businesses

   B. General economic conditions

   C. Tactics to be used to overcome competitive threats

IV. Marketing Plan

   A. Goals and objectives of marketing plan

      1. Target market

      2. Secondary market

   B. Specific tactics

      1. Advertising

      2. Direct mail

      3. Directory advertising (Yellow Pages, industry)

      4. Promotions

      5. Public relations

V. Operational Plan

   A. Organizational chart

   B. Service standards/training

   C. Expansion plans

   D. Prospective suppliers and terms for payment

VI. Budgets and Cash Flow Analysis (years 1, 2, 3)

VII. List of actual and prospective investors

VIII. Appendix

   A. Sample marketing materials

   B. Sample products/services (photos)

   C. Testimonials from investors

C. _Sample Event Organization Employment Contract_

This contract dated _____,20_____ is made BETWEEN

_____ whose address is _____

referred to as the "Company," AND _____ whose

address is _____ referred to as the "Employee."

1. Employment

The Company hereby employs the Employee as a _____
and the Employee hereby accepts such employment in
accordance with the terms and conditions of this contract.

2. Duties of Employee

A. _Job Assignment._ The duties of the Employee are generally
described as follows: The powers and duties of the Employee
are to be more specifically determined and set by the Company
from time to time.

COMMENTS

Employee job descriptions and titles serve to indicate the level
of authority or responsibility of the Employee. The job
description, itself, should not be so detailed that the Employee
may decide to decline duties which are not specifically set
forth. If there is sufficient flexibility in the terminology used,
additional duties to those listed can easily be added. The
following clauses are of a general nature.

B. _Additional Duties._ The Employee shall perform such
additional work as may be required by the Company from time
to time under the terms and conditions and according to the
directions, instructions, and control of the Company. However,
the Employee is not required to perform any duties outside of
the times and places of employment set forth in this contract.

C. _Change of Duties._ The duties of the Employee may be
changed from time to time without having any effect upon any
other terms of this contract.

D. _Company's Rules and Regulations._ The Employee shall strictly
adhere to all of the rules and regulations of the Company
which are presently in force or which may be established
hereafter with respect to the conduct of Employees. The
Employee shall also strictly follow the directions of the

Company with respect to the methods to be used in performing his or her duties. The Employee is responsible to continue and maintain the Company's standards of uniformity, purity, and quality with respect to all products manufactured by the Company. The Company's practices or policy manuals, price lists, general letters and other written publications are all made a part of this contract. The Company shall have the right to amend, revise or discontinue the policies or procedures as the Company deems necessary from time to time. Any such change in such policies or procedures will be effective upon issuance of same by the Company, unless the Company declares otherwise.

3. Power of Employee to Bind Company

(First Alternative) The Employee may not enter into any contract or otherwise bind the Company in any way without written authority from the Company. Any contracts which the Employee enters into without written authorization will not be binding upon the Company.

(Second Alternative) No order shall be binding upon the Company until accepted by the Company in writing. The Company reserves the right to reject any order or to cancel any order or part thereof after acceptance, for credit or for any other reason whatsoever which the Company deems sufficient.

(Third Alternative) The Company may, at its sole discretion, for any reason decline to accept any order for products, systems, or services obtained by the Employee or may cancel in whole or in part any order accepted, and in such case the Employee shall not be entitled to any bonus and/or commission or payment with respect to such order or the portion canceled.

(Fourth Alternative) All orders are subject to approval of items, price, and credit by the Company, and confirmation by purchasers. All quotations for sales made by Employees to customers or prospective customers must be made expressly subject to the approval and confirmation by the Company and are not final until such approval is given in writing by the Company.

4. Other Employment

(First Alternative) The Company agrees that the Employee may continue to (practice law, teach adult education, etc.); however, the Employee is only allowed to pursue such other

activities to the extent to which such pursuits would not interfere with the Employee's obligations under this contract.

(Second Alternative) The Employee is required to refrain from acting in any other work capacity or employment without having first obtained the written consent of the Company. It is the Company's intention that the Employee devote all of the Employee's work effort toward the fulfillment of the Employee's obligations under this contract.

5. **Place of Employment**

(First Alternative) The Employee's initial place of work is _____. However, the Company may require that the Employee work at such other place or places as the Company may direct. However, if the Employee is required to relocate, the Company shall pay the Employee's reasonable expenses in that regard.

(Second Alternative) The Employee will serve as a sales representative for a sales territory consisting of
_____.

(Third Alternative) The Employee shall assume and perform the assigned duties and responsibilities in the territory which is described in the schedule and rider attached hereto and signed at the time of this contract. This territory may be changed at any time and from time to time by the execution of supplementary contracts.

(Fourth Alternative) The Company hereby agrees that the Employee shall have the right to represent the Company as exclusive sales representative in the territory described as follows: _____. The Employee shall have the exclusive right to take orders in the above territory for all _____ *[describe products]* manufactured or sold by the Company.

6. **Employee's Hours of Work**

A. Weekly Schedule. The Employee is expected to work 8 hours per day and 40 hours per week, Monday through Friday. The working hours are normally nine to five but may be determined differently by the Company from time to time. The Employee is to be allowed ____ minutes for lunch with the time designated for lunch to be determined by the Company.

B. Overtime. **All Overtime Must Be Authorized.** The Employee is not allowed to work overtime unless the

Employee receives authorization in advance by the Company. Employees are also responsible to keep overtime to the minimum.

7. Compensation of Employee

(First Alternative) The Company shall pay the Employee the sum of $_____ per _____ as salary in accordance with this contract. The payments will be made on the _____ day of each _____.

(Second Alternative) The Company shall provide the Employee the salary, bonus and/or commission, or other form or type of compensation as may from time to time be established, altered, increased, or decreased by the Company. If the Employee is entitled to receive any bonus and/or commission, an account will be established to record all transactions between the Company and the Employee. Unless otherwise specified, any debit balance of the account shall not be considered an account receivable of the Company but shall nevertheless be carried forward on all subsequent net earnings determinations, until the account shall be settled at the terms and under the conditions as provided from time to time by the Company.

B. *Bonus Plan.*

(First Alternative) The Employee will be paid a bonus in the amount of $_____ for each _____ sold in excess of _____ units per _____. An additional bonus will be provided in the amount of $_____ for each unit sold in excess of _____ units per _____. The bonus period shall begin on _____ and shall end on _____.

(Second Alternative) The Employee shall receive a bonus equal to _____ % of the net profits of the business of the Company. Said sums will be payable within _____ days following the end of the fiscal year and will be determined in accordance with the uniform standards and practices developed by the Company. A more complete description of the Company's accounting methods will be available upon request.

8. Employee Benefits

A. *Holidays.*

1. The Employee will be entitled to _____ paid holidays each year plus _____ personal days. The Company will notify the Employee as much in advance as practical with respect to the holiday schedule. The holidays which are

generally observed by the Company are as follows: New Year's Day, Washington's Birthday, Good Friday, Memorial Day, Independence Day, Labor Day, Columbus Day, Thanksgiving Day, the Friday following Thanksgiving, and Christmas Day. Additional holidays may be allowed in connection with holidays which fall on a weekend.

2. The personal holidays are to be scheduled in advance to the mutual convenience of the Employee and the Company. Such holidays must be taken during the calendar year and cannot be carried forward into the next year.

3. The Employee will not be entitled to any personal holidays unless the Employee has been employed for a period of _____ during the calendar year. If the Employee has been employed for less than the required time, the Company may, at its own discretion, allow the Employee a reduced number of personal days.

B. *Vacations.*

1. The Employee will be entitled to vacations after the first six (6) months of employment with the Company as of May 31 of any year, as follows:

Length of Service	**Days of Vacation**
Six months but less than one year	2 days
One year but less than two years	5 days
Two years but less than five years	10 days
Five years but less than ten years	15 days
Ten years or more	20 days

2. Vacation pay is based on normal pay for a 40-hour workweek without consideration for bonuses or other supplemental compensation.

C. *Leaves of Absence.*

1. Sickness. The Employee is allowed _____ sick days per year. Sick days are not cumulative and may not be carried from year to year.

2. Maternity Leave. Maternity leave is treated the same as any other short-term disability. This means that the Employee will be paid in the same manner as if the Employee was ill or otherwise disabled.

3. Jury Duty. Employees will be given time off for jury duty up to three weeks in any given year.

4. Emergency Leave. If a member of the Employee's immediate family dies or becomes critically ill, the Employee will be allowed up to three days of leave with pay. Additional time may be granted, without pay, upon approval of the Company.

Note: *Leaves of absence may be provided for with or without pay. A leave without pay is used to protect the Employee's right to return to work without loss of rights or benefits.*

Pregnancy must be treated like other disabilities for the purposes of leave of absence and other benefits in accordance with federal laws and the laws of several states.

D. *Medical and Dental Benefits.* The Company agrees to include the Employee in the following medical and dental benefit plans: _____. The Employee should refer to the plans for additional information with respect to coverage and handling of claims.

E. *Moving Expenses.* If the Company transfers the Employee to a new place of work, the Company shall pay the Employee for moving and traveling expenses that are authorized in advance in writing by the Company in accordance with the Company's policy on this subject, which is more fully set forth in the following descriptive memorandum: _____.

F. *Employee Expenses.*

1. No Expenses Allowed. The Employee is not permitted to incur any expenses which are to be charged against the Company without written consent of the Company.

2. Expenses to Be Reimbursed. The Company will reimburse the Employee for all reasonable expenses incurred by the Employee in connection with the performance of the Employee's duties under this contract. The payments will be made within __ days after the Employee provides the Company with an itemized statement of all charges. The expenses to be incurred by the Employee include entertainment, travel, meals, lodging, and related expenses incurred by the Employee in the interest of the business of the Company.

9. Employee Not to Compete with Company

(*First Alternative*) The Employee shall not within _____ years after the termination of employment, directly or indirectly, as principal agent, servant or otherwise, carry on or be concerned or interested in any _____ business within _____ miles from (location), or directly or indirectly solicit or endeavor to obtain as customers any person or corporation who was a customer of the employer during such employment.

(*Second Alternative*) Now, Therefore, It Is Agreed between the parties as follows:

1. During employment with _____ and for a period of _____ (_____) (months/years) after termination of employment, the Employee will not directly or indirectly own, manage, operate, control, participate in, or be connected in any manner with the ownership, management, operation, or control of any business similar to the type of business conducted by _____ at the time of termination of employment.

2. This agreement shall be binding on the Employee only in the areas of past, present, and future employment with _____.

10. Employee Not to Disclose Confidential Information

(*First Alternative*) The Employee agrees that any information received by the Employee during his or her employment, which concerns the personal, financial, or other affairs of the Company, will be treated by the Employee in full confidence and will not be revealed to any other persons, firms, or organizations.

(Second Alternative) The Employee agrees to keep secret and not disclose to others nor make personal use of any confidential information concerning the Company's business, which may become known to the Employee during the course of the Employee's employment with the Company.

11. Terms of Employment

The term of employment shall begin _____ 20___ and extend to and be automatically extended for successive periods of one year each upon the same terms and conditions set forth in this contract unless this contract is terminated by either party as herein provided.

12. **Termination of Employment—General Provisions**

(*First Alternative*) This contract may be terminated by either party on not less than 14 (fourteen) days advance written notice thereof, or on verbal notice confirmed in writing within such 14 (fourteen) day period to the other party. However, the Company may terminate the employment hereunder immediately if necessary in its best judgment in order to protect its business or its good name. If the Employee elects to terminate his or her employment without advance notice, the Company shall have the right to make no further credits to the account of the Employee after the last day worked, notwithstanding the right to such credits had advanced notice been given.

Upon termination of this contract, whether or not by the Company, subsequent credits to the Employee's account with respect to orders then taken will be determined solely by the Company's policies then in effect. The Company will not be obligated to the Employee for bonuses or commissions in relation to accounts not yet closed out for payment, chargeoff, or cancellation.

(*Second Alternative*) If the Employee violates any of the provisions of this contract, the Company may terminate the employment hereunder immediately without further obligation except to pay the Employee for compensation earned prior to the termination of this contract.

13. **Termination of Employment—Illness of Employee**

If the Employee shall become unable to attend to the duties of employment as required by this contract and it becomes necessary for the Company to replace the Employee either temporarily or permanently, the Company may do so and at the same time may suspend all further payments to the Employee for salary or bonuses and all other related compensation. In that event the Employee may still be entitled to long-term disability if such a policy is in effect. The Company will recommence the payment of salaries, bonuses, and other compensation at such date as the Employee shall resume and perform the Employee's duties under this contract. The right of the Company as set forth above is in addition to the right of the Company to terminate this contract at any time as set forth above.

14. Termination of Employment—Relation to Compensation

If this contract is terminated, all compensation, additional compensation, and other benefits shall accrue and be paid to the Employee to the date of the termination. Payments will be made with respect to each item of compensation or benefit as soon as the amount due is determined, except that in the event the termination is due to the Employee's misconduct, the Company shall have the right to withhold any and all monies due to the Employee and shall apply same as an offset against any monies due to the Company from the Employee as a result of the Employee's misconduct.

15. Termination of Employment—Death of Employee

If the Employee dies while being employed by the Company, this contract shall automatically terminate. However, the Company shall pay the estate of the Employee a sum equal to _____. This payment is in addition to any other rights that the Employee may have with respect to pensions, profit sharing, or other Employee benefits.

16. Remedies for Breach of Contract

A. In the event of the breach or threatened breach of any provision of the contract by the Employee, the Company shall be entitled to injunctions, both preliminary and final, enjoining and restraining such breach or threatened breach. Such remedies shall be in addition to all other remedies available at law or in equity including the Company's right to recover from the Employee any and all damages that may be sustained as a result of the Employee's breach of contract.

B. In addition to any other remedies the Company may have available to it under the terms of this contract, the Company shall be entitled to stop the Employee, by means of injunction, from violating any part of this agreement, and to recover, by means of an accounting, any profits the Employee may have obtained in violation of this contract. The Company shall be entitled to recover its attorney's fees and expenses in any successful action by the Company to enforce this agreement.

17. Arbitration of Disputes

Any controversy or claim arising out of or relating to this contract, or the breach thereof, shall be settled by arbitration in accordance with the rules of the American Arbitration Association. Judgment upon the award rendered by the arbitrator may be entered in any court having jurisdiction thereof.

However, in the event of noncompliance or violation, as the case may be, of paragraphs __ __ __ of this contract (provisions relating to confidential information, trade secrets, and other restrictive stipulations), the Company may alternatively apply to the court of competent jurisdiction for a temporary restraining order injunctively, and/or such other legal and equitable remedies as may be appropriate, since the Company would have no adequate remedy at law for such violation on noncompliance.

18. Severability; Governing Law

A. If any clause or provision herein shall be adjudged invalid or unenforceable by a court of competent jurisdiction or by operation of any applicable law, it shall not affect the validity of any other clause or provision, which shall remain in full force and effect. The contract shall be governed by the laws of the state of _____. The _____ court of the state of _____ shall have jurisdiction over any dispute which arises under this contract, and each of the parties shall submit and hereby consent to such court's exercise of jurisdiction. In any successful action by the Company to enforce this contract, the Company shall be entitled to recover its attorney's fees and expenses incurred in such action.

B. Each of the provisions of this agreement shall be enforceable independently of any other provision of this contract and independent of any other claim or cause of action. In the event of any dispute arising under this agreement, it is agreed between the parties that the law of the state of _____ will govern the interpretation, validity, and effect of this contract without regard to the place of execution or place of performance thereof.

19. Complete Agreement

This contract supersedes all prior contracts and understandings between the Employee and the Company and may not be modified, changed, or altered by any promise or statement by whomsoever made; nor shall any modification of it be binding upon the Company until such written modification shall have been approved in writing by an officer of the Company.

20. Waiver of Breach

The waiver by the Company of a breach of any provision of this contract by the Employee shall not operate or be construed as a waiver of any subsequent breach by the Employee.

21. Employment by Subsidiary

If the Company owns, acquires, or forms subsidiary companies or becomes connected with other affiliate companies, the Employee agrees to be employed by any of the same and in such event all of the terms and conditions set forth herein shall bind the parties.

22. Number and Gender

In the above contract the use of any particular gender or the plural or singular number is intended to include the other gender or number as the text of this contract may require.

23. Signatures

A. In Witness Whereof, the undersigned has executed this contract the date and year first above written.

Attest: *[Name of Company]*

_____ By _____
Secretary   President

Witness:

_____   _____
[Name of Witness]   Employee

B. Both the Employee and the Company agree to the above.

Witnessed or Attested by:

_____   _____

_____   _____

D. *Sample First-Year Budget for Special Events Consulting Practice*

Income

100	Consulting fees	
101	Proposal writing	$25,000
102	Planning	$50,000
103	Coordination	$300,000
104	Evaluation	$15,000
110	Products and Services Other than Consulting	
111	Entertainment	$95,000
112	Decor	$100,000
113	Amusement games	$25,000
114	Advertising specialties	$10,000
115	Costumes	$15,000
116	Miscellaneous	$5,000
	Total Income	$640,000

Expense

100	Administration	
101	Full time salaries	$50,000
102	Part time salaries	$25,000
103	Benefits	$15,000
200	Consultants	
201	Accounting	$1,000
202	Legal	$500
203	Marketing	$2,000
300	Office Lease and Equipment	
301	Lease	$12,000
302	Furnishings	$5,000
303	Computers	$10,000
304	Telephone	$15,000

400	Marketing	
401	Yellow Pages	$6,000
402	Newspaper	$5,000
403	Directories	$1,000
404	Radio	$10,000
500	Insurance	
501	Comprehensive General Liability	$3,000
502	Automotive Liability	$1,000
503	Workman's Compensation	$5,000
600	Fees, Taxes	
601	Business license	$500
602	Corporation fee	$100
603	Corporate taxes	$0
604	Sales taxes	$5,000
700	Production Costs	
701	Total production costs	$270,000

Total Expense	$442,100
Excess over expense:	$197,900

E. *Sample Marketing Materials*

YELLOW PAGES (Include logos of organizations where you are a member)

Category: Convention Services

Dependable, Reliable, and FAST

The Event Company is your #1 Choice for (Entertainment, Decor, Planning, etc.)

For 24 hour service Call 1-800-EVENT US! (800-383-6887)

Category: Catering

Traditional or Imaginative or Both?

Call Taste of the Town Caterers

For a Sumptuous World of Possibilities and Great Value from our Award Winning Chef!

(301) 994-1010

Category: Party Rental Store

Easy, Convenient, and Great $avings: Your Formula for a Successful Party or Event Starts with calling

ABC Party Rent-All to receive our FREE LIST of Winning Event Ideas

The Choice of Professional Event Planners-Featured in XYZ Magazine

Call 24 hours to receive your Free List! Mention this ad and $ave 10% on your first order.

(301) 222-1111

3200 Bellaire (Westlake Shopping Center)

NEWSPAPER AD (Make certain you code the ad to track response)

Business: Entertainment

Take A Bow! Let Easy Entertainment Provide High Quality, Tasteful, and Successful Entertainers for Your Next Event and You will Receive Rave Reviews from Your Guests. Music, Variety, Games & More! Call (212) 687-9090 24 hours and $ave 10% off your first order. Code #101

F. *Event Management Business Software*

Most software is available via local computer retailers or through the Internet.

ACCOUNTING/FINANCIAL MANAGEMENT
QuickBooks 5.0
Quicken Basic 98

Quick Pay 3.0

Turbo Tax for Business

Visual AccountMate 3.1

Small Business Financial Manager 97

Money 97

M.Y.O.B. (Mind Your Own Business)

DATABASE

Claris FileMaker Pro

Microsoft Access 97

Lotus Approach 97

PRESENTATION AND GRAPHICS

Visio 5.0

Lotus Freelance Graphics

PowerPoint 97

RENTAL MANAGEMENT SYSTEMS

ALERT Computer Systems, Colorado Springs, Colorado

AlphaSoft, Inc. Minneapolis, Minnesota

Automation Plus, Ft. Lauderdale, Florida

Codesmiths, Inc., Champaign, Illinois

Computer Ease, Novato, California

Creative Business Services, Manchester, Missouri

Operation Management System, Stockton, California

Quality Software Products, Arvada, Colorado

R.E.N.T.S. Computer Systems, Sioux Falls, South Dakota

Solutions by Computer, Springfield, Massachusetts

The Woodward Group, Glendora, California

Unique Business Systems, Santa Monica, California

SPECIAL EVENTS PLANNING AND MANAGEMENT

Advanced Solutions International, Alexandria, Virginia

Business Computer Solutions, Columbia, Maryland

Catermate, Indianapolis, Indiana

Culinary Software Services, Boulder, Colorado

ErgoSoft, Inc. Columbia, Maryland

EventMaker Pro, Nashua, New Hampshire

I Do, The Ultimate Wedding Planner, Mappetus, California

InScribe, Inc., Cambridge, Massachussetts

MeetingPRO, Peopleware, Inc. Bellevue, Washington

Microchips, Inc., St. Louis, Missouri

Mom 'N Pops Software, Springhill, Florida

QuickSilver Software, Sussex, Wisconsin

RE: Event, Blackbaud, Inc., Charleston, South Carolina

ROOMER 3 (computer assisted design), Henry M. Hufnagel

Room Viewer (computer assisted design), TimeSaver Software,
   info@timesaver.com

Smart-N-Easy Wedding Planner

Social Software, New York, New York

Synergy Software International, Arlington, Virginia

Terapin Systems, Silver Springs, Maryland

The Event Edge, ErgoSoft, Inc., Columbia, Maryland

The Event Management System Version 5.3, Dean Evans &
   Associates, Englewood, California

The Wedding Planner, Ninga Software, Calgary, Alberta, Canada

Wedding Workshop, MicroPrecision Software, Santa Clara,
   California

Zea Software, Alexandria, Virginia

SPREADSHEETS

Microsoft Excel 97

Lotus 1-2-3 97

WORD PROCESSING

Microsoft Word 97

Lotus Word Pro 97

OFFICE SUITES

Corel WordPerfect Suite 7

Lotus SmartSuite

Microsoft Office 97, Professional Edition
Microsoft Office 97, Standard Edition

CONTACT MANAGEMENT
Act! 3.0
GoldMine
Sharkware
TeleMagic Progfessional

Index